The Two Princes of Mpfumo

THE EARLY MODERN AMERICAS

Peter C. Mancall, Series Editor

Volumes in the series explore neglected aspects of
early modern history in the western hemisphere.
Interdisciplinary in character, and with a special
emphasis on the Atlantic World from 1450 to 1850,
the series is published in partnership with the
USC-Huntington Early Modern Studies Institute.

The Two Princes of Mpfumo

An Early Eighteenth-Century Journey into and out of Slavery

Lindsay O'Neill

PENN

UNIVERSITY OF PENNSYLVANIA PRESS

PHILADELPHIA

Published by
University of Pennsylvania Press
Philadelphia, Pennsylvania 19104-4112
www.pennpress.org

Printed in the United States of America on acid-free paper
10 9 8 7 6 5 4 3 2 1

A Cataloging-in-Publication record is
available from the Library of Congress.

Hardcover ISBN: 978-1-5128-2720-0
Ebook ISBN: 978-1-5128-2719-4

For Damon

CONTENTS

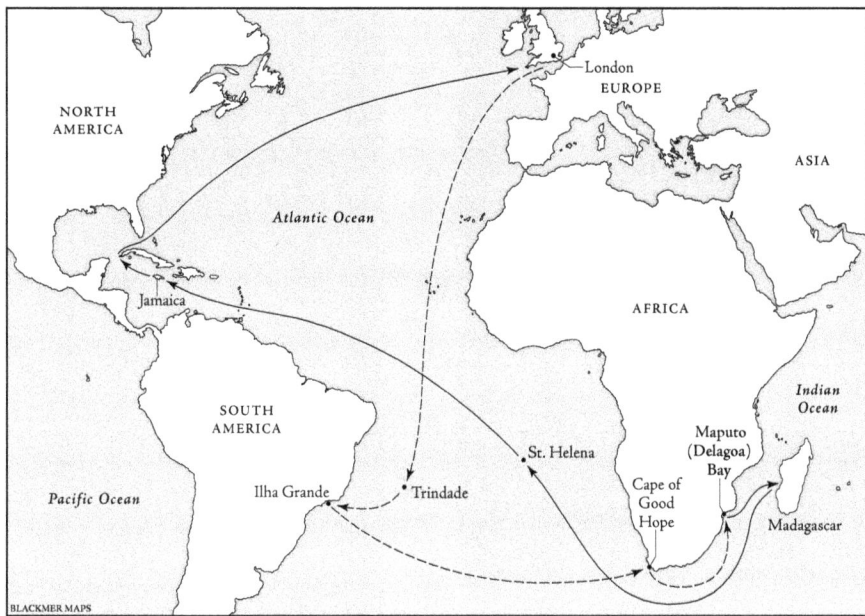

Figure 1. This map traces the journeys taken by Prince James and Prince John. The solid line, starting in Maputo (Delagoa) Bay, traces their path to London. It begins with the voyage of the *Mercury*, on which the princes traveled until Jamaica. Then it traces the short voyage of the *Lewis*, which left Jamaica but was wrecked in a hurricane off Cuba. And finally it follows the route of the ship that eventually took them from Cuba to London. The dashed line traces the voyage of the *Northampton* from London back to Maputo (Delagoa) Bay. Blackmer Maps.

Prologue

For one man, known to the British as Prince James Chandos Maffoom, it ended something like this: On the night of 1 May 1722, he found himself in a field near an apple tree close to Exmouth, on the southwestern English coast. He was far from home. He hailed from Mpfumo on the southeastern coast of Africa, where Maputo, the capital of Mozambique, now stands, but he had been gone almost six years.[1] When he left home he had looked for change, now he simply wanted peace. Here in this field near the English coast it was quiet. There were no shouts of anger and no fists raised, just the muted sounds of the English countryside near midnight. It was a peaceful place to die. He glanced down at his European garb. It was so much more restraining than what he had worn in Africa and so much more complex than what the British forced him to wear when they enslaved him in Jamaica. He freed his garters from his stockings and held the long strips of cloth in his hands.[2] Their length and the tree above him would be the means of his final escape.[3]

Eight months later, his brother, known as Prince John Twogood Maffoom, clothed in similar finery, set foot once more in Mpfumo. His escape from British influence took longer. He had returned on board a British ship, the *Northampton*, ready to facilitate trade between the British and his people. The Dutch, who had set up a trading post in Mpfumo since Prince John's departure, watched him arrive. They noted, somewhat condescendingly, that he had "been treated like a little prince" in Britain and been given "a fine outfit . . . in clothing and otherwise." They thought it would be an adjustment for a man who was "used to eating good food, to now eat rumen, intestines, etc. again."[4] This "little prince," however, soon acclimated and started causing trouble for the Dutch. He had the ear of his uncle, the ruler of Mpfumo, and was trying to convince him to throw the Dutch out and favor the British.[5] Six weeks later, though, things had changed. Prince John turned against the crew of the *Northampton*. The ruler of Mpfumo, with the help of another local polity, took members of the British crew captive and threatened to cut off the captain's head.[6] Unlike Prince John's brother, these men survived, but here Prince John cut ties with the British.[7]

In the beginning, these dark endings did not taint the dreams nurtured by the two men. When Prince James and Prince John boarded the British ship the *Mercury* in 1716 to sail to London, they probably thought they were embarking on a journey of triumph, one that would bring prosperity to them and their people. The captain of the ship had assured their relative, the ruler of Mpfumo, that he would care for them, and the two princes wanted to return with strengthened ties to British traders to help their struggling polity.[8] Mpfumo had once been among the most dominant polities around Maputo Bay, but it had lost much of its status in recent years, coming under the control of one of its neighbors.[9] The princes most likely hoped that a special relationship with the British would reestablish Mpfumo's standing. Instead, they found slavery. This they escaped, but even in freedom they saw their dreams of equality and influence slowly dwindle. Their topsy-turvy experience as they traveled from Mpfumo to Jamaica, to London, and back toward home would stretch and strain one brother's sense of identity until it snapped, and the other would reject his ties to the British.[10]

Once the *Mercury* left Mpfumo, the two men struggled to control the paths their lives took. In British eyes, they were but pawns in a larger game of imperial wealth. Their loss of power is evident in the archives that recount their story. We do not even know their names. We only know what the British called them once they were baptized, almost a year after they arrived in London: Prince James Chandos Maffoom and Prince John Twogood Maffoom.[11] Their names in Africa, in Jamaica, and during their early days in London are lost to us. Furthermore, their motivations, feelings, and reactions to events are often buried by the bias inherent in the European records that detail their travels.[12] British motivations, feelings, and reactions are easier to trace. The reasons why British traders wished to travel to Mpfumo survive in the East India Company papers, which also hold a memorial by the princes' patron telling of their travails.[13] The princes surface in a book written by a sailor shipwrecked on Madagascar.[14] British newspapers reported on their time in Jamaica and on other aspects of their journey.[15] Once the two arrived in London, members of the British elite would write letters telling their tale and detailing the plans circulating about them.[16] Those plans are elaborated on in the records of the trading companies and institutions planning their return voyage: the East India Company, the Royal African Company, and the Society for Promoting Christian Knowledge.[17] After the British ship chartered for their return sailed into Maputo Bay, the Dutch East India Company records pick up the story.[18] British records speculate on the reasons behind Prince James's suicide.[19] His voice is silent. Prince John's actions once he returned to Mpfumo surface in the Dutch East India Company records, but his reasons for turning against the British are opaque.[20] He did not record them. Only two formulaic letters of thanks written by the two men survive. These are copied into a letter book, denying us their handwriting and signatures.[21] They composed no records detailing their story. No accounts were written and retained that tell of their travels from the African perspective.

If we approach the sources carefully, however, the princes' attempts to steer the course of their lives and their centrality to British plans surface. Unearthing their story from beneath the weight of European sources is a complicated and delicate task. As some scholars have rightly cautioned, we need to couple these attempts at recovery with a consideration of the structures of power that intentionally muted or twisted their stories.[22] Much is gained, however, by listening for their side of the story.[23] They boarded the *Mercury* not to please the British but to further their own agenda. Their opinions and actions shaped British plans and often determined their success or failure. To reveal this, I have read the primary sources carefully, looking for cracks where their voices or actions emerge. When a source reported that princes "said" something or "did" something, my eyes paused and noted. I chose, at times, to attempt to recreate their reactions to certain events. To provide a note of caution, I pepper these moments with speculative terms: probably, perhaps, most likely.[24] This helps to put the princes at the center of the story, to remind of us of their constant presence, but also to keep in mind that the sources hide as much as they reveal.

Following the two men on their travels also allows us to see British expansion from a new angle. Rather than focusing on the actions of the English East India Company or the Royal African Company or the Society for Promoting Christian Knowledge, the princes show us the intersections and divergences between these groups.[25] Their story also reveals who had power within these groups and the links between not just institutions but also individuals. We can see that those pushing for imperial expansion were a hodgepodge of different institutions, networks, and interests that were vying to extract the most profit from imperial ventures, either in pounds or in souls. Their interactions with the princes reinforce that most Britons focused on the profit emanating from enslaved bodies, although new ideas about how to exploit Africa were also surfacing. Such desires pushed these different interest groups—be they trading companies, religious organizations, enslavers, or colonists—to rethink the geographic scope and economic focus of their endeavors. They often did so not out of optimism but out of need. Groups, from independent traders to London weavers, were attacking the monopolies and trading rights of the East India Company and the Royal African Company.[26] This pushed these companies to consider new avenues of trade, often in new places that were not as tightly connected to established networks of empire. East Africa and Madagascar, thought to be rich in gold or in captives, beckoned. Connections in the west were becoming linked to those in the east. These new plans brought the companies into contact with the two princes and their world.

While it was Mpfumo's ivory rather than its access to enslavable bodies that drew the British, the European desire for enslaved labor helped determine the trajectory of the princes' lives. The drumbeat of demand for enslaved men, women, and children that echoed from the Caribbean and North America was increasing in tempo, and many traders listened. In the 150-year span between 1550 and 1700 the British enslaved over 260,000 Africans. Close to that same number were sent from Africa in the next twenty years alone.[27] Most of this trade centered on the west coast of Africa, especially the Gold Coast and the Bight of Benin, but some traders began to look farther afield.[28] Starting in the 1680s ships from England and its colonies began to sail to Madagascar.[29] The island was never a main conduit for the slave trade; of the more than one million enslaved men, women, and children transported by the British between 1650 and 1750, only 1 percent came from East Africa or the Indian Ocean islands.[30] In the last decades of the seventeenth century and the early decades of the eighteenth century, however, Madagascar was a tempting alternative for those lusting for enslavable bodies.[31] Indeed, the *Mercury* stopped in Mpfumo only because it was on its way to purchase enslaved laborers in Madagascar.

The racial ideologies the British increasingly used to justify the enslavement of Africans haunted all the interactions the princes would have with the British. As the princes moved through different parts of the British Empire, however, it becomes clear the populations in each place saw them through different lenses. Slave traders, especially those who had worked along the West African coast, knew that they needed to keep elite Africans happy if they wanted access to captives.[32] Plantation owners, however, simply knew that they needed more enslaved bodies. Thus, as the princes traveled from

Mpfumo to Madagascar, to Jamaica, and finally to London their status altered. In the Indian Ocean world, they were more valuable as princes, but once in Jamaica they would bring more profit as enslaved men. In Britain, their royal stature would draw more interest than their enslavement.[33] Even when British officials recognized them as princes, however, such standing did not mean their British patrons saw them as equals. They were curiosities to be viewed, not men to be respected. These cultural blinkers would give the British an unduly optimistic view of what the engagement with Africans in Mpfumo would entail. For while the princes were pawns moved by many British interests in London, in Mpfumo it was the British who were the pawns. The African polities around Maputo Bay knew they held the upper hand. They enjoyed playing the British and the Dutch against each other and when they decided they wanted the British gone, that too was easily done.

The princes' story reveals the violent fragility of British imperial expansion and southeastern Africa's place within it. It also reminds us that the British were open to new exploitative possibilities. This book, along with the princes' voyage, starts in what is now Maputo and next visits Madagascar, locations rarely brought into the imperial story. The princes' travels show us that the East India Company was considering expansion into the Atlantic, bridging two imperial worlds often treated separately.[34] And while their story affirms the economic importance and horrific reality of the trade in enslaved bodies, it also shows that Britons longed for African gold as well, the original commodity they had sought on the African continent.[35] These unexpected moments in the princes' story reveal cracks in the standard narrative we tell. Here the Atlantic world, and its triangle trade between Britain, Africa, and the Americas, is pulled east into the Indian Ocean, questioning the borders we draw between them. The old assumptions and structures reassert themselves in the end. The old borders, in fact, are strengthened. The princes' journeys did not transform the world. Telling their story, however, destabilizes and makes more complex what we know about British expansion in the early eighteenth century and the place of Africans in it. It was an expansion based on unlikely projects, untrustworthy figures, violent means and ends. It was also a push that could be stopped. It ended in death for one prince, but also in the captivity and expulsion of the British. And Prince John made it home.

CHAPTER 1

Leaving Mpfumo

Mpfumo, Southeastern Africa, 1716

Prince James and Prince John could have been watching when the *Mercury*, Captain Thomas White in command, laid anchor at Mpfumo.[1] As one British seaman noted, "The best Anchoring is about 6 or 7 miles up the River, over against a little Town on a hill on the Starboard side call'd Mafooma."[2] This was the princes' home, and this ship would transform their lives. It would take them to Madagascar, St. Helena, and Jamaica and would see them go from honored guests to enslaved property. To Captain White the two men were always possible commodities, but it is unlikely that they knew this. Their sparse knowledge of the transatlantic slave trade, and the racist ideology underlining it, probably blinded them to the possibility of their own enslavement. They did not possess the networks of trade and information that bound and informed European and African slave traders on the west coast of Africa. White did have such knowledge and connections. Chattel slavery, as practiced in the Americas, would have been unfamiliar to the princes as well. Mpfuman society had hierarchies and ties of dependency, and the Indian Ocean world had an active trade in enslaved bodies and many different forms of enslavement, but it was more nuanced, varied, and less based on race.[3] With White and ships like the *Mercury*, European ideas about slavery and the slave trade were creeping into the Indian Ocean.[4]

When the princes encountered Captain White, their main concern was the status of Mpfumo. The past few years had not been kind to the princes and their people. Mpfumo had once been a powerhouse in the region but had recently lost power. The bay near where the princes lived, today the site of Maputo, the capital of Mozambique, and known to the British as Delagoa Bay, was a competitive enclave (fig. 2). The princes' kingdom of Mpfumo sat

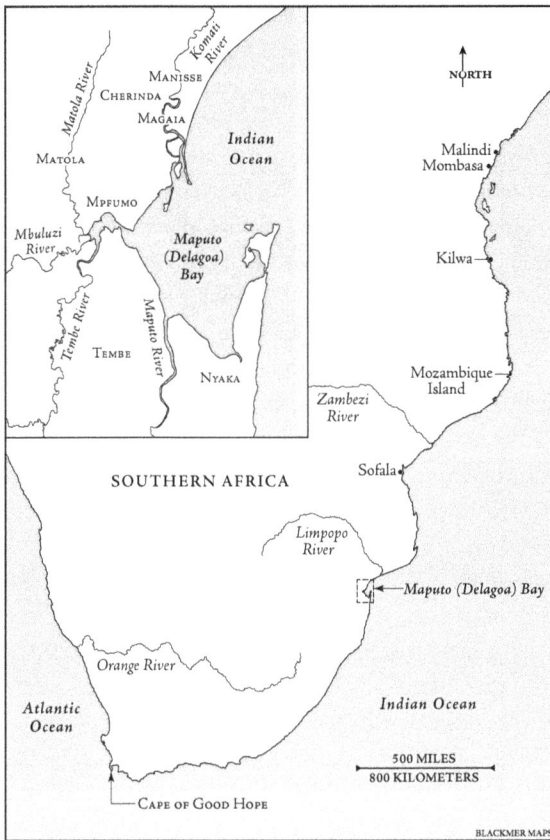

Figure 2. This map shows the major ports along the southeastern coast of Africa in the early eighteenth century. The insert is a detail of the polities around Maputo (Delagoa) Bay during the same period, including the princes' home of Mpfumo toward the center. Blackmer Maps.

near the center of the bay. The polities of Manisse, Cherinda, Magaia, and Matola lay to the north, and Tembe and Nyaka to the south.[5] All the inhabitants of the region were members of the same Ronga language group, but this did not translate to political unity. They could, however, understand the insults they hurled at one another.[6] Over the years the people of Mpfumo had watched as their kingdom's influence plummeted. Tembe, the kingdom to the south, and Magaia, the polity to the north, were now in control of the region.[7] Mpfumo had gone to war once too often. It lost to Manisse and then went to war with Magaia. This seemed like a good idea, since it had the kingdom of Tembe as an ally, but even that was not enough to keep Magaia from victory. In the end, Magaia claimed much of Mpfumo's land and made it a tributary state. Magaia's ruler gave the ceded land to one of his war leaders, Mateke, who, over the coming years, would slowly attempt to carve out his own independent polity. Things were not looking good for Mpfumo, but trade with Europeans could offer succor.[8]

Access to European trade goods meant more cattle and more cattle meant more wealth and status in Mpfumo.[9] Most villages had a cattle enclosure in the center, surrounded by the homes of the village leader's wives and dependents, and protected by an outer fence. It was these cattle that allowed the village leader to expand his power by exchanging them for more wives and using them to weave webs of dependence and power.[10] Trade with the interior augmented this wealth by allowing the region access to more goods and more cattle.[11] The Dutch and English noted that African traders arrived at the bay with copper and tin to trade and that those around the bay would make collars out of the copper, sometimes with tin added, and these were sold as trade goods.[12] The fertile opportunities for trade, agriculture, and cattle caused the polities around the bay to grabble for control.[13] And when the Europeans arrived, who controlled access to their trade goods became a point of contention.

Seaborne trade was infrequent. While the inhabitants along the bay had canoes that could hold up to fourteen people for fishing, whale hunting, and local transport, they were not a maritime people.[14] They stood on the outskirts of the trade networks that were tightening across the Indian Ocean basin. To the north was the Swahili coast, dominated by the great trading cities of Malindi and Mombasa. To the south was the newly emergent Dutch settlement at the Cape of Good Hope, begun in 1652 (fig. 2). To the east lay the vibrant trading world of South Asia. But the winds did not favor those from Maputo Bay. They sat just below the monsoon winds, and many traders in the Indian Ocean worried that if they traded that far south they would never return home.[15]

For a long time, Europeans just glanced at the area as they sailed by toward the riches of the Spice Islands, the Indian subcontinent, or the more profitable ports along the Swahili coast. The first European to stop in the bay was the Portuguese captain Lourenço Marques in 1544, but he too continued on and settled in the north. The Portuguese would set up their main trading post in the area on Mozambique Island and eventually established quasi-feudal land settlements along the Zambezi River, known as the Portuguese *prazos*, but these centers of power lay hundreds of miles north (fig. 2).[16] Nonetheless Portuguese influence, both formal and informal, slowly made its way south.[17] By 1589 the Portuguese were sending regular ships to the bay for ivory. That ivory came from elephants hunted in the interior, and trade in it was controlled by the African rulers who sent the tusks.[18] The interior polities hunted elephants for their meat; the tusks were a by-product that they sometimes used for fences. Exchanging them for beads and cloth was a boon.[19] The Portuguese were pleased as well. They found they could get forty thousand *reis* worth of ivory for fifty *reis* worth of beads.[20] The European demand for ivory did not transform the economic or social contours of the bay, but it did give the area's rulers other goods besides cattle to deploy as they jockeyed for power. It also pushed them to develop new diplomatic and commercial skills as they processed European norms.[21]

Encounters with the Portuguese were common for 150 years and would have marked the memories of the Mpfumans. Most years the Portuguese sailed into the harbor in early winter along with the winds and would stay at least four months. Ships' crews would set up on a small island in the bay and then sail up and down the rivers collecting ivory at way stations and stashing it back at their headquarters. Trading did not always go smoothly. Locals plundered ships due to suspected wrongs, they executed traders and priests accused of murder, and tensions could force the Portuguese to look for new allies or suspend the trade for years on end. These tensions could change power relations within the bay. Initially, the Portuguese mostly traded with Nyaka in the south, fueling its expansion. In 1621, however, the Portuguese turned from Nyaka and began to favor Tembe, the other power to the south, which allowed that polity to gain power.[22] The ability of the Portuguese to sway conditions in the bay would wane by the end of the seventeenth century as Dutch and English captains began to show an interest in the area.

The princes' parents or grandparents witnessed this growing European competition for trade in the bay. Throughout the 1680s English ships sailed in and out of Maputo Bay. In one year, five English ships came to trade.[23] From the Cape of Good Hope the Dutch warily eyed the burgeoning trade with the English. Positive reports from English captains who stopped by the Cape on their way home made the Dutch curious about the possibilities of Maputo Bay, a port they were nicely situated to exploit.[24] In 1688 there were English, Dutch, and Portuguese ships in the bay. Such demand gave the local leaders more power as they played the Europeans off one another.[25] The stiff competition, however, caused the Dutch and the Portuguese to rethink trading in the bay. For the Dutch, the expensive ivory did not seem worth the effort.[26] Plagued by other problems in their wide empire and ships empty of ivory returning from Maputo, the Portuguese abandoned the trade to English in 1703, around the time the princes were born.[27] But even English ships rarely came to the bay after the turn of the century, although interest remained.[28] This hurt the Mpfumans and other polities around the bay. Ivory piled up, and rulers lacked European goods to form or pay ties of obligation.[29] The hope for European ships probably haunted the princes' childhood, although they may have seen a ship or two enter the bay. People with connections to the trade remained. When the Dutch arrived in Maputo Bay in 1721, they found an old man who spoke Portuguese. He had been born on the island of Mozambique, a Portuguese stronghold to the north, and had come to Maputo Bay on one of the trading vessels.[30] This man, or others like him, could have told the young princes' stories about Europeans and their trading ways.

The people of Mpfumo, in particular, had long-standing ties with European traders. The north side of the bay had the deepest water and made an obvious place to anchor. Thus, Mpfumo often surfaces as a power player in English observations of the area. In the early eighteenth century, an English traveler let his readers know that the most powerful ruler "on ye northside" was "King Mafomo."[31] Furthermore, in a "Vocabulary of Delagoa" from the same period, the only place name listed with a translation was "the Country of Mafomo," which in the local language was "Misabah a Mafomo."[32] Thus, it was probably the Mpfumans whom Captain White approached first when looking to trade.

If White followed the instructions of a later visitor, he would have laid out "a Tarpaulin or Carpett," placed his goods upon it, and waited until the leader of Mpfumo joined him upon it, perhaps with the princes waiting at a distance. Then, White would have presented him with some gifts, and the tit for tat of trade would have commenced.[33] Each side knew what the other desired. The British wanted ivory. They coveted it for what they could transform it into. They carved it into intricate pieces of art, shaped it into dice, transformed it into piano keys, formed the delicate frames of fashionable fans with it, and allowed it to anchor the hair of upper-class women. Traders also wanted ambergris, produced in the bowels of sperm whale, as a spice and as a fixative for perfume. Traders found it wherever sperm whales traveled, and the coast of East Africa was a prime location from which to gather it.[34] The Mpfumans also knew that a European crew might hunt for the whales that often took shelter in the bay.[35]

In return, the people of Mpfumo wanted, according to one observer, "Glass-beads, Knives, Scizers, Needles, Thread and small Looking-glasses." These, he stated, "they are very fond of."[36] Another European visitor related that they wanted brass, beads, and cloth and that they were picky: "The Brass

must be made into round Collars just fit for their Necks, bright and well pol-
ished," and the beads "yellow or deep blew and a pearl colour'd white, all of
the bigness of a white pea."[37] For both sides this was a luxury trade. Just as the
Europeans did not *need* any of the Mpfuman goods, the Mpfumans did not
need the European goods. No one starved if a cargo of ivory and ambergris
did not make it to port, and the societies around the bay would not have
fallen apart without beads and mirrors. These goods were not necessary on
either side, but they were desired.[38]

Later reports suggest that it was through these trading rituals that the two
princes came to know White. He had them and the ruler of Mpfumo on board
his ship. There he "[entertained] them with great Civilityes."[39] Such attention
was not unusual on the African coast. Traders often brought local notables on
board ship during their stay to curry favor. It was part of the dance of trade. A
Dutch ship anchored in Madagascar around the same time was sure to invite
the king and his family on board. The captain served them wine, "caressed
their ears with our Dutch music," and gave the wives cloth as a party favor.[40]
Similarly, slave-trading captains on the west coast of Africa often hosted gath-
erings of the power players aboard ship, where wine flowed freely.[41] In fact,
in 1688 an English author published the story of a fictional African prince,
Oroonoko, who was enslaved when an immoral captain invited him onto his
ship for dinner and served him "all sorts of fine wines" before clapping him
and his followers in irons.[42] The Mpfumans did not know this story, but they
still might have been wary of these strangers bearing gifts. Thirty years before,
Englishmen had taken local leaders captive when they came aboard to inspect
a ship.[43] But this seems not to have deterred the princes. And, while it is not
mentioned, the ruler of Mpfumo probably entertained White on shore in
exchange, perhaps with his own music and spirits.[44] Such interactions would
have strengthened the bond between White and the ruler of Mpfumo. By the
time the *Mercury* was ready to sail, the princes had hatched a plan.

While we are not privy to their thoughts, circumstances suggest that the
two men had decided that the best way to improve Mpfumo's standing in the
bay was to travel to London with White. There they would gain more knowledge and favor than their neighbors could dream of. According to British
accounts, they convinced the ruler of Mpfumo to give them leave "to Sail as
passengers under the Care of the said Captain White."[45] The deal appealed
to White, and he agreed. It did not hurt that the ruler then provided him
with "great Quantities of Elephant Teeth and Ambergreece."[46] One wonders
why these men were chosen. Had the princes gone on diplomatic missions

before? Were they deeply trusted envoys or were they men the ruler was happy to see far from his shores? Relatives of rulers often had a fragile and menacing position in the African societies around the bay. Uncles often took control from young princes, and brothers often deposed brothers.[47] The ruler of Mpfumo probably watched the two men warily.[48] They do not appear deeply integrated into their community at this point. No mention is made of them having wives or children, the sign of power and maturity in this society. Such ties would have made it difficult to contemplate leaving for a long voyage. They were old enough to have established themselves more solidly, though. According to numbers later provided by the British, Prince James was around twenty-four years old in 1716, when they boarded the *Mercury*, and his brother, John, was not yet twenty.[49] They probably lived in the ruler of Mpfumo's village at his beck and call.[50] But they probably thought less about improving their own lot and more about improving that of their kinship group. These ties, not individual interests, were the main nodes of power and consideration in most African polities.[51] Perhaps the ruler of Mpfumo suggested they go on this voyage.

Taking high-status Africans on board a ship bound for Europe was hardly novel. For centuries African rulers had been sending their sons and relatives to Europe as diplomats or as individuals in search of knowledge.[52] The Temme kings, who ruled what is now Sierra Leone toward the end of the seventeenth century, received a Jesuit education in Portugal, and in 1701 the ruler of Bonny, what is now Nigeria, sent his nephew to London to, he hoped, further the Niger trade.[53] Especially on the west coast, many members of the African elite knew that their wealth and status hinged on the control of trade with Europeans and that more knowledge of these interlopers would strengthen their hold on it. European products had become signs of status, and European connections signs of power. Sending sons and relatives to Britain was a way to strengthen these ties and to gain information on the other nation.[54] It also allowed rulers to manipulate the competing Europeans. One ruler sent one of his sons to Britain and another to France to gain traction with these powers, all the while knowing that due to their matrilineal family structure neither son would become very powerful, dashing European hopes of influence through the men.[55]

The Mpfuman princes' decision to travel to London would have made sense to the British elite as well. Traipsing across continents and countries in search of new knowledge and new social polish was the mark of a well-educated member of the British elite in the early eighteenth century. The

Grand Tour, as the British termed the elite parade through the capitals of Europe, gained in popularity as the eighteenth century rolled along.[56] On it, young noblemen saw new countries, in their eyes became more civilized, and judged the attributes of their European competitors. One of the princes' eventual supporters, Sir John Perceval, set out "on his travels abroad and saw a good part of Europe" at the age of twenty-two.[57] He too was curious about the world beyond his own shores and he too faced danger on his travels. At one point, he barely escaped being taken captive when a French or Turkish privateer menaced the ship he was on.[58] The British would play up the princes' disinterested curiosity when telling their tale. British sources held that the men had a "desire to see England," a craving "to see new Countrys," or a longing to see "the grandeur of the King of great Brittain."[59] Framing the princes' motivation for the voyage in this way drew parallels between the princes and the British elite. Such parallels had their limits, though. Princes they might be, but, for the British, they still came from a barbarous land.

The line between the princes and enslaved Africans was probably always thin in Captain White's mind. He had been a slave trader on the West African coast. Elite Africans had probably been on board his ship before, and such guests were not always free to leave. African leaders on the west coast sometimes followed the practice of "pawnage," where people under their rule were held as hostages by other powers until a debt was paid. In the case of the transatlantic slave trade, this usually meant until the enslaved Africans the Europeans had purchased were loaded aboard. At times, European traders kidnapped those pawns and sold them into slavery.[60] Moreover, there is an interesting statement in the Dutch archives that notes that, after Prince John's return, the African leaders declared that the Dutch should allow them to kill the British because they were "the ones who had taken their uncle and other people away from here."[61] While the returning prince had not previously been referred to as an uncle, it does seem that people had been kidnapped in the past. Thus, it is not outside the realm of possibility that the princes might have been unwilling passengers.

Nonetheless, most documents support the view that the princes boarded the *Mercury* voluntarily as high-ranking men, blind to the fact that White might see them differently. They brought gifts and six or seven attendants to travel with them and attend to their needs.[62] These men expected to be treated as honored passengers; the idea that they could be enslaved was probably unfathomable to them at this point. If they had lived on the west coast of Africa, their attitude might have been different. But the trade in enslaved bodies had yet to seep its way deeply into Mpfumo and would not become embedded in the economy until much later.[63] No sources mention the purchase of enslaved people from the bay until the Dutch tried and failed to introduce the trade in the 1720s.[64] We do get glimmers, however, that Europeans were beginning to see southeast Africa as a place to trade in enslaved Africans. In 1708, for example, Thomas Bowrey listed "Negro Slaves" among the "present products for trade" there, and six years later another ship pondered purchasing enslaved Africans there.[65] But there is no evidence that the slave trade existed in the bay at the time of the princes' voyage, and even if it did, it consisted of isolated exchanges that did not define the way the people of the bay thought about trade with the Europeans. They may have been asked to sell people and may have had an idea of the trade in enslaved bodies in Madagascar, but it did not dominate their trade.[66] Once the princes boarded the *Mercury*, they even may have seen implements of the slave trade on board, but they would not have connected them to their own fate.

Such implements signaled the desire for enslaved bodies that caused White to voyage into the Indian Ocean. By the early eighteenth century, the trade in enslaved African bodies was well established in the Atlantic.[67] The harsh climate and labor demands of the Caribbean plantations created a charnel house for those enslaved, especially the newly arrived. Only a quarter to a half survived their first three years in the West Indies.[68] Those who traded in enslaved Africans fed the constant demand for men, women, and children that emanated from the planters looking to keep their populations steady. This kind of chattel slavery, and the profits it attached to Black bodies, would have surprised the princes. But it was this desire that caused White to look for permission to trade in enslaved labor in Madagascar and it took him to Mpfumo.

For White, Mpfumo was only a stop on the way to his real goal: Madagascar. For most European traders, Madagascar—about eight hundred miles from Mpfumo across what is today known as the Mozambique Channel—was an outpost for supplies and an eastern entrepôt for the trade in enslaved bodies. Unlike the Mpfumans, the Malagasy had long been entangled with the trade. Swahili-Arab traders, known as the Antalaotra, came to Madagascar and started a number of settlements in the late sixteenth century in the northwest of the island. They brought enslaved Malagasy to locations around the Indian Ocean world.[69] Through their hands enslaved people and goods from Madagascar found their way to the Swahili coast, southern Arabia, and the Comoros.[70] Throughout the seventeenth century the Antalaotra annually exported around three thousand enslaved Malagasy.[71] Then Europeans began to trade in enslaved Malagasy. The Dutch needed labor for their expanding settlement at the Cape and on islands like Mauritius. The white inhabitants of the Cape faced chronic labor shortages, and the local populations did not fill their needs; and so they turned to Madagascar, which lay close at hand and had a slave-trading infrastructure.[72] Many a Dutch ship made the relatively short journey. The British also needed enslaved labor within the Indian Ocean basin. The East India Company brought enslaved Malagasy to their holdings in places like St. Helena and Bengkulu, their foothold in Sumatra, known to the English as Bencoolen.[73] Demand also came from the west. British slave-trading voyages to Madagascar peaked twice during this period: once from the 1670s through 1698 and once from 1716 to 1721.[74] The first push was cut short in 1698 when the East India Company's rights to restrict trade through its monopoly were reasserted and it clamped down on the merchants who were trading in the area.[75] The second push would give birth the voyage of the *Mercury*.

London, England, 1715

It was the East India Company's need for enslaved bodies that first brought Thomas White into their orbit. In the years preceding his meeting with the princes, the company's officials at St. Helena, an island in the middle of the South Atlantic, often asked their superiors to send them more enslaved laborers.[76] The company's first solution to this request was to send enslaved people from the West African coast.[77] In October 1713, they accepted a proposal from the owner of a slave-trading ship to deliver fifty or sixty enslaved West Africans to St. Helena.[78] In the end, they received forty-three enslaved Africans from a ship named the *Mercury*.[79] The captain of the ship was Thomas White.[80]

In St. Helena, White became aware the East India Company's desire for enslaved bodies, and now this West African slave trader began to look eastward. In July 1715 he applied to the company "for leave to proceed with two Ships, and a Sloop with a proper Cargo to Madagascar, and Delagoa to purchase Slaves & Elephants Teeth to be carried from thence to The West India Plantations."[81] The company rejected his proposal in less than a month.[82] White's request that he "purchase Slaves . . . to be carried from thence to the West India Plantations" would never be approved. The company's charter forbade it from transferring goods directly from the east to British colonies in the west. Everything had to pass through Britain. The government allowed the company to be the sole British traders to the east, on the condition that those goods be "brought to some port of Great Britain and there put on shore."[83] The "West India Plantations" spoken of by White were not a "port of Great Britain." The company's monopoly gave bite to its requests to the government to clamp down on pirates and unlicensed traders in the area and its officials did not wish to risk it. White's proposal was tempting, however.

The captain did not give up. He simply got sneaky. In October, White submitted his proposal again. This time, however, he left out a number of telling details. He asked for a license for three ships and a sloop "to trade to Delagoa & Madagascar, for Whale Fishing, Teeth, and other Commodityes of said places."[84] Two ships had become three, enslaved Africans had become "other commodityes," and the West Indies had dropped from sight. Suddenly, the voyage became a possibility, and it was the addition of Delagoa (Maputo), not a stop on the slave trading circuit, that made it credible. If it was "Whale Fishing" and "Teeth" a trader was after, it was to Maputo he went, not Madagascar. White had crafted a credible smoke screen for what the phrase "other Commodityes" stood for.

Those "other Commodityes" still worried the company men. So, when they received White's second proposal, they decided they had to seek legal opinions on the charter and slavery. White's proposal soon graced the desks of John Hungerford, the East India Company's legal counsel, and Edward Northey, the attorney general. The first query the company had for its advisers was whether it could "grant such a License knowing beforehand that the Ship intends to proceed from Madagascar to the West Indies & there deliver her Slaves."[85] Company officials knew that allowing White to ship human cargo from Madagascar to the West Indies was against the rules laid down in their charter. The lawyers gave them a slippery solution. Northey agreed that "it will not be proper for the Company to grant a Licence to send a Ship to Madagascar for purchasing of Slaves for the use of the West India plantations." "But," he added (and it was a pretty big but), there was no reason the officials could not license a ship to trade with Madagascar "within the Limits of their Charter" and to trade for goods "generally." This, Northey thought, would "be better than expressly to license the trading for Slaves."[86] The message was clear—vagueness would be the officials' guide. They were simply licensing the ship to trade within their sphere of influence. If that ship's captain happened to trade for enslaved people and happened to take those captives to the West Indies, the infraction would be his, not theirs. As

Hungerford, who agreed wholeheartedly with Northey, said, if trouble raised its head, "the Trader and not the Company is answerable for it."[87] For the company, the less detail written down, the better.[88]

The need for secrecy and plausible deniability on the matter of destination and cargo mooted the importance of the company's second query, about the status of enslaved bodies. It does show, however, the company's deep knowledge of and engagement with the slave trade. The officials asked the legal minds "whether the words—Goods Wares Merchandizes and Commoditys may be construed to include Slaves."[89] Seemingly, debate had sprung up about the status of the enslaved. Were they really the same as the other commodities that the company's monopoly forbade to be imported straight to the colonies? The moral niceties of seeing human beings as goods did not motivate or even surface in this discussion, but the officials did feel that enslaved people were different from calicoes or spices. Like their concerns, the legal answers were nebulous. Northey stated that enslaved people were certainly seen as commodities in the North American colonies and in the Caribbean. He stated that even in England if individuals stole enslaved persons, they would be liable to pay damages to the original owners. Here he was relying on a legal decision made in 1677, which did define the enslaved as property in England. He could, however, also have turned to a legal decision from 1696 which said the opposite, that in England no man could own another as property. What the East India Company sensed was that the legal status of the enslaved in England was unstable, and perhaps they saw this as an opening for reimagining the status of the enslaved with regard to the company's charter.[90] Northey even stated that he did not think that enslaved people were "within the intent" of the act passed to define the company's charter. Hungerford concurred. He admitted, "It is certain that Slaves are in some cases accounted Chattells and part of a Mans personal estate. But it is as certain that they are neither Silks or Callicoes or any of the Goods or Merchandizes intended by the two Million Act."[91] The understanding of the enslaved as commodities rather than human beings, which was so central to chattel slavery, was unsettled, but not enough to cause any concern about engaging in the trade.

As soon as the company granted White his license, the savvy merchant community of London caught wind of this new opportunity. White's strategic silences fooled no one. Suddenly requests for licenses deluged the company. William Heysham and his company, who were active Atlantic slave traders, wanted a license to trade with Madagascar.[92] In late February of 1716, John Merewether asked for one, and less than a month later Sir Randolph Knipe and Sir John Fryer requested the freedom to send their ship "to Madagascar or Mozambickque for negroes."[93] Though Merewether's name disappears from the records, Heysham, Knipe, and Fryer got their licenses.[94] As soon as the company granted them, however, they slammed the door of opportunity shut by resolving to "not grant Licence for this year to any other private Persons to trade to Madagascar."[95] In the end, the ships given permission to trade to Madagascar included the *Mercury* and its sloop, the *Henry*, the *Drake*, the *Sarah Galley*, and the *Hamilton*.[96]

The discussions regarding the terms of these licenses make it clear that these voyages were for enslaved labor and that the East India Company was well versed in the ways of the slave trade. William Heysham tried to use his deep knowledge of the Atlantic trade to get better terms. He first offered to pay the company 8 percent of the value of his outward cargo for the privilege to trade. The company frowned on this, and he raised his offer to 10 percent. To justify this number, Heysham reminded the company that 10 percent was "the most that was ever paid to the African company for a Voyage of the like nature." He reminded the company officials that the voyage to Madagascar was not only longer but also more dangerous than that to the West African coast, and thus their payment for the license should be less.[97] It was to the Royal African Company, which had once held the monopoly on the slave trade to the West African coast, that he turned for comparison, and it was the trade on the West African coast that served as a point of reference. The East India Company did not accept the comparison, and the lowest it offered was 20 percent.[98]

As negotiations proceeded, it became clear that the company officials had continued to think about slavery. They had plantation societies to supply. And, as White knew, St. Helena was desperate for enslaved labor.[99] The East India Company had begun a settlement there in 1659 to offer an alternative stop to the Dutch settlement at the Cape. The company also established it as an experimental plantation colony that could link east and west.[100] The results did not live up to expectations, and the colony never became as prosperous or as central to shipping as the Cape. They were not self-sustaining, and goods from Europe, or elsewhere, were in short supply. They also needed enslaved labor. Plantations bespeckled the island, and suspected rebellions by the enslaved haunted the imaginations of its slaveholders.[101] Few slave-trading voyages stopped at the island, however, and their need for enslaved labor grew.

The East India Company had not forgotten the needs of St. Helena. Sparked by the discussions surrounding the licenses and the silent presence of enslaved labor in the negotiations, the committee in charge of the licenses put the desires of St. Helena together with the plans of the merchants. In March 1716 they offered two ideas to the Court of Directors: one, the private traders could pay 20 percent on the value of their outgoing cargo or, two, they could deliver a designated number of enslaved Malagasy to St. Helena, determined by the value of their cargo.[102] It was the second option that the court embraced.

The directors were not, however, finished with discussing the people they sought to buy and sell. Numbers came next. How many enslaved bodies should the private traders leave in St. Helena? How many pounds sterling worth of cargo equaled a human life? The company was unsure. Perhaps one enslaved individual for every £50? The number seemed low to some. Nine enslaved individuals for every £500, or about £55 per person, suggested another voice. This made sense, and the directors inked it onto the license. One dilemma remained: What if the values did not work out smoothly? What if the ship owed a fraction of a person? They found a horrifying answer: "In case the sum to be sent out should make it a fractionall part, That then the Master is to deliver a Boy or Girl instead of a grown Person."[103]

Once the directors had decided upon the number, they discussed quality. They knew the ships' captains would try to use this directive to unload undesirable enslaved Malagasy and decided to prevent this up front. The enslaved laborers, besides the fractional children, should be in the prime of their lives or between sixteen and thirty years of age. Men should outnumber women by a third. Furthermore, they should "be all Natives of Madagascar, and sound and healthy and every way merchantable."[104] The governor of the island was to stand as judge, and if the ship was short of enslaved Malagasy, then the license holders owed the company thirty pounds per head. Next came the vote; it was "Resolved that this Court do approve thereof."[105] In the end, the governor of St. Helena was told to expect between six and seventeen enslaved men and women from each licensed ship, depending on its size.[106] After a week more of haggling, the licenses became official.

The dispatches sent to officials in St. Helena around this time reveal the deep thought the company put into how to manage a slave society. It was important to them that their officials there recognized that the enslaved were rational human beings. Twice they told officials to "Remember they are Men."[107] They recommended that no one but overseers should strike the enslaved and that overseers should not "tyrannize over them." The enslaved should have Sundays off, should not be overworked, and should be given adequate food and clothing. The officials believed that since the enslaved "are endued with reason as well as you and they can discern the difference between Wrong and Right," such treatment would create a docile enslaved population. For if they were to rebel after such "rational" treatment "they will stand self condemned in their own consciences."[108] Here the enslaved were not only numbers and fractional objects but also rational beings. This recognition of their humanity, however, was deployed to control the population of enslaved laborers, not to question the morality of the institution. In fact, the company officials wanted the enslaved to be complicit in justifying their status—they should use their rational minds to see that they should not resist and to grasp that they were part of a rational system of labor management. While the officials may have seen the enslaved as human, they did not see them as equals and they did not question the institution of slavery.

Eavesdropping on the East India Company's discussions about slavery also highlights the diversity of people the company enslaved. Men, women, and children from West Africa were sent to St. Helena, as were those from Madagascar. The company transported enslaved Malagasy to Bengkulu, where they also brought enslaved people from throughout South Asia.[109] The island of Nias, off the coast of Sumatra, had provided enslaved labor to their settlement at Bengkulu since 1705, and areas of the Indian subcontinent had provided enslaved labor for the settlement since the seventeenth century.[110] As one scholar has noted, "The Atlantic trades consumed mostly Africans, while those in the Indian Ocean drew in men, women, and children from a multitude of ethnic and cultural backgrounds in South and Southeast Asia as well as eastern and western Africa."[111] Slavery here did not just mean the enslavement of Africans. This complicates the idea of race-based slavery. Much ink has been spilled determining how Europeans justified the enslavement of Africans, but here we are reminded of the diversity of the peoples Europeans enslaved and how generalizing blackness was one way to ease the divide. The enslaved Malagasy were not just called "slaves," they were also referred to as "Madagascar Blacks."[112]

East India Company officials did believe that certain peoples made better enslaved laborers, however. Since the 1680s the company had seen enslaved Malagasy as desirable. They were believed to be more intelligent and productive.[113] When instructing its officials in Bengkulu about the enslaved Malagasy who would be arriving, a company representative said that the officials there should not use them as footmen or servants, because "they being able body'd can better perform the more laborious employs than the Nais or Coast or other Indian Slaves."[114] The officials at St. Helena preferred enslaved Malagasy to enslaved West Africans. When White arrived in St. Helena with enslaved Malagasy, slaveholders there exchanged a number of enslaved West Africans for the newly arrived Malagasy. White, however, did not share their beliefs. He held that the enslaved from the West African coast were more valuable than the enslaved Malagasy.[115] Another slave trader concurred, stating the enslaved from Africa were "better Slaves for working, than those of *Madagascar*, being stronger, also blacker."[116] Thus, a broad link between blackness and enslavement, which stretched beyond Africa, provided a way for the British to think about the enslavement of a very diverse set of people; but that diversity still mattered, and it changed the fates of those enslaved.

Morondava, Madagascar, 1716

When White and the princes arrived at Morondava in the Kingdom of Menabe, located in the center of Madagascar's western coast, they found that another ship had arrived before them. Captain William Mackett of the *Drake* had not stopped in Mpfumo, and thus by the time the *Mercury* arrived he was already deeply engaged in trading for enslaved Malagasy.[117] He had also ransomed an English sailor, Robert Drury, who had been shipwrecked and then enslaved on the island for fifteen years. Drury, in an account of his time on Madagascar, published in 1729 (fig. 3), noted the arrival of the princes and their attendants.[118] He observed that when the ship "call'd *The Mercury*, Capt. White, Commander," arrived in Madagascar, it had "on Board eight or nine Natives of Dillagoe in Africa, who liv'd very merrily."[119] Whether that sense of merriment faded during the four to five months they spent in Madagascar we will never know. But this was their first look at the workings of an established trade in enslaved peoples.[120]

Learning about the slave trade in Madagascar would have differed from being introduced to it on the western coast of Africa. If White had gone northward, they would have seen a much more culturally diverse trade. There Arab, Asian, and African traders jockeyed with Europeans for enslaved Malagasy and other goods.[121] But farther south, in Menabe, the princes were unlikely to have seen these competitors, and here the trade in enslaved Malagasy did not dominate the economy. For the most part, rulers throughout Madagascar looked to sell foodstuffs and provisions rather than enslaved Malagasy.[122] It was often hard for slave traders to fill their ships.[123] Many spent months

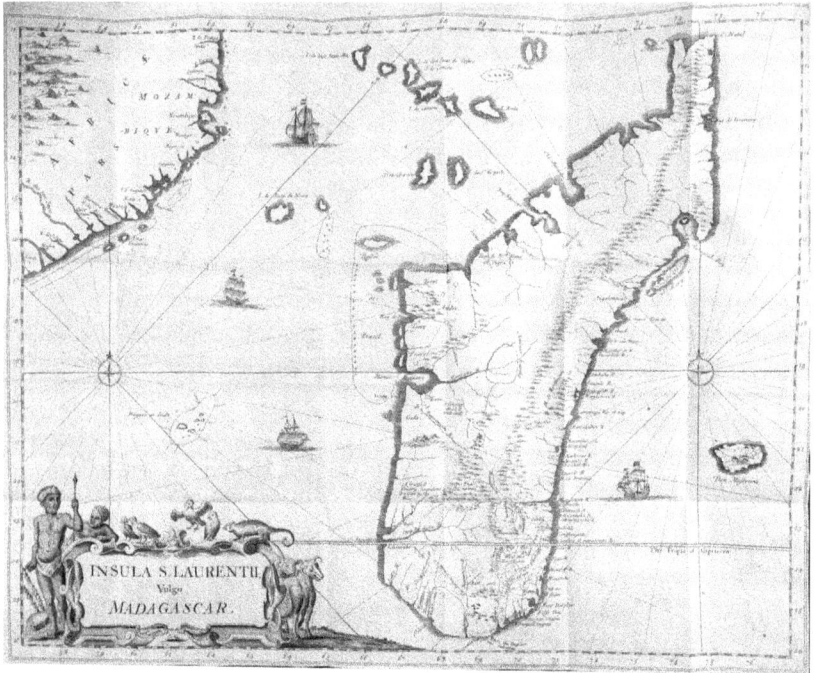

Figure 3. When Robert Drury's journal was published in 1729, a map of Madagascar was included toward the front of the book. It was large and had to be
unfolded. The way the ships sailing near Madagascar are dwarfed by the island
brings home the large size and, thus, geographic and political diversity of Madagascar. Robert Drury, *Madagascar: Or Robert Drury's Journal* (London, 1729),
HEH RB 122787. Reproduced by permission of the Huntington Library, San
Marino, California.

sailing up and down the coast searching for rulers who could fulfill their
needs. Drury and Mackett left Morondava soon after the *Mercury* arrived, to
search for more enslaved Malagasy in the north at Massaliege in the Kingdom of Boina. To their disappointment, they found no trade could be done
until the king returned from the wars he was waging.[124] They waited. It took a
month for him to return. Then they waited another month to acquire enough
enslaved Malagasy to fill their hold.[125] In the end, the ruler at Massaliege had
more than enough captives to sell, but it was a slow business. Back in Morondava, White was struggling to find enough Malagasy to buy. When Drury and
Mackett returned, they found White still trying to get his "his Complement of

Slaves."[126] Thus, though a trade in enslaved bodies happened in Madagascar, it was on a smaller scale, less integrated into the economy, and more international in flavor than that on the western coast of Africa.

The trade was in flux during this period, though. The rulers whom White, Mackett, and possibly the princes encountered controlled the Sakalava kingdoms, which were reconfiguring life on the western coast of Madagascar. Their power had originated in the kingdom of Menabe, in the center of the western coast, but soon scions of the royal family were pushing both northward and southward. This expansion was fueled by royal rivalries. Near the end of the seventeenth century, the ruler of Menabe expelled two of his brothers who threatened his rule. One went south, seeking to establish a power base near Saint-Augustin Bay. The other brother went north and eventually established the Sakalava kingdom of Boina, displacing and then incorporating the Muslim merchants who provided access to the trading worlds of the Comoros and the Swahili coast.[127] This expansion changed the power structures in this area and altered the trade in enslaved Malagasy. Unsurprisingly, it was during their rise that the trade in enslaved Malagasy with Europeans peaked—both in the later seventeenth century and again in the early eighteenth.[128]

The upheaval these conflicts caused led to the capture of more people who could be sold into slavery and, even more significantly, led to economic instability in many areas, which caused communities to sell their enslaved people due to the lack of other goods to exchange.[129] Drury directly connects this warfare with the growth of the trade in the enslaved, stating, "The epidemical Evil of this Island is, Their *frequent Quarrels with one another*; and the very cause so many of them are sold to the *Europeans* for Slaves."[130] It was also around this time that Malagasy rulers began to demand guns from those who desired enslaved Malagasy.[131] These firearms may have exacerbated these conflicts. Drury did recall a Sakalava prince declaring that it was due to "English-men's Guns" that they overcame their enemies.[132] But many of the guns the Sakalava received seem to have served ceremonial purposes, rather than being transformative weapons in the wars of expansion.[133] Nonetheless, Mackett and White arrived at an opportune time to fill their holds with enslaved Malagasy.

The origins of the enslaved Malagasy who ended up in chains aboard the *Drake* and the *Mercury* are obscure. Drury himself is vague on who these enslaved were. When Europeans came to trade, Drury simply stated that "Slaves were sent down to be sold" or that a ruler was eager to trade, "he having a great many Slaves to sell."[134] While slavery was deeply embedded in Malagasy

society, it appears that most rulers sold those who were not their own dependents but came from other communities farther inland. To the south, near
Saint-Augustin Bay, the rulers usually relied upon inland trading networks; the
enslaved from those areas would make their way to the coast with rice, cattle,
or other provisions and, in turn, be sold to the Europeans.[135] To the north, the
Sakalava rulers expanded their control of inland kingdoms, demanding tribute,
which often included enslaved Malagasy.[136] But during their wars of expansion
it appears that a number of those sold were captives taken in war.[137] This would
have been a change, since in the past most men taken captive in war were killed
or ransomed back to their people.[138] Thus, those trapped in the holds of these
British ships had already traveled a long and hard road, and that journey was
about to take a turn for the worse.

As the princes and their attendants watched either from the deck of the
Mercury or from the shore, they would have had a glimpse of the Malagasy
slave trade at work. On the coast there would have been several huts built by
locals to provide milk and other provisions for the Europeans, and a number
of the crew would have been on shore to manage makeshift structures they
had erected for the incoming human cargo. Then the princes would have witnessed as the crew brought these men, women, and children on board the
Mercury. They must have been present as the crew jammed these individuals
into the hold. There is no record of the number of enslaved people held
within the *Mercury* on this voyage, but a few years later, in 1720, it carried
674 enslaved Malagasy to Virginia, 466 of whom survived.[139] Next, the ship
would have set sail for St. Helena. The princes must have heard the groans
that emanated from the hold during the voyage, the songs of lamentation.
Every day as the ship moved around the Cape towards St. Helena, they must
have watched as the sailors herded the women and children unshackled onto
the quarter deck and gathered the men onto the main deck, chains intact.[140]
They would have watched the frenzied fight for food. Have observed as some,
bent on survival, desperately reached for the buckets of gruel thrust at the
huddled groups. Have seen as others ignored the buckets and fought not to
eat. They would have witnessed these resisters having their mouths pried
open and food jammed into them or facing the lash for their refusal.[141] Next,
the princes would have watched as the slavers played music and insisted the
enslaved move to keep up their physical condition. Perhaps they saw some
who danced to express their fury and their desperation and perhaps they
shivered when the crew cracked the whip at those who remained immo-
bile.[142] The violence and horror of the voyage would not have been hidden

from them. As the days rolled by, the horrors of European slavery would have become increasingly clear. And when the princes arrived in St. Helena and White unloaded the enslaved Malagasy the East India Company had demanded, they would have understood, to a degree, that Europeans saw the people in the hold not as human beings but as objects to be bought and sold. What did the princes think of these discoveries? Did they feel a sense of connection with those in the hold? A throb of pity? Or would their sense of themselves as honored guests, as men apart, have caused them to dismiss it all? One thing is for certain, worry and concern should have crept in, if not for the fate of those shackled below them, then for their own.

CHAPTER 2

Being Enslaved

Port Royal Harbor, Jamaica, 1717

When the princes first glimpsed Jamaica from the *Mercury*, the island may have looked inviting. As a contemporary observed, "At a little Distance, this Island makes a grand Appearance, the high-rising Mountains ever green, and cover'd with Wood" (fig. 4).[1] But for all its beauties, Jamaica was a dark place. Even before the princes stepped on shore its dependence on enslaved bodies would have been revealed to them. As soon as the ship anchored, word circulated about the new ship with enslaved Malagasy. Next, small boats approached the *Mercury*, holding the wealthiest slave owners and officials wanting to make a purchase.[2] The crew then brought the enslaved Malagasy who had survived the journey to the deck, where the Jamaican buyers inspected them like cattle and chose the most ideal for themselves.

Whether the princes knew it or not, this was the point where the line between them and the men and women in the hold was beginning to erode. According to a later newspaper account, when the Jamaican planters saw the princes, they saw enslavable bodies—desirable ones at that. The princes would have felt the calculating eyes upon them, estimating their age, tracing their unravaged physiques, adding up their price. The planters thought the princes were "of a better personage and Look than the others," and they pestered Captain White with offers. Luckily for the princes, White held his ground, and his "Answer was made, That they were not to be Sold, as the other Negroes were."[3]

The princes' status appeared clear. But, if you listen closely, according to the newspaper, they were not princes, they were now, at least linguistically, lumped with "the other Negroes." They watched from their lofty (albeit increasingly unstable) perch as a factor (broker) cleared the ship of the rest

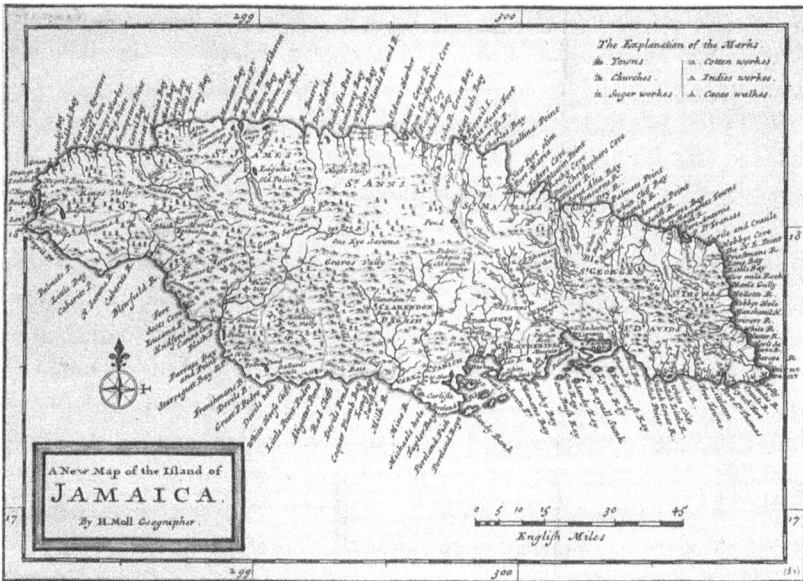

Figure 4. This map gives a view of Jamaica as it was during the princes' enslavement. The fact that it was made in the 1720s speaks to the growing interest in the island as its sugar production began to grow. Herman Moll, *A New Map of Jamaica* (London, c. 1720), Huntington Library, HEH Rare Books 183337. Reproduced by permission of the Huntington Library, San Marino, California.

of the captive Malagasy, whom White sold at a public auction. Meanwhile, it appears that he allowed the princes to move freely.[4] The future looked bright for the two men. The longest part of their journey had been completed. They were seeing places and meeting people that their rivals back home could not imagine. And soon they would be off to London. Or so they thought.

White's need to turn a profit got in the way. According to a newspaper report, the sole detailed account of the princes' time in Jamaica, "one Day being on Shore to divert themselves, they saw their Ship under Sail, going out of the Port-Royal Harbour, and walk'd towards her, along the Sea-side, thinking the Master would every Minute send the Boat on Shore for them." This was not to be. The two men then "retir'd to the Town in very Great Concern." Their worry was not misplaced. White and his factor had hatched a plan. They had agreed that once the *Mercury* was loaded with cargo and ready to set sail, White would send the princes ashore and he would weigh anchor and sail to London. That time had come. Once the princes returned to town, the factor collected them and then sold them to the highest bidder. In the end, the two men were sold for "about 40 pistoles each," which was almost double the average price paid for an enslaved man or women at the time.[5]

Why did White change his mind? We will never really know. He was not taken to task for his actions or given a chance to explain them. By the late summer of 1719 he was dead. He perished on the French island of Réunion on his next slave-trading voyage to the Indian Ocean.[6] This meant no one could question him when the princes' story came to light in London in 1720. We are left with suppositions. His decision probably boiled down to money. The *Mercury* had arrived in Jamaica at an inauspicious time. It was often difficult to sell enslaved laborers in late June. The harvest was over, and the demand was not strong.[7] Furthermore, William Mackett and the *Drake* had just left after selling its cargo of enslaved Malagasy, possibly flooding the market.[8] White also arrived in a year when prices for enslaved individuals were abnormally low. Scholars estimate that between 1715 and 1719 the average price was just over £18, the lowest estimated price during the entirety of the eighteenth century.[9] Most likely, White examined these numbers, looked at the princes and their attendants, and decided that they were more valuable as enslaved bodies. Whether he considered his own profit or that of the ship's owners is unclear.[10] Perhaps he did not get a full complement of enslaved Malagasy and needed to make the voyage more profitable for the owners, so they would employ him in the future, or perhaps the princes were his own guests and he decided he would make more profit selling them rather than displaying them as curiosities in London. The specific details are lost to time and forever debatable.

In fact, Robert Drury, the shipwrecked sailor who had been ransomed in Madagascar, made a statement that redeems White's character on this point. After his return to London, Drury decided to go to sea again after hearing that Captain White and the *Mercury* were to return to Madagascar. They set sail in September 1718.[11] They arrived at the Cape of Good Hope the next April and, a few days later, laid anchor along the coast of Natal, far south of Mpfumo. Here they sold trade goods and took on board some enslaved Africans. They left more than brass rings and beads on that coast, however. According to Drury, "Captain White put on Shoar here six Natives of Dillagoe, which he took with him the former Voyage." He provided them with "Guns, Ammunition, Hatchets, and brass Collars," as "they had two or three Kings Dominions to go thorow, before they came to their own Country, and were in some Fear they might be intercepted."[12] This observation complicates things. Could the princes' Jamaican story be a hoax? It is possible, but not likely. Other sources assert that a relative of the ruler of Mpfumo did return to his homeland in 1723 on a ship named the *Northampton*, and that the relative was known as John.[13]

All told, the evidence about the princes' time in Jamaica is sparse and sometimes contradictory. The most detailed account of their time in Jamaica comes from a London paper, the *Weekly Journal: or, British Gazetteer*, published in late 1720, about two years after the princes' initial enslavement. While the article survives in a London paper, it does assert that it had first been published in a Jamaican newspaper, although a copy of that paper does not survive.[14] While other sources corroborate many of the details in the London article, some aspects conflict with other sources, casting doubt on its credibility. The report begins by stating that White, who was trading in Madagascar (not Mpfumo), "became accidentlly acquainted with two Sons, and two Nephews, of a King of some Part of the Country," whom he agreed to take to Britain.[15] The name of the captain is correct, and the general story matches. But there are now four high-ranking men from Madagascar and not Mpfumo, and it never mentions the rest of the attendants Drury saw on board. The waxing and waning of the number of Mpfumans, along with Drury's assertation that six made it back to Africa earlier, causes concern, as does the fact that the article assumes the men were from Madagascar. The general approach of the report, however, presents a picture of Jamaica that is compatible with what scholars know of life on the island at the time.

It is not surprising that White would sell the two men, for when the *Mercury* entered the Caribbean the status and worth of the princes altered. In Africa they were worth more to White as princes, as men who could ease the give-and-take of trade. In Britain, their social status would give them value. There African princes were curiosities and men who could be valuable trading connections. Those in the metropole had been deeply involved in discussing the best way to organize the slave trade for the past twenty years at least. Debates had raged in Parliament and in the press over who should control the trade: an organized monopoly, in this case the Royal African Company, or independent traders. In the end, the Royal African Company lost, and the independent traders came to dominate the trade.[16] These debates meant that Britons were well versed in the workings of the trade and would know the importance of elite African facilitators. In Britain, their princely status would outweigh their racial origin. But in Jamaica their princely status was valued much less than the labor they could provide. Here they became "Negroes." While the Indian Ocean world was shot through with different forms of enslavement, here there was one kind—and it was increasingly defined by race.

The princes arrived in Jamaica during a time of transition. The number of enslaved Africans almost doubled between 1700 and 1720, and Jamaica was becoming a key node in the slave trade.[17] During this period, Britain had been given the asiento, the right to ship enslaved laborers to the Spanish colonies, and soon Jamaica would become a way station in this trade, a place where ships full of enslaved Africans would stop before they were sent to the Spanish colonies. But this was still to come.[18] Sugar production was on the rise, however, and smaller landholdings were giving way to larger integrated plantations. Enslaved labor was the lifeblood of the colony. To strengthen their hold over enslaved Africans, the members of Jamaica's Assembly passed laws looking to separate the free from the enslaved via race.[19] Fissures still showed, however, in the wall separating white from Black. Free people of color walked the streets and had rights. They owned enslaved people. Furthermore, white Jamaicans were often related to these free people of color (and to those they enslaved). Racial identities blurred, and familial networks that crossed racial divides helped the colony function.[20] This remaining racial fluidity still existed when the princes arrived, although lines were hardening.

The majority of the enslaved population labored on plantations, which were growing in size.[21] The princes could have been enslaved on one of these. Sugar was becoming a more popular crop, but its dominance would come slowly. Jamaica, with its varied geographies, also produced ginger, cocoa, indigo, and cotton.[22] But all its plantations were dangerous places. Few enslaved people on a plantation lived to old age, especially those who worked in the fields. The horror of the work surfaces in plantation records. "A List of Negroes on Mesopotamia Estate" from 1762 lists two enslaved women, Leah and Margaritta, as having no hands.[23] Even in this horrific state, they still lived longer than most enslaved men and women. Records from the Mesopotamia estate note their existence in 1734. They had lived this horror for almost thirty years. In fact, they could have been at Mesopotamia when the princes arrived in Jamaica fourteen years before. The fate of these two women could have been the princes' story as well.

The princes' ability to tell their story and find someone to free them, however, indicates that they were not isolated on a plantation. It is more likely that they were enslaved in an urban setting or in a pen, where livestock were raised, near a city. If they did end up enslaved in Spanish Town, Port Royal, or Kingston, this was a slightly unusual fate for the two men. While enslaved men and women were a compact, mobile, and usually profitable investment for urban dwellers, especially for women, the princes' age and lack of skills would have been a hard sell.[24] They were not blacksmiths or coopers and, at around twenty or twenty-five years of age, were too old to be trained in these trades. They could have been put to work in the home, but even there their skills were lacking. They would have been more at home tending cattle and perhaps hunting, duties often given to young men in Mpfumo.[25] Perhaps they ended up watching livestock in a pen near a city.[26] It could be that their notoriety made them desirable as curiosities. Whatever the reason, if they were purchased by an urban dweller they would have been more in the public eye and in a space to push for their freedom, although this position could have made them vulnerable to surveillance and punishment.[27]

If the London newspaper account is to be believed, the two men did experience the violence often faced by the enslaved. Yet their enslavers punished them not because they rejected their enslaved status but rather because they did not see themselves as equal to other enslaved Africans. The *Weekly Journal* told its readers that "in the Time of their Slavery, being near 18 Months, they readily attended and obey'd their respective Masters." The newspaper also stated, however, that they "always treated the other Negroes with an Air of Scorn and Contempt, never conversing with them." This defiance and assertion of status caused white Jamaicans to act. The paper declared that "the Planters had been so often impos'd on by Stories of Slaves being Princes, so immediately determin'd this to be a Trick, and advis'd their Masters to have their Pride whipt out of them; accordingly they were frequently severely Lash'd."[28] The planters wanted the two men to accept their status as equal to that of other enslaved Africans. They sought to reduce their sense of difference and to assert control through violence. The princes, however, came from a place where degrees of status mattered more than the stark division between free and unfree. They would have identified themselves as elite men who should form ties with those above them, those with power, rather than with those they saw as occupying a lesser station. These African ideas of power could have allowed them to accept a relationship of dependency in which they would seek ties to their patron or those in power over forming relationships with others who faced enslavement.[29]

The British in London might have seen things differently as well. In London the play *Oroonoko*, adapted by Thomas Southerne in 1695 from Aphra Behn's 1688 novel, was quite popular.[30] It told the tragic story of Oroonoko, a noble African prince from Angola, who was sold into slavery by a captain he trusted. But from the moment the ship docked and the planters became aware of the prince's presence, the captain's actions were condemned by the characters the audience was supposed to admire in the play. Oroonoko was sold to the governor, who was absent from the colony, but Blanford, the governor's agent, assures Oroonoko that the governor "is too generous not to feel your wrongs" and that he himself will do all he can to "find the means to send you home again."[31] At first, Oroonoko did not mix and mingle with the other enslaved men and women, asserting, "I am above the rank of common Slaves." But after his patience with the white planters ran out, he did form a common cause with the other captives and led them in a revolt against the planters. The rebellion failed, however, due to the cowardliness of the other enslaved men, and he quickly saw the error of his ways. He lamented that he ever thought he "cou'd design to make those free Who were by Nature Slaves; Wretches design'd To be their Masters Dogs, and lick their Feet."[32] In British imaginings of enslavement, status was more important than race. Things were more complicated in Jamaica.

In the late seventeenth and early eighteenth centuries, white Jamaicans faced earthquakes, worried about invasions from without and attacks from within, and watched warily as the number of white residents fell and the size of the enslaved Black population grew. The island was an uneasy place.[33] This sense of strain among white Jamaicans augmented their desire to control their enslaved population. Between 1700 and 1720 the number of enslaved rose from 42,000 to 79,600. The white population remained relatively steady at around 7,300.[34] As a minority population who based their power on terror, whites were constantly haunted by the nightmare of revolt. As Charles Leslie, who published a history of Jamaica in 1740, stated of the enslaved: "They are so far superior in Number to the Whites, that one should think it would be unsafe, considering all Circumstances, to live amongst them."[35] White Jamaicans responded with violence. Leslie detailed horrific punishments. He saw "their Bodies all in a Gore of Blood, the Skin tore off their Backs with the cruel Whip" and reported that slave owners "beat Pepper and Salt in the Wounds."[36] With this before them, he pondered, it was no wonder the enslaved might rebel.[37] But he also saw the logic of white violence. He thought "such Severities may in some Shape be excused, when we consider the State of the Country." For how could the white population "live amidst such Numbers of Slaves, without . . . punishing their Faults with the utmost Severity."[38] Violence was a necessary tool of domination.[39] If they held this mind-set, it is no wonder that the planters had the princes "severely lash'd" for their pride.

The presence of maroon colonies, settlements of runaway enslaved laborers, amplified the planters' fear of enslaved men and women. Maroon communities had existed since the defeat of the Spanish. Those who had been enslaved by the Spanish on Jamaica fled to the interior of the island and began their own settlements. Soon enslaved men and women who had fled English plantations joined them or set up separate communities.[40] Small settlements dotted the island, but two groups dominated. The Leeward maroons lived on the western side of the island and included many formerly enslaved workers who had escaped from nearby parishes. Cudjoe, their leader, was centralizing his power in the early eighteenth century, and this worried white planters and the authorities in Spanish Town. The Windward maroons lived in the mountainous regions on the east end of the island. This group was less centralized, but their position, closer to the cultivated areas of the island, thrust them into conflict more regularly with the European population.[41] Thus, as planters began to expand outward toward untapped lands, they increasingly came into conflict with these maroon communities.

The Assembly passed a number of laws to try to destabilize the maroons. The Slave Act of 1696 looked to stop maroons by giving rewards to those who killed or captured formerly enslaved Africans who had left their plantations at least twelve months before.[42] By 1718 the Assembly was pressing to pass a bill "for the encouragement of voluntary parties to suppress rebellious and runaway negroes."[43] By the time the princes left the island, conflict with the maroons was escalating. As they sailed away, reinforcements hired by the governor of Jamaica arrived—in the form of Moskito Indians from the coast of Honduras.[44]

The governor had to call upon distant Indigenous allies because he had few white troops at his command, a fact that led to further anxieties on the part of the colonizers. This had been a problem before. At the end of the seventeenth century and into the next, European war after European war rolled through the Caribbean, and as hostile fleets roamed the sea the metropole left the colonies to defend themselves. If the French or Spanish invaded, Jamaicans had only their own militia to look to for defense. This was a problem because the population of white settlers was small and getting smaller. Between 1674 and 1720 the white population had dropped by more than six hundred people, from 7,768 to 7,100.[45] These diminishing numbers and their military implications worried the governors of Jamaica. Naval impressment, which would take white Jamaicans, caused great concern. They desperately needed such manpower and they complained to the metropolitan authorities.[46] Such complaints fell on deaf ears.

The threat of invasion, conflict with the maroon colonies, and the general discomfort with an enslaved majority caused the Jamaican Assembly to continuously promote white settlement in the colony. During the princes' time on the island, the Assembly was almost constantly proposing and debating such bills. In 1716, just before the princes arrived, it passed one bill to "encourage the bringing over and settling white people in this island."[47] In 1720 the governor joined the fray and suggested transporting settlers from the Virgin Islands to Jamaica for the island's "strength and security."[48] None of these plans made a dent in the numerical disparity between the white and Black populations or eased the fear of the maroons. White Jamaicans would continue to fret and tighten their control over the increasingly large enslaved African population while they looked to suppress the maroons, who threatened their growing plantations and tempted their enslaved laborers to flee.

Besides importing white settlers, another way to ease planter concerns was to increase the divide between the white and Black populations and strictly control the enslaved population. Laws drawing a line between white and Black had come early to Jamaica. In 1664 Jamaicans copied Barbados's slave code almost word for word. Then in 1681, in a law about servitude, racial language began to surface connecting servants to the white population.[49] When the slave code was revised in 1684, it was made clear that the enslaved were chattel, objects to exchange like livestock.[50] The next decade saw a number of uprisings by the enslaved, and so in 1696 more brutal laws were added. For example, an enslaved African who struck a white man or even thought of murdering a member of the white population would be executed.[51] The Assembly also passed deficiency bills, which stipulated that a number of white people, defined in proportion to the number of enslaved on the land, had to live on a plantation if the owner wished to avoid fines. Besides increasing the white population on plantations, these laws drew stricter lines between Black and white by defining who counted as white.[52] While these laws were often hard to enforce, the idea that whites and Blacks should be separate had gained traction.

This idea of racial separation did not always fit the realities of Jamaica. There was a relatively large population of free mixed-race Jamaicans and a community of free people of color. This group troubled white Jamaicans. On the one hand, many of these people were family, and they could serve as a bulwark against the rising number of enslaved. But, on the other hand, their race made them suspect. Would they, in a time of crisis, actually side with the white population?[53] White Jamaicans were unsure. At times, they drew free people of color closer. During the period the princes were in Jamaica, any man with an estate of more than £10 could vote.[54] In 1705 mixed-race free-man could earn privileges if they joined the militia.[55] But on other occasions white Jamaicans clamped down on privileges. In 1715, the Assembly denied many forms of employment to free people of color. This was an attempt to keep them from earning money and joining the middling sort and thus caus-ing tensions with the white population, who embraced the color line.[56] On the whole, white Jamaicans were willing to accept some elite, wealthy people of color, usually those with whom they had kinship ties. These people they could trust. Those lower down the social scale they looked to control and lump with the enslaved population.[57]

The story of the Williams family shows both the inclusion and the exclu-sion of free people of color by white Jamaican society. John Williams, a suc-cessful Black Jamaican merchant who had won his freedom "for his fidelity and good service," had to work for the same rights as white freemen.[58] When enslaved Black men and women gained their freedom, they did not become equal to white Jamaicans. They simply received the right to own property rather than be it.[59] A jury of their peers did not judge free people of African descent. The law protected other free men from the testimony of the enslaved but not them.[60] Williams sought to change this, at least for his family. He knew that the Jamaican Assembly could pass special bills that provided free Blacks with additional rights.[61] It was unusual, but it happened. Such bills would grow in number after 1733, but by then they were almost always restricted to those with blood ties among the white Jamaican elite, which Williams did not possess.[62] In 1708, he asked the Assembly to grant him the right "to be tried by a jury, as a white man," and to have the same exclusion of the testimony of the enslaved allowed to white men. He told the Assembly he feared that his enslaved laborers could bring him to ruin through unfounded accusations. The act passed. In 1711, he pushed further. He convinced the British Parlia-ment to pass an act that not only kept enslaved men and woman from giving evidence against him but also gave him, and the rest of his family, the ability to give evidence in civil cases. By 1716 the Jamaican Assembly agreed that those enslaved could not give evidence against any member of his family.[63] This was approved by the British attorney general, Edward Northey, who had recently commented on slavery for the East India Company.[64] But Williams was an outlier. In 1708 when he first petitioned for rights, several other men of color put forth their case. Only one other petition, that of Manuel Bartholomew, was approved. White Jamaicans were willing to accept a few families of color into the fold, but not too many.

Williams's son, Francis, would remain in this marginal space, and his status would decline during the course of his life. A portrait of Francis, painted in the 1740s, now in the Victoria and Albert Museum in London, shows a successful Black man (fig. 5). Unlike other portraits that include Black figures, the painter does not dress Francis in exotic finery or have him offering grapes, coral, or adoring glances to a master or mistress; he has him look directly at the viewer. He stands alone. His white wig is straight, his blue coat refined. Books, sumptuously bound in precious leather, line the walls of his study. A hand rests on an open copy of "Newton's Philosophy," and the world, in the shape of the globe, sits at his feet.[65] It might not be as finely wrought as a Kneller portrait, but if you exclude the palm trees outside the window and turn the Black body white, it could be a portrait of any member of the British gentry. And like the sons of wealthy white planters, Francis went to London to be molded into a proper English gentleman. He studied law at Lincoln's Inn and, like many sons of gentlemen, learned the classics, poetry, and mathematics. He returned to Jamaica by 1724, most likely due to the death of his father, in the summer of 1723.[66] He could have crossed paths with the princes when they arrived in London. Upon his return, however, the limits of inclusion became clear.

In the autumn of 1724, an argument erupted between Francis Williams and a prominent Jamaican, William Brodrick. Records leave out what precipitated the argument, but it appears that Brodrick verbally attacked Williams's status as a free Black man with special privileges. What resulted was an outright brawl. Williams rushed Brodrick "in a passion," Brodrick violently pushed back, and Williams struck him. Insults flew. Williams called Brodrick a "white dog," and Brodrick labeled Williams a "black dog." Broderick was left with a torn shirt and neckcloth, and Williams received a bloody mouth.[67] For Williams, the sharp, metallic taste of that blood would linger. The incident caused the Jamaican Assembly to attempt to revoke the special privileges Williams possessed. His "behavior is of great encouragement to the negroes of this island in general," the Assembly opined, "and may be attended with ill consequences to the white people thereof."[68] Fighting tooth and nail, and petitioning the English Privy Council, Williams kept his special status, but just barely. It was a sign of things to come. In the 1730s free people of color would lose the right to vote, and after Tacky's Revolt in 1760 even more

Figure 5. Scholars estimate that this painting of Francis Williams was done in the 1740s, but by whom or even where is unknown. Interestingly, the painting appears to have ended up in the collection of a distant descendant of Edward Long, who wrote scathingly about Williams in his *History of Jamaica*, published in 1774. Unknown artist, *Portrait of Francis Williams*, c. 1745, Victoria and Albert Museum, P.83&A-1928. Reproduced by permission of the Victoria and Albert Museum, London, United Kingdom.

restrictions would be imposed.[69] By the time Francis Williams died in the 1770s, white Jamaicans had solidified the lines between Black and white. But during the years that the princes lived in Jamaica, his father John Williams still freely walked the streets.

The princes would have encountered other free men of color if they were enslaved in Port Royal, Spanish Town, or Kingston, the urban centers of Jamaica. Here they would have discovered a jumble of different sorts of people, both Black and white. In 1730 a quarter of the population of free people of color lived in Kingston. In Spanish Town in 1754, Black and mixed-race men and women owned property and ran businesses, usually working in the retail and the building trades.[70] Spanish Town was especially diverse.[71] Here women rented rooms to Jewish men, who in turn did business with women of African descent.[72] Many of those the princes would have encountered would have been Black women.[73] While records often sexualized these Black women, concentrating on the fact they were often mistresses of white men, they often had businesses and networks not based upon sex or intimate relationships with white men.[74] In these towns the princes could have learned that in Jamaica those of African descent could live as free men and women and be embedded in the larger society.

It was in Spanish Town that the two men found Joshua Bowes, a white lawyer, who listened to and believed their story. The surviving sources do not detail how they met. According to the London newspaper report, he watched the princes' harsh treatment and was moved by compassion. A later account held that he watched them and "observing such a Discontent in them as betoken'd some great Disapointment, and having got some Information on their Case from the Ship's Crew, Bought them of their New Master, most Charitably designing, to bring them himself to England."[75] In these tellings, Bowes is a "white savior" figure: a person who out of charity and a feeling of shared humanity saves the princes. They become passive receivers of his benevolent actions. Another source, however, contended that the princes took action, that their enslavement lasted until "jabbering a little English they told their story, & were freed by means of a Lawyer."[76] Here the princes took the reins. They learned English and repeated their story until someone listened. How Bowes came to hear their story is unclear. Did they meet at the house of their enslaver? On the street? Did the princes' laments cause someone to mention them to Bowes? Did they seek him out, or vice versa? The nature of their initial encounter and their relationship during their time together is lost to us, but it seems clear that the princes spent their time in Jamaica constantly telling their story until doing so produced results, even if they were lashed for telling it.

Most of what we know of Bowes comes from the will he drew up in 1718 and continued to add to until he left Jamaica. The first bequest in the will is to his brother John, who lived in the north of England, which was probably Joshua Bowes's own place of birth. The will does not say why he came to Jamaica or when.[77] He was a barrister, called to the bar in London in 1708, and so the litigious nature of Jamaica's elite would have provided him with opportunities, as the supply of lawyers there was low.[78] He left his law books and manuscripts to two "Friends and Fellow Labourers" who had been at Middle Temple with him.[79] He had married in London in 1712, but by 1718 his wife, Mary, had died.[80] He must have missed her terribly: he bought a portrait of an unknown woman, he wrote, "for the sake of some resemblance it had of my late dear Wife." Even though "the face is less than was the life and wants that good Complexion and fine black hair." It hung in his study.[81] He also felt the need to declare the status of his faith in his will: "Seeing some have been very inquisitive touching my Creed and others have mistaken it. I tell them once for all I am a Christian and I hope an Orthodox one." But little seems to separate him drastically from other white Jamaicans, except his actions toward those he enslaved.[82]

Bowes mentioned owning nine enslaved men and women in his will.[83] Of those noted, Bowes gave the name of all but two, and he planned to free them all. Two, Temple and Peggy, he had purchased before 1718 and he had thought long and hard about their fate. He freed both eight years after his death. His will implies that he delayed their liberty because he did not want to throw them out into the world without prospects. Both were young: he called Temple his "Negro Boy" and Peggy his "Negro Girl," terms he does not use when describing other enslaved peoples. He wanted Temple taught "some useful trade or employment" and given "a little money to begin with." He also asked that he would be "instructed in the Generall principles of Christianity." His wishes for Peggy were the same, but in her case he added more stipulations. He was concerned about any children she might have during those years of waiting. So, he added that if she became "with Child within the said Eight years," at the time of her marriage or when she reached her seventh month of pregnancy "she be sett at liberty."[84] Bowes knew that if the child came into this world while Peggy was still enslaved, the child would share that fate. It is possible that Temple and Peggy were his own children. His attempts to provide for their future echoes the steps taken by fathers who freed their children in their wills.[85]

Bowes's actions in freeing all those he had enslaved is out of the ordinary, however. Only 15 percent of male slaveholders freed at least one their captives in their wills, and these were usually their children.[86] In a sample of wills from 1674 to 1765, 48 percent of those freed by men were children, 37 percent adult women, and 15 percent adult men.[87] Bowes bought six men and women around August 1719. He mentioned them by name in his will: Atlas and his wife, Abinowa, Harry, Ando, Achilles, and Betty. He freed them, and any of their issue, ten years after his death. A month later, he added instructions regarding two further individuals he had just purchased. These are the only two enslaved laborers left unnamed; he referred to them as "two Madagascar Negroes viz. a Man and a Women." He wished them freed in ten years as well. A few months later he amended this. The "Madagascar Woman" had died, and now, he stipulated, he wanted to "give the Man his freedom at the end of three years after my decease."[88] In freeing all his enslaved laborers, even ten years after his death, Bowes was swimming against the Jamaican tide, and one wonders if his executors followed his stipulations.[89] When his heirs complained that his executor had not given them all that was due to them, the executor claimed that he sold the pen Bowes had owned and the enslaved men and women. The case makes no mention of Temple, Peggy, Atlas, Abinowa, Harry, Ando, Achilles, or Betty, but most likely they remained in bondage.[90]

Bowes never detailed why he wished to free the men, women, and children he had purchased. His detailed instructions suggest a tempered dislike of the institution. He did not totally reject slavery. He bought enslaved laborers. He even bought into a pen, a piece of land where owners raised livestock and grew crops, which had enslaved laborers working on it.[91] He benefited from their work and did not plan on freeing them until long after his own death. Yet even this was a radical move at this time, and he seems to have cared both for their souls and their futures. These manumissions and the freeing of the princes were different from the majority of manumissions in Jamaica at the time. Usually, men and women freed their captives to fortify interracial networks, and thus those freed often had complex ties to the person who freed them.[92] Bowes and the princes had no such connections.

He appears to have freed them because he saw their enslavement as wrong. He purchased them for forty pistoles each and, according to the newspaper account, was "resolved to hazard his Person and Fortune towards getting them Justice."[93] He dressed them in "silken Mantles" to emphasize their status and took them to wait on the governor, to whom they "set forth their Case." The governor, Nicholas Lawes, in return, offered his protection.[94] The two men, and Bowes, expected redress. There was little the governor could do. There were no official laws on unlawful enslavement.[95] But, as was becoming clear, there were unwritten ones, and some in Jamaican society were willing to admit that Captain White violated those rules.[96] The rules that had been broken, though, were the rules of the slave trade, not the rules of slavery itself.

Thomas White is always presented as the villain in the princes' tale, not the planters who purchased them. "Villainy and Treachery" defined *his* actions, not theirs.[97] White's major crime was that he had betrayed the trust of his trading partners in Africa. This echoes Oroonoko's dismissal of the captain who had betrayed him. In the play, Oroonoko turned to the captain and said, "Men live and prosper but in Mutual Trust."[98] The playwright had the captain blush in shame. Most trade with African countries was done through the African elite of those areas. If too many captains shattered that trust, fewer enslaved bodies would fill ships' holds. In the *Weekly Journal* account, the princes make this clear. When presenting their case to the governor, they supposedly said "they did not so much regard their own Misfortunes, as the Welfare of the English, who might hereafter Trade to Madagascar, being certain that such People would receive ill Treatment on their Accounts." In fact, according to the *Weekly Journal*, Robert Baldwin, the editor of the *Weekly Jamaican Courant*, first published the story in Jamaica so "fair Trading People might not suffer by such base and inhuman Practices."[99] In buying Africans, even high-status individuals, Jamaican planters were within their rights; it was the captains, whose actions threatened the trade in enslaved people, who had crossed the line. But the planters of Jamaica did not really care if the princes were wrongly enslaved or not; they still valued them more as enslaved labor than as members of the African elite. It took the princes years to convince someone to free them. In persuading Bowes to purchase them, free them, and take them to London, they reasserted that their value lay in their elite status, a valuation that was much more welcome in London than it was in Jamaica.

By the spring of 1720 the princes were free. They had no wish to remain on the island, and white Jamaicans were happy to see them go. The fewer men like John Williams, the better. Bowes and the princes prepared to set sail. On 12 June 1720, all three men boarded the *Lewis,* bound for London.[100] It would be a short and tragic journey. June marked the beginning of hurricane season.[101]

The *Lewis,* the *Milford* (the ship the Royal Navy had sent as an escort), and a fleet of thirteen other ships had been at sea for six days when disaster struck.[102] The weather shifted as the rocks of Cape Corrientes off the westernmost end of Cuba came into view. What happened next probably echoes the account given by Charles Leslie of hurricanes on Jamaica. First, he said, the sea became calm, "smooth as Glass." Then the air darkened, and clouds "thick and gloomy" crowded the sky. The princes probably warily watched the heavens. The period of foreboding was short for soon "'tis all as [if] it were on Fire." The storm attacked sight, sound, and any sense of stability. "Dreadful Lightnings" scarred the skies, and then came "horrible Claps of Thunder." Next the wind, which "blow[s] with such Impetuosity and Force, that it . . . destroys everything within its Whirl." The storm could last for hours, making "the whole Round of the Heavens" and blowing "from every Point of the Compass." As the princes sailed within this maelstrom, it would have seemed to them "as if the Heavens were rent asunder."[103] Meanwhile, slowly, inexorably, horribly the rocks of Cape Corrientes came closer and closer until the winds and waves threw the ships upon them. They splintered. The riches of

Jamaica bled into the Caribbean Sea. The living and the dead became flotsam and jetsam tossed and turned by the waves. Two ships, jammed onto the rocks, remained whole, the rest shattered along the coast. Some 450 men, women, and children perished; among them was Joshua Bowes.[104]

The princes survived. They probably clung to the rocks as the splintered remnants of the ships and the dead flowed around them.[105] Luckily for them, another homeward fleet had set sail from Jamaica only a few days after them. As this fleet approached Cuba, devastation stretched as far as the eye could see. Dead bodies and skeletons of buildings lined the coast. "The Waves have so far exceeded their usual Bounds," reported the *London Journal*, that "the adjacent Lands are all under Water."[106] The *Mermaid*, the naval ship leading the new fleet, found thirteen survivors from the *Milford* on the rocks, fed them, and took them to Britain.[107] A small boat stopped a sloop bound for New York and relayed the tragedy. The captain of the sloop and his men went ashore and found fifty more survivors and heard that one hundred more had made their way to Havana.[108] Eventually, the new fleet took those who had survived to Britain.[109] This fleet arrived unharmed. By August the survivors had reached Bristol, and by September they were in London. Among those who survived were "33 Sailers out of the Man of War, Capt. Laming, Capt. Kingston, Colonel Towgood, Mr. Goddard and his Wife, and one Child, and the three Black Princes which were Passengers."[110] Their survival prompted the *Weekly Journal* to tell their story in more detail to a London audience. It ended, "Mr. Bowes and two of these unfortunate People being Drown'd, the other two it's reported, are now in London; and if any more of their story can be brought to Light, it shall be sent you."[111] After their arrival in London there is no more mention of additional princes or attendants. Eight or nine had become four, and those four had become three and finally only two. These two men would look for justice and a way home by presenting their case to the trading companies of London, hoping that their value as trading partners would hold strong in the center of the British Empire. Luckily for them, both the East India Company and the Royal African Company were rethinking the nature of their trading patterns in ways that looked to embrace the area they knew as Delagoa and that the princes knew as Mpfumo.

CHAPTER 3

_____

Doing Business

London, England, 1720

The princes' early days in London would have been spent at the Spread Eagle Inn, off Gracechurch Street in the center of the city (fig. 6). The inn was tucked away off the street, its three-story gallery surrounding a courtyard where coaches and locals could come to escape the commotion of central London. It was popular, busy, and not cheap. It was from within one of these rooms, or perhaps on one of the balconies, that the princes could hear the sounds of the city. The cacophony of noises that floated into the inn could both oppress and excite. It was certainly louder than the shores of Maputo Bay. Instead of the murmur of water, the faint cries of birds, and the subtle bustle of human life, here noise and life surged, surrounded, and sometimes choked. Gracechurch Street was a major London artery running directly toward London Bridge, the only span across the great river Thames in the city, and so visitors, carriers, and cargo charged up and down the street. The clattering of horses' hooves and the shouts of drivers and pedestrians must have met the princes' ears. Competing with the roar of the street traffic was the hustle and bustle of Leadenhall Market, which surrounded the inn: the herb market to the south, the fish market, connected by a passageway, to the east, and the leather market to the north. The grumbling of crowds, the calls of the merchants, and the arrival of merchandise in the wee hours must have been audible. When the din quieted and the princes strained their ears, they could probably have made out the "curious Ring of Bells, esteemed the best in the City," that rang out from St. Michael's Cornhill just down the way.[1] But at most times of the day the comings and goings within the yard itself probably drowned out such subtle sounds. Coaches rumbled in and out with great regularity, bringing people with them.[2] Such sounds might have defined

Figure 6. This image of the Spread Eagle Inn from 1814, almost a century after the princes' stay, shows its many stories lined with balconies over which Prince James and Prince John could have leaned, to watch the carriages come and go. It would not be demolished until 1865 and was one of the most famous coaching inns in London. *Gracechurch Street*, by Robert Blemmell Schnebbelie, image © London Metropolitan Archives (City of London).

the princes' early experience of London; according to one observer, "For the first 6 months that they were in London they were kept like prisoners at the Spread Eagle Inn in [Gracechurch] street where they saw none but those who by chance found 'em out."[3] How curtailed their movements were, or why they were restricted, is not clear. What *is* known, is that during their first months in London their presence was not much in demand. East India Company officials were interested in what the princes could do for them, but not necessarily in the men themselves. A simple lack of invitations might have caused their isolation. They may also have been wary since earlier encounters with the British had not gone well. Visitors did come to find them, however, bringing different concerns and agendas with them.

Their main connection to the outside world was John Toogood, who, after Joshua Bowes had perished, became their new patron. Toogood had survived the hurricane alongside the two men and saw opportunity in them.[4] He himself is a shadowy figure. Even his name is unstable, morphing from John

Toogood to John Twogood to John Towgood, and back again. Sometimes he was a colonel, sometimes not.[5] We do know that Toogood liked to invest in unusual endeavors. At least, he subscribed for shares in a project to exploit the mines of Jamaica.[6] In July 1720 the king had granted a group of projectors, led by Charles Long of Jamaica, "the liberty of searching for, digging, and opening All Mines of Gold & Silver and Royal Mines in his Island of Jamaica" for thirty-one years, in exchange for one-fifth of what they found.[7] Interest in these mines and this project may have been one of the reasons Toogood was sailing between London and Jamaica.

The princes came to London right when interest in projects and investments was reaching a fever pitch. One of their future patrons, James Brydges, first Duke of Chandos, even wrote to the princes' old friend, Nicholas Lawes, the governor of Jamaica, in September 1720, a month after they arrived in London: "The humour of the age hath made people of all degrees so fond of Projects which we call here by the Name of Bubbles that for these 8 months past nothing could be proposed . . . [that] was not greedily enter'd into." He then segued into his next topic: the state of the mines in Jamaica. He had heard of the new scheme and wanted Lawes's opinion.[8] One opportunity, though, dominated public discourse at the time: the South Sea Company. When founded in 1711 the South Sea Company had promised another way to fund the national debt, which multiple wars had increased by leaps and bounds. Other financial institutions, like the Bank of England, were dominated by Whig supporters, and the South Sea Company would offer a Tory alternative. Investment in it was based on its access to trade with the Spanish colonies; that promise increased in 1713 when the company was granted the asiento, the monopoly on the trade in enslaved bodies to the Spanish colonies.[9] In late January 1720, the government had accepted the company's proposal to take on some of the national debt, making it a trading company that acted like a bank.[10] A frenzy of speculation ensued, which peaked just as the princes arrived.

The excitement surrounding the South Sea Company stock shows both the emergence of a new financial world and interest in the profit to be found in global exploitation. The South Sea Company was not the only company involved in such projects. New schemes like that exploring the mines of Jamaica were emerging, but the older trading companies were also on the hunt. By the time the princes arrived in London in the late summer of 1720 both the East India Company and the Royal African Company were facing challenges and rethinking the direction and nature of their trading patterns.

Both were thinking about Africa in new ways. They saw it as a location from which to feed the colonial desire for enslaved bodies, but they also believed that Africa, especially the east coast, could enrich them in other ways—mainly through access to gold. For this reason, both would listen, at least for a while, when Toogood came calling.

He initially approached the East India Company. It was the obvious first stop for support. It had given a license to Thomas White, who had betrayed the princes, so who better to facilitate their return home? In fact, Toogood probably picked the Spread Eagle because it was only a three-minute walk from East India House on Leadenhall Street. The princes never visited East India House, but Toogood did, and he brought a petition with him. The paper he used was large, his handwriting ornate, and his lines perfectly straight.[11] It laid before the Court of Directors of the East India Company "the suffereing and deplorable case of these Injur'd princes." The actions of Captain White, Toogood implied, had tainted the honor of the company, which had to be redeemed. Furthermore, it certainly did not hurt, he suggested, that saving the company's honor would secure "the trade in their Brothers Dominions and in that part of the world."[12] Luckily for Toogood, "that part of the world" interested the company in the late summer of 1720.

Toogood had angry English weavers, who did not appreciate the expansion into this global economy, to thank for the East India Company's interest.[13] English weavers were looking to stop the East India Company's importation of calicoes. Ever since the East India Company had begun to import this printed cotton cloth from India, cloth manufacturers in England had worried about the competition they posed. Its importation became a scapegoat for the pinch of the general economic downswing at the turn of the century. By 1700 Parliament had passed an act banning the importation of printed calicoes to England, although plain white cotton cloth was still allowed, since it helped stimulate English cotton printing. This was not enough for the weavers. Ships smuggled in calico, and there was no penalty for wearing it. By 1719 weavers began to take matters into their own hands, and it became dangerous to wear calico, especially near Spitalfields, where the weavers congregated.[14]

Elizabeth Price, perhaps blissfully unaware of the simmering tensions, stepped out of her house on a June day wearing her fashionable calico gown covered by her cloak. For her, such a grown was probably a fashion coup. It allowed her to mimic the embroidered silk of the elite and it spoke of foreign climes far beyond the streets of London.[15] She and her acquaintance, Mary Williamson, were looking for housing, and perhaps she thought the gown would impress the landlord. She was wrong. As she made her way down the street someone lifted her cloak and saw the gown beneath. A call of "Callicoe, Callicoe; Weavers, Weavers" echoed down the street, and one woman yelled "Callicoe Bitch!" Soon Price was surrounded by a swarm of boys and girls who "tore her Gown off all but the Sleeve, her Pocket, the Head of her Riding Hood, and abus'd her very much."[16] Rosamond Becket's calico gown led her into danger as well.[17] According to one witness, a man approached Becket and her friends, rubbed against one of them, and then exclaimed, "D—m you, you have a Callicoe Gown. I'll have the Tail of it." He then pulled a knife, wet it on his shoe, and struck at her. As she ran into a house, he yelled that he "would cut her soul from her body."[18] Other witnesses denied this account, but taken together with the other incident it becomes clear that fashion had become dangerous.

The violence peaked on 11 and 12 June 1719. A mob of thousands roamed through Spitalfields looking for calico wearers.[19] They clad themselves in scraps of the hated cloth, waved pieces over their heads, and cried: "Down with the Callicoes!"[20] No one was safe, not even "those of the best fashion." The protestors tore clothes and doused bystanders with ink or aqua fortis, which today we call nitric acid. The streets filled with smoke as they burned cloth taken from shops.[21] On 12 June they threatened to pull down a house to get at the calico wearers inside.[22] The disorder almost flowed out of the city as the rioters called for the destruction of the printing presses located just beyond the city limits that were used to add images to the imported cloth.[23] In the end, the government called out the troops, who killed one man, wounded another, and dispersed the rest.[24] Calico was no longer just a piece of cloth, it was trouble; and the East India Company was its main purveyor.[25]

Thus, by the summer of 1719 the company knew calicoes were again going to be a problem. By July the Board of Trade was discussing halting the importation of unprinted calicoes, and by October it was asking the company for its thoughts on the matter. In November, the disgruntled merchants tersely replied and attempted to protect their profits.[26] In May 1720 the House of Lords would actually reject a ban on the importation of unprinted calicoes as a way to help protect the profits of the company.[27] But the issue would continue to plague the company into 1721 and would force it to keep a keen eye out for new trading opportunities.[28]

In May 1720 two men approached the East India Company with a plan that might solve its problems, offering a solution that would make the company see the princes' presence as a welcome possibility. The Reverend

William Gordon and Mr. John Huggins wished to open a whole new trade in an area under the company's purview—the southeastern coast of Africa. Gordon imagined the area to be filled with gold and silver, and he believed that the Africans would sell the two for the same price.[29] The former Barbadian clergyman spread rumors of gold mines in southeastern Africa that were "immensely rich," and he wished to share this windfall with the East India Company.[30] He and his partner would be happy to exploit this glittering trade themselves, but they knew it stood within the East India Company's monopoly, and so they hoped to cut a deal. If the company did not wish to embark on the trade themselves, Gordon and Huggins wanted a license for thirty-one years. They would pay three hundred thousand pounds for the privilege and provide the company with 10 percent of the profit. If, however, their proposal inspired the company to take on the trade, they expected to be paid ten thousand pounds for their trouble.[31]

The company quickly thrust aside any idea of giving the two men a license as the idea of expanding a trade into southeastern Africa did tempt them.[32] The gold glittered, but developing the area also promised a way to deal with Madagascar, which had long been a thorn in the company's side. Company officials knew that pirates found a haven there, although their numbers were declining, and unlicensed ships sneaked in and out for enslaved Malagasy.[33] Here was an opportunity to tame and control the island in a profitable manner. The company knew there was demand: the minutes of the Court of Directors include thirteen requests for licenses to trade to Madagascar between the time of White's first voyage and Gordon's proposal.[34] By June, after a discussion in the Court of Directors and the General Court, which many attended, it was decided that the company would embark on the trade itself and give Gordon and Huggins a fitting gratuity, a decision it later allowed to lapse.[35] This decision caught the attention of the city. The *London Journal* reported on the matter, stating that the idea of setting up "a new Trade to the South East parts of Africa" had "set the whole Town in Expectation of mighty Things from that Part of the World."[36]

That summer the East India Company swung into action. It formed a committee to consider the opening of trade in the area, and the committee members gathered information on Madagascar and the southeastern coast of Africa.[37] The whole committee devoured an account of "the Island and Trade of Madagascar and also an account of the Trade of Delagoa on the Coast of Monopatapa."[38] The same day, they brought in Captain Matthew Kent, who had traded in enslaved bodies in Madagascar under the company's license in 1718, to inform the committee of "the Places he traded at there and the manner of purchasing Slaves and where he disposed of them as also what sort of ships were properest to be sent thither for ye slaving trade."[39] In the end, the company resolved to send three or four ships to Madagascar to trade in enslaved men and women, which it knew would be profitable, but it also wanted to send along smaller vessels that could go "to The South East Coast of Africa to make Discoveryes and carry on a Trade Thither."[40] Here was, possibly, a new opportunity, and, if Gordon was right, a golden one. It seemed like an opportune time for such a voyage, as the government had agreed to send out a number of men-of-war to suppress piracy in the East Indies, and these would make a perfect convoy for the exploratory ships.[41] Next, the company officials went public. A publication requesting proposals from ship owners and commanders who wished to join them on this adventure graced tables at the Royal Exchange and at East India House. Interested parties had to turn in their proposals by 12 August 1720, the day before the princes arrived in Bristol.[42] Thus, when the princes set foot in England, their homeland was on people's minds, and the East India Company was ready to listen to Toogood's petition on their behalf.

Toogood sent two petitions to the Court of Directors, one in late September and one in early November 1720. There was a reason, however, the Company did not pounce on the first one. Between those two dates the company's big dreams to establish a rich and profitable trade in Madagascar and southeastern Africa crumbled. Six days after the company read Toogood's first petition, it received a letter from the king of Portugal's envoy in London about the "rumour spread here for some time that the East India Company intended to set up a new Trade to the South Coast of Africa beyond the Cape of Good Hope."[43] That area, he reminded the company, was under the control of the Portuguese. The company easily dismissed this claim, but the problems began to add up.[44] First, none of the men they talked to who had been along the southeastern coast agreed with Gordon and Huggins. Ships from Madras and Bombay had traded in ivory and ambergris there, but never gold. The commanders of ships with licenses to trade there concurred. Gordon insisted the British did not frequent the part of the coast that had the gold, but the company found him less and less convincing.[45] But, more important, September was the month the South Sea Bubble, one of the first big financial bubbles, popped. The financial market was in turmoil. Credit, public credit in particular, was frozen. By mid-September Parliament was leaning on the East India Company take on some of the debt of the South Sea Company to help stabilize the economy.[46] By October East India stock was worth half of what it had been in August.[47] This was nothing compared to the losses the South Sea Company faced, but it hurt nonetheless. On 18 October, the day after East India stock hit its lowest point, the committee decided not to open the trade with southeastern Africa, at least not until the next season, due to "the present Exigency."[48]

The financial turmoil and the dismissal of these larger plans did not condemn the princes to a life at the Spread Eagle—they still interested the company. In November, after Toogood's second petition, officials pondered sending a ship to Maputo Bay "to try if any Trade can be gotten in or about that place." The man they had in mind to command the voyage was none other than William Mackett, who had been at Madagascar when White arrived with the princes.[49] By this time Mackett had become a familiar name to the directors. He had taken the *Drake* on another voyage to Madagascar under their license, and he had been open about the interlopers he saw there.[50] In December, a voyage to Mpfumo to return the princes, with Mackett commanding, was coming together. The company discussed expenses with Toogood, both for his past outlays of funds and for future expenses for the princes until they could be sent home.[51]

Interest in this voyage remained, thanks to the debates surrounding calico that still simmered. A bill that sought to ban the importation of all calico, both printed and nonprinted, was in the making. The Board of Trade valued the East India Company, however, and was willing to talk. The board wanted to know other ways it could help the company in its time of need. Among its desired concessions, the company included the establishment of a settlement at Madagascar and the "liberty to send the slaves procured there, wherever they shall find most beneficial without bringing them first to Europe."[52] Later, the company officials were even more blatant, asking the king to grant them "leave to import such slaves as they shall purchase there directly to the West Indies."[53] This expansion of their trade was not to be. Parliament was not feeling that permissive. Rather than loosening the borders of their monopoly, by allowing the East India Company to join the trans-Atlantic slave trade, the concessions granted tightened it. The name says it all: it was "An Act for the Further Preventing of His Majesty's Subjects from Trading to the East-Indies under Foreign Commissions; and for Encouraging and Further Securing the Lawful Trade Thereto."[54] A few months before, the act banning the importation of calico was also passed.[55] The company had lost its fight against the weavers, but it was closer than ever to defeating the interlopers and pirates. The opening for the company to trade directly in enslaved labor to the western colonies, however, closed— as did its interest in the princes.[56]

During a debate in late March, the East India officials admitted that since Parliament was not willing "to allow The Company Liberty to send Slaves to The West Indies," they were not willing to send a ship to Maputo Bay. Instead, they resolved that the princes "be sent to Bombay on one of the Ships now outward-bound thither with directions to The President & Councill to take Care of sending them home as soon as they can."[57] This did not please the princes or Toogood. They rejected the offer.[58] The company shrugged and told them that if that was their attitude, Toogood could have "the future care of them on his own account."[59]

Southeast Africa had interested the East India Company for two reasons: access to enslaved bodies and access to gold. The buying and selling of enslaved Africans was the usual way to make a profit in Africa. As we have seen, it was the desire for enslaved Africans that caused the company to issue the licenses to trade in Madagascar, and here we see it wanting, however briefly, to blur the boundaries of its monopoly to get in on the game. The East India Company, the Royal African Company, and the South Sea Company knew the profit to be had in enslaved Africans. But neither the East India Company nor the Royal African Company had forgotten that gold had been one of the early commodities that had drawn Europeans to Africa. The East India Company had evaluated this trade and rejected it, but the Royal African Company remained intrigued—and for good reason.

Gold had flowed out of Africa for a long time and had marked European ideas of Africa. The 1375 Catalan Atlas showed Mansa Musa, king of the ancient kingdom of Mali, holding an orb of gold. The massive amounts of gold he had carried with him on his way to Mecca, twenty-five years before, had left a mark on European conceptions of Africa.[60] Stories of a golden Africa filled English ears again in the mid-sixteenth century and then again in the early eighteenth century.[61] This gold was no fairy tale. In the west, it came from the Akan goldfields in what is now Ghana, the Bure goldfields in what is now Guinea, and the Bambuk goldfields in what is now Mali.[62] But gold did not come only from the west. Gold from eastern Africa had seeped into Egypt from Ethiopia as early as the second millennium B.C.E., and the Zimbabwe Plateau, not too far distant from the princes' homeland, became a major source of gold between the eleventh and fifteenth centuries.[63] This is the gold London trading companies thought the princes could help them access.

In fact, African gold tantalized the British in 1720. Newspapers reported that William Gordon had found the ancient mines of Ophir mentioned it the Bible and that those attracted to his project "amuse themselves with Hopes of equalling Solomon in Riches, tho' not in Wisdom."[64] The Royal African Company was sending out miners to its trading posts to dig for gold and other minerals. They even had hopes that at Cape Coast Castle, in what is now Ghana, "the very Mountains in that piece of ground, which is call'd the Company's Garden contains Mines within them."[65] Even the fiction of the time highlighted Africa's golden possibilities. Daniel Defoe made such riches the centerpiece of his new novel, *Captain Singleton*, published in 1720. The novel tells the story of John Singleton, who is part of an ill-fated mutiny and finds himself marooned in Madagascar. He and some of the surviving crew precariously float across the channel on a makeshift raft to modern-day Mozambique, whence they walk across the continent on foot. Along the way, they stumble across great quantities of gold, which brings them fantastic wealth when they return home. And their guide through the center of Africa is a local prince from the eastern coast. He joins them after seeing the power of Singleton's guns and his surgeon's healing prowess.[66] One wonders if the princes heard the story once they arrived in London. In 1720, many Britons believed that the African interior was a place of wealth, mystery, and possibility, and some thought African princes could unlock it. James Brydges, first Duke of Chandos, would bring two such princes to the attention of the Royal African Company (fig. 7).

The Duke of Chandos had a dream. Well, he had multiple dreams. He was always on the lookout for the next big thing and never met a project he did not like. One historian has described him as "one of the most notorious embezzlers and projectors of the eighteenth century."[67] He invested in the Mississippi Company, South Sea Company, and many others, but the Royal African Company dominated his time in 1720.[68] And to save this company he had to dream big, since its present and future leaned toward the nightmarish for its supporters. The company had lost their monopoly to control the West African slave trade in 1698, and by 1712 even the duty that free traders had been required to pay it when they arrived in Africa had lapsed. The company had transported almost 175,000 enslaved bodies between 1673 and 1720, but not even that number was enough.[69] The plantation owners wanted enslaved Africans, and the company did not have the ability to put together enough voyages to fulfill their needs, especially now that independent traders were in on the game.[70] It was time, in Chandos's eyes, for the company to get a makeover, perhaps one less dependent on voyages for enslaved Africans. Chandos had begun to invest in the company in 1717, and by 1720 he had a place on

Figure 7. James Brydges,
first Duke of Chandos,
in all his pomp. He had
become a duke a few years
earlier, in 1719, not long
before the princes arrived
in London. He made his
fortune, and obtained his
dukedom, through his
services as the paymaster
of the queen's forces from
1705 to 1713. John Simon,
Duke of Chandos, 1722,
Yale Center for British
Art, transfer from the Yale
University Library and the
Yale University Art Gallery,
B1994.4.1377. Reproduced
by permission of Yale
Center for British Art, New
Haven, Connecticut.

the Court of Assistants and Committee of Correspondence—and he did not
take his positions lightly.[71] He had a new vision for the company. He thought
it should transform its slave-trading outposts into productive settlements
that grew and sold goods. They would be more like the American colonies.
Profit would come from plantations that grew cotton, indigo, or spices. Then,
he believed that establishing trading ties with the African interior would be
worthwhile. He also hoped that gold or other minerals would be found and
could be traded. These pathways would guide the company to success and
give its structure as a company meaning. Independent traders could not start
settlements or open whole trades, but companies could.[72]

It was probably the mines of Jamaica that brought Toogood and, eventually, the princes into Chandos's orbit. Both men were investors in the project
to exploit the Royal Mines of Jamaica. Toogood's name and the "Duke of
Chandois" appear in the account book of the Royal Mines as subscribers.[73]
It was to this known speculator and acquaintance that Toogood turned as
the East India Company's interest in the princes waned.[74] In fact, Chandos
had been watching the men. In November 1720, just after Toogood had sent
his second petition to the East India Company, Chandos had issued a dinner

invitation to "Coll: Towgood and the Indian Princes."[75] By January 1721 Chandos was making use of his knowledge of the princes. At the time, the Royal African Company was establishing a settlement in Angola at Cabinda, on the southwestern coast of Africa, and Chandos had special instructions for its first governor.[76] He wanted him to look closely when he sailed between the latitudes 22 and 25 degrees south, as a contact had told him there was a river there whence they could access the African empire of Monomotapa, a region thought to be rich in gold. And Chandos believed that "the Emperor of this Country [was] a brother to the two Princes of Lagos, who were barbarously trespass'd away by Capt White." The governor, if possible, should find a translator and send an embassy to tell the emperor of his brothers' survival. In his joy at the news, the emperor might reward them with trading rights and a settlement along the river.[77] For Chandos the princes were key to accessing the empire of Monomotapa, which he thought was "very rich in Gold, teeth, & other valuable Commodities."[78]

Monomotapa was a much talked about but little seen empire in the center of southern Africa that had long intrigued Europeans. Rumor had it that this was where Solomon's famous mines were.[79] And these mines were synonymous with gold in English minds.[80] As early as 1613, Samuel Purchas was talking about them, and the way he structured his description sums up English attitudes toward the area. His account begins with the mines, shifts away, but ends with the declaration: "But to returne (and who will not returne?) to the Mines."[81] When thinking of the interior of Africa, and Monomotapa in particular, British thoughts, especially Chandos's, always returned to the mines.

The polity Europeans knew as Monomotapa is known today as the Mutapa Kingdom, which rose to power in the fifteenth century.[82] Some of the gold-producing areas that Europeans associated with the kingdom did lie within Mutapa territory, and others lay within tributary kingdoms.[83] The people who lived on the gold-producing plateau did not, however, see gold as their main source of wealth. Rather they were agricultural communities who turned to gold mining in the dry season to make ends meet. They would collect it from riverbeds or find pieces of quartz bearing gold and dig down, sometimes to a depth of thirty meters, carving footholds as they went. They would then use fire to separate the gold from the stone and grind it down to dust that could be transported via porcupine quills and vulture feathers.[84] At its height, more than a ton of gold a year was exported from the plateau.[85] Before the Portuguese arrived, this gold would make its way to the southeastern coast at Sofala and then be transferred by local Swahili traders to Kilwa in the north, where traders

Figure 8. This detail of Africa is taken from Herman Moll's *A new and correct map of the whole world*. In this map, Monomotapa is the oval country in the very south with no coastline. Maputo Bay is not labeled but is located not far south of the Tropic of Capricorn, the thick line that bisects Monomotapa. Detail taken from Herman Moll, *A new and correct map of the whole world* (London, 1719), Huntington Library, HEH RB 493935. Reproduced by permission of the Huntington Library, San Marino, California.

from around the Afrasian Sea could access it.[86] The Portuguese attempted to tap this trade but soon found that the supply of gold was waning in the face of conflict in the interior, depleted mines, and their own interference.[87] Throughout the seventeenth century, both Portuguese influence in the area and Mutapan power were faltering. The Kingdom of Butwa, south and west of the Mutapan centers of power, was on the rise.[88] In reality, by the time the princes made it to Britain, a connection with a Mutapan ruler was not what it once was.

British knowledge of the area was outdated. Chandos did not seem to have a strong grasp of what was truly happening there. He was not alone. For many Europeans, knowledge of the area came from romantic accounts like Vincent le Blanc's *The World Surveyed*, written in French in 1648, published in English in 1660, and based on a Portuguese account from a century earlier. Le Blanc's book would influence works published into the eighteenth century.[89] The maps of the time were misleading as well. Herman Moll's 1719 map of the world shows Monomotapa much farther south than it actually was (fig. 8). Judging by this map, however, making contact with Monomotapa from Maputo Bay looked almost easy. The Santo Espiritu River is shown as flowing straight from the bay to the capital of Monomotapa, and from there the western coast looks easily accessible.[90] It is telling, though, that the East India Company, with is wide-ranging networks and eyewitness accounts of the area, decided against initiating trade there. Perhaps it knew things that the others did not. The Royal African Company, on the other hand, continued on—it, or at least Chandos, was more willing to embrace voyages or causes more, shall we say, speculative.

While the East India Company's information came from captains who had sailed the waters around Mpfumo, Chandos's intelligence came mostly from the two princes themselves. It must have been them who had told him that their brother was the emperor of Monomotapa; the information is never mentioned in any of the petitions that Toogood sent to the East India Company. In general, however, the Royal African Company was more interested in listening to the two men than the East India Company ever was. The two never attended a meeting at East India House. No directors gave dinners in their honor. It was during their first six months in London, when negotiations with the East India Company took place, that "they were kept like prisoners."[91] This was all to change. For Chandos's plans to prosper, the princes' information and presence was crucial. It was time for them to leave the Spread Eagle Inn.

CHAPTER 4

Becoming Celebrities

Cannons, Middlesex, England, 24 September 1721

The princes arrived at Cannons, the estate of the Duke of Chandos, as the sun began to drop lower in the sky (fig. 9). Their carriage would have traveled up a grand avenue a mile long and broad enough for three carriages to travel side by side.[1] Soon the looming façade of the house would appear with its great ionic columns and a roof crowned with statuary. Chandos had been working on constructing his estate since 1713, and in 1721 he was putting on the final touches. The finished results impressed many. Daniel Defoe declared: "So Beautiful in its Situation, so Lofty, so Majestick the Appearance of it, that a pen can but ill describe it, the pencil not much better."[2] John Macky thought that once finished it would "be inferior to few Royal Palaces in Europe."[3] It was here, in the lap of English luxury, that the princes were guests of honor.

Once they arrived, a servant ushered them into the Great Hall, where they would have gazed upon the massive unfinished marble staircase and a ceiling painted to represent "the Triumph of Victory."[4] Next, walking to the right they would have passed through the Stone Gallery, the longest passageway on the ground floor.[5] Finally they would have reached the spacious dining room.[6] On the left, when they entered, the gleaming plate inside the buffet room would have caught their eye, as would its ceiling, which showed Bacchus offering Ariadne grapes, a fitting addition for a room that also held the wine coolers.[7] To the right was the music room, where strains of the finest music could have floated from the instruments of Chandos's private orchestra.[8] Then there was the massive dining room itself, capped with a huge painting depicting the five senses. Chandos wanted this room to stimulate them all.[9] Eyes enjoyed the massive paintings and the light bouncing off the

The Elevation of a New House Intended for His Grace ye Duke of Chandos, in Mary Bone Fields.
Design'd by John Price, Architect, 1720.
Is most humbly Inscribed To her Grace the Dutchess of Chandos.

Figure 9. The Duke of Chandos's estate, Cannons, which the princes visited in 1721. The home was celebrated at the time as the height of luxury, but Chandos's spending and his losses in the South Sea Bubble would lead to his heir selling the house and its contents in 1747. Henry Hulsberg, *The Elevation of a New House Intended for his Grace ye Duke of Chandos, in Mary Bone Fields*, 1720, Yale Center for British Art, Paul Mellon Collection, B1977.14.17525. Reproduced by permission of Yale Center for British Art, New Haven, Connecticut.

silver plate.[10] Smooth wood and crisp linen met the fingers of guests. Music and voices poured into their ears. Finally, the smell of multiple dishes, all richly prepared, tempted their taste buds.

The princes doubtless met with an array of tempting morsels. The staff would have laid out all the dishes for the first course by the time the princes entered the room. An impressive dish in the middle of the table probably met their eyes first. A book once suggested placing here a large root vegetable shaped like a castle and surrounded by carved vegetable trees decorated with herbs and flowers.[11] While the centerpiece the princes saw was probably not so grand, it would still be surrounded by a number of smaller dishes. Since the guests could not always reach the dishes on the other side of the table, the plates offered usually mimicked each other. Those on one side got boiled tongue, those on the other boiled chicken. By not simply doubling the dishes hosts showed the creativity of their kitchen and their own munificence.[12] Only the most well-oiled kitchens operating on large budgets could accomplish such feats. Chandos knew the name of the game, and as one visitor recorded: "He spares no Expence to have the best."[13] We do not know the number or content of the dishes laid before the princes that Sunday, but we do know what Chandos offered at a similar-sized dinner party almost exactly a year later.[14] The centerpiece of the first course was a "Sallet." Above this salad, near the host, sat "oyster pottage," a dish not unlike our modern oyster soup.[15] At some point during the meal, a servant removed the soup and replaced it with "breast of Veal ragoo'd," or a breast of veal that had been boiled, breaded, broiled, and served with a thin sauce and garnish.[16] At the other end of the table lay the roast mutton.[17] Filling in the gaps in between were, on one side, fish and boiled tongue and, on the other, "Chicken boyl'd" and pudding.

Next came the second course and, at Cannons, it often arrived in style. On Sundays, Chandos's usher of the hall "with his gown on and staff in his hand" led in the second course.[18] This second course was usually sweeter and lighter than the first. The menu for 23 September 1722 called for tarts at the center.[19] Six dishes encircled the tarts. At the head and the foot of the table sat the partridge and the duck. The avian feast continued on one side of the table with a serving of larks and one of pigeons in jelly. The other side held a dish of sturgeon and one of apple fritters.[20] While the menu does not mention this, the second course could have been followed by a dessert course consisting of raw and dried fruits and perhaps creams of all sorts.[21] The princes would not have left hungry.

By the time the princes came to Cannons for dinner they knew it was their royal status that kept them apart from others of African descent in London. They were aware that their worth to the British, and thus their ride home, depended on them maintaining that status. They made sure they played their part well. Years later, an observer would state they "were well Cloath'd and Rigg'd, and were ty'd to Swords." They cultivated an attitude to match, for the same man noted that they "must be saluted, forsooth, by the title of their Highnesses."[22] The princes knew they had to prove their status and Chandos wanted to increase their profile to gather support for his new scheme for the Royal African Company.

They were hardly the first elite men from a non-European country to make a splash in London, but public interest in these visits grew in the eighteenth century.[23] In 1710 the "Four Indian Kings" came to London from America and were a public sensation, much more than the "princes of Delagoa" would be. They were on an official diplomatic visit organized by the governor of New York, who was asking for support against the French during the War of the Spanish Succession and for Protestant missionaries to counter the Jesuit presence in the region. The "Indian Kings" had an audience with the queen herself and were taken to all the major sites of London. Their portraits were painted and entered the Royal Collection, and a performance of *Macbeth* was put on in their honor, but the audience really just wanted to see the four men, and they were brought up on stage. They had poetry, ballads, and pamphlets written about them.[24] At a time of British imperial expansion and in a period that saw the development of the public sphere, the British were interested in the peoples who populated the wider world and had the means to talk about them. These men (it was almost always men) provided the British public with a way to talk about their ideas—positive and negative—about empire and power. The men themselves were acknowledged as elites, but they were always objectified and treated as curiosities rather than as respected leaders of their nation.

The two princes from Mpfumo had a much less stable position than other visitors. They were not on a diplomatic mission from their ruler and had no money of their own. Chandos knew, however, that they had to be accepted and celebrated as princes to convince others that his plan to use them to access trade was viable. So, like the "Indian Kings," they had theater performances put on for them. Months before they dined at Cannons, from late April 1721 to late May of that year, "His Majesty's Company of Comedians" at the Theatre Royal Drury Lane put on three different performances "at the Desire of the Two Princes, Brothers to the King of Delago in Africa," and a company of comedians at the theater in Lincoln's Inn Fields also put on one for their "entertainment."[25] Such benefits were common.[26] Newspaper advertisements often stated that a theater company was to perform a play "at the particular Desire of several Persons of Quality."[27] Sometimes theater managers advertised this to drum up support, but they could reflect actual requests.[28] It is unlikely that the two princes had enough social power at this time to request performances on their own, but Chandos did. He had connections to the Theatre Royal though one of its mangers, Richard Steele, who was an acquaintance.[29] If Chandos did set these theater benefits in motion, part of his agenda was to increase the princes' importance in London society; two days before the first benefit, the Royal African Company read the petition asking for assistance in sending the princes' home.[30] Perhaps Chandos pushed these benefits along to help show the princes' popularity and status.

And popular they were by this point: all the theater advertisements but one use the definite article to refer to the men. They are *the* Indian princes and *the* two princes, implying that readers knew them.

When high-ranking visitors, who seemed exotic to Londoners, came to the metropole, it was not uncommon for a theater company to put on a performance for them. In 1702 Drury Lane performed Aphra Behn's *Emperor of the Moon* "For the Entertainment of an African Prince lately arrived here, being Nephew to the King of Bauday."[31] In 1703 the envoy of the "King of Persia" saw the same play. Five years later, a company treated the Moroccan ambassador to a performance of *Othello*.[32] After the princes' visit, in April 1731, the envoy of the emperor of Dahomey saw a performance of John Fletcher's *Rule a Wife and Have a Wife*. The advertisement read that the play was for "Adomo, Oronoco Tomo Caboshirre of the Great Country of Dawhomay," which was ruled by "the Mighty Trudo Audato Povesaw Danjer Enjow Suveveto, Emperor of Pawpaw in Africa, who lately conquer'd the great Kingdom of Ardah and Whidah."[33] The litany of African titles and names marks this visitor as different and suggests that he too might be a spectacle. To a degree, these visitors' presence drew people to the theater because they were exotic and watching them was a performance in itself, but other dignitaries also went to see plays put on in their honor. During the princes' time in London, the envoy from the king of Sardinia had Shakespeare's *King Henry the Eighth* put on at his "particular desire."[34] This, however, was the only other time during the princes' stay in London that another named individual had a play put on for his entertainment. The princes had four.

While the "Indian Kings" were brought on stage, it appears that the princes were not, and the plays put on for them had no connection to their story. They simply saw the current offerings of the theater companies. They could have been treated to *Oroonoko* or *Othello*, both of which were being performed at the time. In fact, *Oroonoko* entertained playgoers thirteen times while the princes were in London.[35] Instead, they saw one of the twenty-seven performances of the popular revival of Shakespeare's *Merry Wives of Windsor* at Lincoln's Inn Fields. They got a fair dose of Restoration comedy with William Congreve's *Love for Love* and John Dryden's *Spanish Fryar*, along with Sir Richard Steele's more recent comedy *The Funeral*. All three plays were part of the repertoire at Drury Lane, performed eight, nine, and four times, respectively, during the princes' visit.[36] Attending these performances had more to do with establishing their credentials as powerful visitors, than with their exotic origins. This disconnect between the play and the story of the "honored guests" would not continue in the years after the princes' departure.

Some twenty years later, in 1749, a troupe performed a play for a wronged African prince, and this time the stories of the visitor and the play intertwined. William Unsah Sessarakoo, who, in a chilling echo of the princes' story, had been sold into slavery by a captain who had promised to take him to Britain for his education, also went to the theater. The crowd was buzzing because this prince and his African companion, who had shared his fate, had not come to see a comedy: they had arrived to watch *Oroonoko*.[37] The spectators knew the parallels between the two stories and were on the edge of their seats to witness the reactions of these wronged men. Upon the arrival of the prince and his companion the crowd applauded, which the prince "acknowledged with a very genteel bow." During the performance, the story, which so echoed his own, overwhelmed the prince, and he left after the fourth act. His companion stayed and "wept the whole time; a circumstance which affected the audience yet more than the play, and doubled the tears which were shed for Oroonoko and Imoinda." The observers greatly admired the Africans' emotional outpouring, which, for them, was a sign that "art had not yet taught them to suppress" their natural feelings. These men were better at being a "noble savage" than even Oroonoko was—and they were real. *Gentleman's Magazine* reported the incident.[38] Sessarakoo's public persona was different from that of the princes of Mpfumo. Interest in Sessarakoo lay in the fact that he had been wronged. That element of the princes' story is rarely mentioned once the Royal African Company became their patron. For the company their worth lay in their elite status, not in the actions taken against them.

Their elite status both highlighted and hid their blackness. The strict racial divide between Black and white and between freeman and enslaved did not exist in Britain to the same extent that it did in the colonies; however, those with black faces were seen as different and lesser than those with white skin. By the sixteenth century, as European colonial expansion grew, literature began to highlight the polarity between dark and light and to tie whiteness to Europeans and darkness to the "other."[39] The medical and scientific communities discussed skin color and difference as well. It was the heat near the equator that caused blackness, said some. But even here judgment lurked, for they also thought that the heat of the "torrid zone" made those living there lazy and lascivious and thus less open to a "civilizing" impetus.[40] The idea of fetal impression, that dark skin resulted when women thought dark thoughts when pregnant, gained traction.[41] By the late seventeenth century, the idea that blackness was an "accidental monstrosity" had taken hold.[42] Humoral theory too argued that one's complexion was a reflection of the state of one's humoral balance, and that this was a state that was difficult, if not impossible, to change.[43] Different ideas peppered European thought, but all believed that God created man white and that some kind of aberration or degeneration caused blackness and that the difference was probably permanent.[44]

Furthermore, Europeans tied darker complexions to those of lower social standing.[45] Since the medieval period, people had created links, visible in literature, between blackness and servitude.[46] Some of these links came from the Bible, especially the story of the curse of Ham.[47] In the Bible, Noah's son Ham uncovers his father's nakedness and Noah declares that Ham's son, Canaan, would be a "servant of servants." The Bible says nothing, however, about Canaan's descendants having darker skin. Europeans constructed this connection as their involvement in the slave trade became increasingly common.[48] The sin of the act would obviously have darkened the skin of the sinner's descendants, they thought.[49] Thus, African princes presented a conundrum—their color suggested servitude, but their status implied otherwise. This made them curiosities, not their color alone.

Londoners were used to seeing Black faces on the streets of the capital. Scholars have found references to more than seven hundred people of color between 1600 and 1710 in London's parish registers of births, baptisms, and deaths.[50] By the late seventeenth century, many aristocrats, members of the gentry, merchants, army officers, naval captains, and absentee planters in London had Black servants and enslaved Africans. Possessing a Black servant had become a symbol of status.[51] Paintings from the seventeenth and eighteenth centuries often depict Black pages or servants floating around the edges of paintings.[52] In some, like that painted by Bartholomew Dandridge around 1725, the enslaved youth is meant to contrast with the white child, upon whom he gazes adorningly (fig. 10).[53] In others, like that showing Elihu Yale and his sons-in-law, painted in 1708, the enslaved (and collared) youth appears as an afterthought, a sign of the ubiquity of enslaved Africans in Britain (fig.11). Even scandalous events could reveal the mundane presence of African servants. While the Mpfuman princes lived at the Spread Eagle, a woman attempted to elope with her lover. Upon hearing the news her family sent "a faithful Negro in pursuit," and "the diligent dog, with the help of some watermen, overtook the lady with her lover," and she agreed to go back

Figure 10. This painting highlights the way the British saw the enslaved as property. Here both the enslaved boy and the dog are depicted with collars. Bartholomew Dandridge, *A Young Girl with an Enslaved Servant and a Dog*, c. 1725, Yale Center for British Art, Paul Mellon Collection, B1981.25.205. Reproduced by permission of Yale Center for British Art, New Haven, Connecticut.

with "the Negro."[54] To see Black faces in London was common by the early eighteenth century. In fact, there were probably a few thousand residing in England during the eighteenth century, and most lived in London.[55]

The princes may have met or seen others of African descent during their time in London. Only a few blocks away from the Spread Eagle Inn lived nineteen-year-old "Agnes," or as he liked to be called, John. He could have run an errand for his master to the Spread Eagle wearing his blue livery, hat, and gray stockings. He seems to have had a unique presence, being described as "of a large size for his age, and pretty fat" and having "a long foot, and his legs almost all bones and sinews, and a long nose for that sort of people." This

Figure 11. This image shows an enslaved boy, with a collar, serving wine to Elihu Yale, his son-in-law, Lord James Cavendish, Cavendish's father, the Duke of Devonshire, and a lawyer. The presence of Yale, who made his fortune working for the East India Company, and the unknown enslaved youth highlights the overlap between the Atlantic and Indian Ocean trades. Unknown artist, *Elihu Yale with Members of his Family and an Enslaved Child*, c. 1719, Yale Center for British Art, gift of Andrew Cavendish, eleventh Duke of Devonshire, B1970.1. Reproduced by permission of Yale Center for British Art, New Haven, Connecticut.

image of him comes from the advertisement printed when he escaped his enslaver; the phrasing of the ad and the description of him as a "Negro Man, or rather great Boy," who is called Agnes but "pretends to be Christned by the name of John," hints at some of the many reasons he might have left.[56] Or perhaps the princes met Nanny, who lived in Mark Lane, a six-minute walk away.[57] Even closer to home was Peggy, a "Negro Woman-Servant," described as "tall, slender, and well shaped," who often wore red and white calico, a "round-ear'd Cap," and a "white short jacket."[58] It is possible that any of these men and women could have encountered the two princes, although their lives were different in many ways.

The status of these Black men and women in England was ambiguous. The word "slave" only slowly worked its way into the London record books, first used in 1662.[59] In fact, in the seventeenth century the English used the term more to refer to themselves when discussing resistance to tyranny than they did in relation to the enslaved people around them.[60] The metropole was also, however, a crucial site for the establishment of racial slavery. The fact that many people had Black servants, who were probably enslaved, normalized it, and even the running of advertisements for enslaved Africans who had absconded advanced the acceptance of slavery and racial difference.[61] The courts were busy as well. Charles II and James II were keen to see enslaved Africans defined as permanent property by law. In 1677, the case *Butts v. Penny* actually defined enslaved people as property. The tables turned in 1696 after the Glorious Revolution when the case *Chamberlayne v. Harvey* found that people could not be property.[62] Thus, when the princes arrived in Britain the question was legally muddled.[63]

Even with a law in place declaring that people could not be property, men and women found it necessary to seek their freedom, and others thought they had the right to advertise for their return. While the princes were in London, newspapers ran advertisements seeking the return of at least eight African servants or enslaved laborers who had reached for their liberty.[64] The advertisements provide a vivid picture of these individuals. There was twenty-two-year-old Dick, who was five foot six inches and of a "yellow complexion." He had "Wool Hair" and the word "HARE" burnt into his right breast.[65] There was also Pompey, a "well set fellow" who played the trumpet and had two jackets, "one a sailor's Pee-Jacket, the other a white cloth," and "a coloured shirt." He also sported "a cross cut in his forehead, and several small scars in his face, and a Cut of one side his neck."[66] These could be marks of white violence, but some of them could be scarification marks made in Africa. Aaron, "a lusty Negro man," absconded from a ship on its way to Jamaica, probably hoping to find a better life in London. He was described as "a sour looked fellow, of a surly dogged Disposition, wearing a Silver laced hat, a black horse hair wig, a grey cloth coat and breeches trimm'd with the same colour, and white block tin buttons."[67] Women too sought their freedom. Kitty, "a negro maid" of twenty-two years, left her mistress. The advertisement for her return described her as "pretty short, inclining to Fat, of a yellowish complexion" and possessing a "down look," which probably had more to do with her situation than her natural disposition.[68] Ann Moor also escaped, until the advertisement posted for her led to her capture.[69] The lives of these men and women were different from those of white servants. Their probable experience of enslavement had marked them, often literally. Furthermore, owners of enslaved Africans in London often sent them to the West Indies, and its even harsher forms of enslavement, if they proved "troublesome." This would haunt them.[70]

Some enslaved Africans looked to fight for their liberty using connections and the law. One such man was Diego. He lived in London during the princes' time there, and his main supporter was Henry Newman, who knew the princes. The death of Diego's owner, Mr. Woodbridge, in England, left him in a precarious position. On their voyage to London, Woodbridge had promised Diego his freedom and had allowed him to train as a bricklayer, but now Diego worried he would be sent back to Barbados, "where," in Newman's words, "he may be liable to be bought & sold as a common Slave." He buttered Newman up by reminding him that in Barbados he would "be more out of ye way of instruction as a Christian wch he desires to enjoy." He then stated his belief that "his being a Christian and upon English Ground" should "entitle him to the Priviledges of an Englishman," which, for him, meant freedom. When Newman raised the point that Mrs. Woodbridge might have a claim on him, Diego "readily answered that the Laws of Barbados might give her a right . . . but the Laws of England give her no such right to him." He knew the legal debates about slavery in the metropole. Diego also looked after his own property. He knew that English law did not allow the owners of the house where he had lived with Woodbridge to withhold his possessions unless he owed them money. He did not owe anything, and if they did not surrender his things, he was ready to have them arrested. Newman acted as the mediator between Diego and Woodbridge's man of affairs. In the end, the Woodbridge family let him go, especially when he expressed a willingness to serve Woodbridge's son when he came of age.[71] Here we see the liminal and unstable world in which these men and women lived. Diego was free, but not. Even when he "won" the right to stay, his ties to the Woodbridge family were not cut.

Diego's case also shows the importance of religion in these debates. Europeans always had a lurking belief that Christians could not be enslaved, as seen in Diego's arguments.[72] Christian baptism, especially into the Anglican Church, increased the sense of sameness between him and white Britons, rather than emphasizing his difference. Religion, however, was deeply tied up in ideas about race and difference. Many of the justifications for judging people of darker hues as inferior to white populations came from the

Bible. Some looked to the curse of Ham.[73] Others saw blackness as the mark of Cain, bestowed on him after he murdered his brother, or the legacy of the daughters of Lot, who raped their father to conceive children when they thought they were the only people left on earth.[74] One thing becomes clear: in British eyes, the sinners of the Bible were the ancestors of those with darker skin. Often, condemnation of a group or area focused on that society's lack of Christianity, which the British would connect with their concept of civility. To British observers, Africans, because they lacked a Christian foundation, were "savage," "rude," and "brutish."[75] They lived wild, uncultivated lives that placed them as close to animals as to man.[76] But they could be saved. Many Britons believed that if Africans embraced Christianity, they would clothe their nakedness, see the error of their ways, and cultivate their fields. They would become "civilized." They would not be equals—their blackness with its ties to ancient sin remained—but ties of similitude would exist.[77]

The princes' souls had been of concern to Londoners since they arrived. One of the first people they met was Joshua Oldfield, a Presbyterian clergyman. He had met the princes "by chance" one day, probably when he stopped by the Spread Eagle Inn on his journey between his academy in Hoxton Square to the north and his flock at the Globe Alley meeting on Maid Lane in Southwark across the river.[78] Their souls interested him, and he hired a tutor to teach them to read and "by proper degrees to instruct 'em in the Christian Religion."[79] Chandos later took over the payment of the tutor.[80] The instruction must have paid off, for in mid-June 1721, a month after the plays in their honor ended and three months before they dined at Cannons, they were baptized. The *London Journal* reported on the event, opining that "the Conversion of Infidels to the Christian Faith must certainly be very acceptable to the Readers of the London Journal."[81] It then detailed the baptismal ceremony. Dr. Pratt, the dean of Rochester, had presided over both the baptism and the service with "the greatest Solemnity" before "a numerous Congregation of Persons of Quality." The witnesses were Viscount Vane, who stood proxy for the Duke of Chandos, Lady Blount, and Colonel Toogood. It was the dean who formally christened them "James Shandois" and "John Twogood."[82] These names tied them to their patrons and two of Jesus's first disciples, the brothers James and John. While the christening was not quite front-page news (the editor placed the story on the fourth page, between a description of the glories of Bristol's spa waters and the elopement of an heiress with a blacksmith), it still received more coverage than most baptisms of the time. The same can be said for the entry in the parish registry. Under christenings, the princes' baptism is inserted between the entry for "Joseph, sonne of Joseph Warrin and Elizabeth his wife" and that for "James, by a Travelling woman." It reads, "James Shandayes & John Twogood, Two Indian princes. Baptized by Doctor Prof Deane of Rochester This 20th day of June of 1721."[83] This was a comparatively elaborate entry, casting those placed before and after it into obscurity.

Their baptism also marks the first time the princes are referred to by a name. The *London Journal* informs us that "the Eldest was named James Shandois and the youngest John Togood."[84] Later they would be referred to as James Maquillan Muffoom and John Chaung Muffoom.[85] But, for the most part, they were still usually referred to as a matched pair—the princes or the two princes. The two trading companies usually expanded on this to add their place of supposed origin. When the East India Company was involved, they were usually called "Indian Princes," "Princes of Delagoa," or the "Delagoa princes," but they were also referred to as the "Black Indian Princes" or "Black princes."[86] In the Royal African Company records, they were almost always the "African Princes." Their choices highlighted the geographical claims of these companies. But these new individualized names gesture to the influence the two men had amassed.

At certain moments, we can peek under the statements made by their patrons and see the princes shaping their journey home. Only they could have agreed that their brother was the emperor of Monomotapa, although this relationship was later downgraded, and they admitted that "their Brother is King Tembo & the Emperor of Monomatapa married their sister."[87] They also began to attend meetings of the Royal African Company. A few weeks before their baptism and a week after a theater benefit, they were present at a meeting of the Court of Assistants, where they met eleven of the members.[88] The *London Journal* reported that they were "daily attending the Directors of the African Company."[89] Their voices must have been heard during these visits.

One reason the Royal African Company listened was because by May 1721 it had decided that linking the princes' desire to go home with the company's own wish for a new settlement on the southwestern coast of Africa would benefit both parties. The plan was that the company's men and the princes would arrive on the west coast and start a new settlement. The princes' presence would ease the concerns of the local Africans. The company assumed that the princes' royal connections meant they were well known, even in western Africa, and if they were not, "the relation of their case and treatment they have met with from the Royall African Company cannot fail so to conciliate the Affections of the Natives to the Company," which in turn would "facilitate the Establishing the Settlement and produce very happy consequences from it."[90] After impressing the Africans on the west coast by arriving with celebrities and a story that highlighted the benevolent ways of the company, an embassy would travel inland to Monomotapa. There the princes would introduce the company's representatives to their brother-in-law, the emperor, and trade between the two groups would blossom. Gold and ivory would flow to the west coast, and the company would prosper as never before. Once the princes had completed this task, they would be free to travel eastward from Monomotapa, which they "represent to be a Moon [a month's travel] from their own Capitall."[91]

The man who had proposed this new settlement was one Captain John Hill, a man the princes had known for a while and seemingly disliked. After their baptism, Colonel Toogood was heard of no more, and the princes were put in the care of Captain Hill. He moved them to Lambeth, just across the river from Parliament, far from the Spread Eagle. Hill had cultivated the princes' interest when Toogood was still attempting to convince the East India Company to take them home. But the East India Company knew of Hill's reputation as "a Rattle and a Rake" and refused to deal with him.[92] This was not known to the men of the Royal African Company, and when he proposed a new settlement on the west coast, not far from the Cape of Good Hope, the company was intrigued. It was to be a substantial factory (trading post), where Hill would be the chief merchant and oversee another merchant, a factor, two writers, two carpenters, two blacksmiths, two masons, four soldiers, and a surgeon.[93] As seen, the princes were key to the whole endeavor, since their social ties would bring in trade from the interior. So, in May, a month before their baptism, the Royal African Company put Hill in charge and began paying him £5 15s. a week for the upkeep of the princes and their servants.[94] By the early summer of 1721, the Royal African Company was serious about setting up a new settlement in southwest Africa and saw the princes as a tool toward that end.

This was not a happy period for the princes, however. When Captain Hill moved them to Lambeth, he cut them off from any social networks they had begun to build in the area. Hill dismissed the clergyman whom Dr. Oldfield had found to live and travel with them because, according to one observer, he wanted "no body near 'em to hinder their learning Swear & Curse &c."[95] The princes were not pleased, but it appears they had learned how to maneuver in British society. They knew that to change their situation they had to find a person of rank to help them. They also knew that they interested men of the cloth, so they found David Wilkins, the archbishop of Canterbury's personal chaplain. Wilkins later wrote that he "became acquainted with the 2 African Princes who live in his Neighbourhood at Standgate under the care of Captain Hill of whom they very much complain."[96] Wilkins then informed the archbishop of the case and wrote to the Society for Promoting Christian Knowledge, which, in turn, told Chandos.[97] The company dismissed Hill from his ship and removed the princes from his care. The princes next fell under the watch of Captain John Sharrow, and the two men moved back near the city center, on Burr Street, close to what is now St. Katherine's Dock. The princes thanked the archbishop.[98]

Captain Sharrow was a remote connection of the Duke of Chandos.[99] It should not be surprising that the two men got along, as both thrived on developing projects. Sharrow had also suggested a settlement on the southwest coast of Africa, to the Royal African Company. This proposal went nowhere, but now he had another plan in mind.[100] It caught Chandos's attention. The duke forwarded it to another active Royal African Company member, stating that he wished "some way could be found to put this design in Execution," as "the Voyage of the African Princes will furnish a very good opportunity & pretence to colour it with."[101] The proposal appears to have concerned the island of Trindade and the possibility of trade with Brazil.[102] Trindade sits more than 750 miles east of Rio de Janeiro in the middle of the Atlantic. According to Chandos, William III had granted the island to Sir John Hoskyns, whose son had married Chandos's sister.[103] It was a family tie the duke now wished to exploit. He began to write to lawyers asking about the legality of the grant and its validity if no settlement existed on the island. He thought it might be rich in gold or silver and, if not, it might serve as a station from which to trade with the Portuguese in Brazil.[104] A side trip to this island was eventually added to the princes' itinerary home.[105] Sharrow's ploy had worked, and by the end of the month he was the commander of the *Northampton* in place of Hill. This was the ship that would set sail for Mpfumo.

The Royal African Company was reevaluating the itinerary of the voyage as a whole. The company had lost interest in establishing a settlement on the southwest coast and linking the princes' trip home to it. The day after they dismissed Hill, the company's Court of Assistants asked the Committee of Trade to tell them "which way they [thought] most proper for sending home the African Princes." Then, tellingly, the members of the court also told the committee that they had the "power to consult & treat with the East India

Company upon this affair."[106] This could mean only one thing—the company wanted to go beyond the Cape of Good Hope into the waters watched over by the East India Company.

Talks between the two companies began in early September when two members of the Royal African Company went down the street to talk to two members of the East India Company at East India House. They began with the easy request. All they wanted was "to send a small Ship . . . to Delagoa to carry the Black Princes thither and dispose of the Cargo." They also wanted the right to "purchase Slaves at Madagascar for The West Indies" in "case of disappointment." They ended, however, by elusively stating that "they had some other Affairs of moment, which they should be enabled to communicate in a little time."[107] It turns out they wanted "an exclusive Licence to purchase Slaves at Madagascar."[108] As we know, the East India Company was not keen on licensing ships to trade with Madagascar at this time. Not only had Parliament just rejected the company's own attempt to send enslaved labor from Madagascar to the West Indies, the company was also trying to shut down illegal trade between the two places.[109] If it granted licenses, it would be easier for unlicensed ships to sneak in and out. Company officials also knew they walked on thin ice when they discussed trade in southeastern Africa. The company had promised Gordon and Huggins a sizable reward if it opened trade in that region, and this was not a charge it was willing to pay simply to help the Royal African Company. It did what any self-respecting company would do—it asked its lawyers. Robert Raymond and Philip Yorke came back with an answer in early October. The Royal African Company could send a ship, but it could not trade in the area. They recommended that the East India Company "insert a clause restrictive of all Trade there in order to prevent its being made use of for that purpose."[110] The company was willing to let the Royal African Company take the princes home, but it was not willing to let them trade. Oddly, the Royal African Company quickly agreed and asked the East India Company to expedite the license.[111] By the new year, the company had it.[112] With the profit to be had by trade removed, it would seem that the Royal African Company now saw this as a benevolent journey. The company hoped, however, that its generosity would bring profit in its wake. First of all, who was to say that the princes' brother could not give them gifts for their trouble? In the instructions sent with the captain of the ship, the company expounded: "it is not to be doubted, but on this occasion the King and Princes will not scruple to fully load your ship home," but to avoid trouble with the East India Company he should have them compose "a letter of thanks" and specify that "what they send home by you as presents to the company [are] in return for those civilitys and the presents which have been made to them."[113]

The princes had no role in these negotiations. Neither their connections nor their competency had any bearing on whether the East India Company was going to allow another company access to their domain. Instead, their late summer and fall was spent maintaining old connections and fostering new ones. Chandos still wanted to keep the interest in the princes high to shore up their importance to the company's plans. This is when he invited them to Cannons.[114] It was a chance to remind those who had an interest in them that these were men they could depend on. Men who knew the rules of British society. Men who could assert power. Men who belonged.

How one ate and where one ate were becoming markers of class in Britain.[115] Unlike in previous centuries, dinning was no longer something the household did together. Servants ate at different tables in different rooms.[116] Elaborate meals like this were stages for the elite. And those at the table judged each other. You could no longer gnaw on bones or throw food on the floor. Eating with your hands was frowned upon. Napkins should only be slightly soiled. The fork, an introduction from the previous century, should be managed with ease and in silence. You should eat without drawing attention to the food. You should not smell it or suck it from the spoon. It was "indecent to fill the Mouth too full; such cramming is more suitable for a Beast than a rational creature," and it was "unseemly to chew your meat with open lips; for it is loathsome and unpleasant to see the Meat in such a frame."[117] Grace should attend one's actions, and rules should be followed. These were rules the princes would have needed to learn. They seem to have embraced them. Years later, Thomas Bray, a religious reformer, would complain that "they look'd upon themselves as affronted, if their Meat was not of the best Kind, and well Drest."[118] The princes knew they had to project authority and that even their actions at a meal needed to reflect their status.

To an extent, though the rules of comportment were different, the princes knew that social meaning saturated food and table etiquette. Dining both in Mpfumo and in London was about community and social power. In Britain, you were not to "sit above your betters," and if a superior offered you a dish, you could not refuse.[119] Women carved the meat and often served it, although this was beginning to go out of fashion.[120] At home in Africa, the princes usually dined once a day in the late afternoon. The women of the village spent much of the day, when they were not working in the fields, preparing cooked

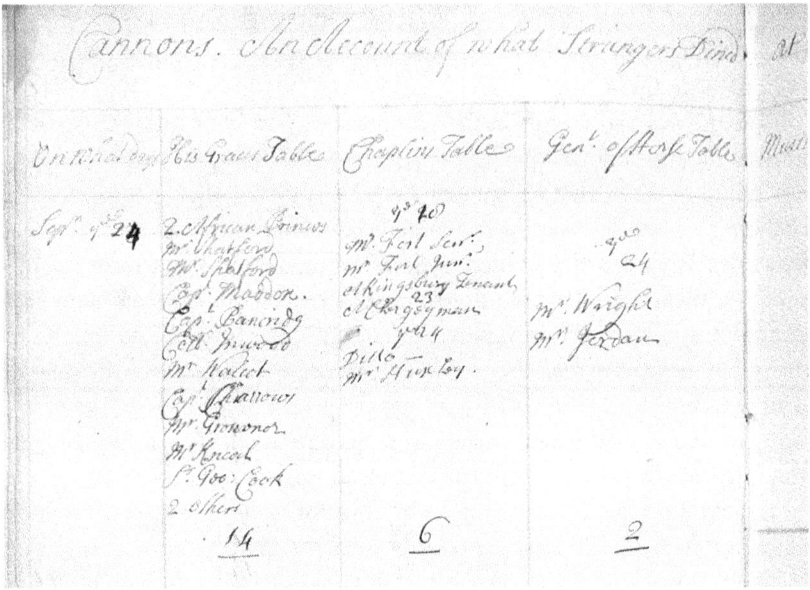

Figure 12. This image comes from "A Book of Strangers," a list of dinner guests at the Duke of Chandos's estate, Cannons. It shows the list of guests at "His Grace's Table" on 24 September 1721, when the princes were guests of honor. We can see that while they are listed first, they are not individualized by name. Captain Sharrow, however, a few rows down, is. "A Book of Strangers," Huntington Library, Stowe Papers, HEH ST 59. Reproduced by permission of the Huntington Library, San Marino, California.

cereals layered with sauces. At mealtime, each woman bought her food to share with the entire village, and the first to eat were always those with the most authority.[121] There were no forks and no separate tables for the elite, but the messages sent through meals were similar.

Even when the princes were guests of honor, however, they were not seen as equals. When their visit was entered into Cannons's "Book of Strangers," a list of dinner guests, the princes appear first, just as the Duke of Manchester, the Duke of Argyll, and the Duke of Newcastle had been on other dates (fig. 12). But unlike the other men of high status noted, the princes were not given names. They are simply "2 African Princes."[122] This marks them as curiosities more than guests. There are other guests left unnamed in the book. There is an "Africa Captain," a "gentlemen," and "others." Many women are simply referred to a "Lady."[123] None of these other individuals, however, was listed first, seemingly as a guest of honor. Furthermore, almost a year earlier, when discussing another dinner invitation, one of the princes' supporters suggested not bringing the two men to dine, "for fear his Lady should have an Aversion to their Colour."[124] In fact, there were no women noted at the princes' dinner. The only woman ever mentioned as being in their orbit was Lady Blount, who was at their baptism, although the records do not note any other interactions with her. Their British world was a very masculine one. These men were too different to mix with the families of their supporters. Converting to Christianity, insisting on being called your highness, and dismissing ill-dressed meat was not enough to break down the wall of difference between them and the Britons with whom they interacted.

CHAPTER 5

Preparing to Leave

London, England, 5 October 1721

In early October 1721, the princes passed by the newly rebuilt cathedral of St. Paul's and arrived at its chapter house. The building, of red brick and Portland stone, with large windows, sat in the shadow of the cathedral and had also been finished just a few years before (fig. 13).[1] The princes traveled about a mile and half to get there from their new lodgings on Burr Street to the east. They had come to meet with members of the Society for Promoting Christian Knowledge (SPCK). The society's main focus was conserving and expanding the Anglican faith and the princes interested them. The society had been aware of the two men since the beginning of the year, if not before, but starting in the fall of 1721 their engagement began to grow and they requested a meeting.[2] With Captain Sharrow, the princes waited outside the closed doors where the meeting was taking place, perhaps sitting, perhaps standing, perhaps pacing. When called into the cold and bright room, they faced twelve men.[3] They were introduced as "James Maquillan Muffoom, and John Chaung Muffoom of Delagoa," an interesting change from their baptismal names and perhaps a suggestion of what they were called in Africa. At first, the princes stayed in the background, letting Sharrow take the floor. He answered questions about the religious books possessed by the princes and the plans of the Royal African Company to send them home. The SPCK, it turns out, wanted to send a religious instructor with the two men to Mpfumo. It was at this point that the princes asserted their presence. They informed the society that "if any Persons would go over with them to instruct them they should be kindly receiv'd, and if they did not like the Country they should be at Liberty to return to England in the same ship that carry'd 'em over."[4] They were the authorities on Africa, and the society listened.

Figure 13. St. Paul's Chapter House was one of the meeting places of the Society for Promoting Christian Knowledge, but it was not the society's favorite. The large windows probably brought in light, but they made the building cold. This produced many complaints from members of the society. Unknown artist, *The Chapter House, St. Pauls*, Yale Center for British Art, Paul Mellon Collection, B1977.14.16221. Reproduced by permission of Yale Center for British Art, New Haven, Connecticut.

The voyage home was becoming a reality, and it took many different voices and groups, working together, to make it possible. At this point, the princes were an active presence in the negotiations, not only with the Royal African Company but also with the Society for Promoting Christian Knowledge. Furthermore, the various London institutions worked together. The SPCK was dependent upon the Royal African Company to send an instructor to Africa, and it probably knew of the princes because their secretary, Henry Newman, knew the Duke of Chandos. The webs of connection were dense and made voyages like the princes' possible. The meeting also highlights that it was not only trading companies that built projects around the princes, religious societies did too. The SPCK was interested in keeping the princes steady in their Anglican faith and in converting other Mpfumans, an unusual aspiration for the society at the time. All of these groups would begin to load their hopes onto the *Northampton*, the ship the Royal African Company had earmarked to send the princes' home.

The Society for Promoting Christian Knowledge had formed in 1698 to address concerns about the spiritual state of England itself, not areas beyond its shores. This group of citizens, some clergymen, some not, believed that "the growth of Vice and Immorality" was slowly choking the nation and that at its root lay English peoples' "gross Ignorance of the Principles of the Christian Religion." The society wanted to fix this. It distributed religious books, started charity schools, and hoped this infrastructure of knowledge, would foster godliness.[5] The society was the brainchild of Thomas Bray, a man of humble origins who understood the struggles of local clergymen and wanted to cultivate educated congregations. He first came to the attention of the public through the publication of his *Catechetical Lectures*, a book that provided clergymen with tools to explain the catechism to their congregations. The popularity of this work brought him to the attention of the bishop of London, who appointed him his commissionary, or agent, in Maryland. The bishop tasked him with nurturing the Anglican clergy in this formerly Catholic colony. This was easier said than done. Bray despaired at the state of the colonial church. Colonial clergy could not even afford the books they needed to enlighten their wandering flocks. He feared that the colonial problem was the same as that plaguing the British Isles: poor clergymen did not have the means to nurture a congregation and help them become well versed in their faith. His concerns, which were shared with others around him, led to the establishment of the SPCK and its sister society, founded a few years later, the Society for the Propagation of the Gospel in Foreign Parts, which was to look after souls in the western colonies.[6] Both societies wanted to foster an educated clergy that could reach out to poor benighted Anglican souls at home and abroad.

The SPCK was more than just a reflection of one man's concerns: it was the product of a church rethinking its position vis-à-vis the nation. After the Glorious Revolution of 1688–89, the Anglican Church split into factions. On one side stood the high churchmen, who wanted to solidify and assert the power of the Anglican Church and its doctrine. This meant reestablishing the power of the bishops and emphasizing the sacraments. Then there were the low churchmen, who wanted to loosen the structure of the church to revitalize the faith of the larger populace. They were more willing to accept those of different denominations in the hope of converting them. The SPCK emerged in response to both desires: through education it would solidify the power of the Anglican Church, but it was also interested in outreach.[7] It wanted to bring people to Christianity and polish their faith to an Anglican gleam.

This was a time when multiple religious societies were bubbling up to support such designs.[8] Among these were the governors of Queen Anne's Bounty, who distributed funds to poor clergymen, and the Commission for Relieving Poor Proselytes, which sought to help those who wished to convert to Anglicanism from Catholicism. The founders of these societies believed that there was more power in the group than in the individual. As the members of the SPCK stated in their first letter to correspondents, "By means of this Society many good Men are become more known and usefull to one another by a Christian Conversation, and Correspondence." Such a group they knew had "a far greater Power by the Grace of God of doing Good by their joint Assistance and Advice than singly can be expected."[9] They made it a point, early on, to establish contacts with like-minded souls throughout Britain, the Continent, and the world beyond.[10]

In many ways, the SPCK encapsulates the spirit of the age. It was a group of men looking for new opportunities, just like the East India Company and the Royal African Company. As one historian has stated, "Religion, it seems, was taken up by the culture of enterprise that had seized much of English society at the end of the seventeenth century."[11] All were looking for new ways to profit, except that for the SPCK the payoff came in souls rather than pounds sterling. Furthermore, these religious men based their push for change not on the state or the official church but on loosely knitted groups of individuals who helped make up the nascent civil society that was taking shape and gaining power.[12] The actions of individual citizens and "the public" mattered, as did the networks woven in between.

The intertwined nature of these networks shaped the experience of the princes. They found that men of godly conversation knew men who talked in pounds and pence, and vice versa. Henry Newman, the secretary of the SPCK and a man who had known the princes since they were under Colonel Toogood's care, spoke both languages. His place as secretary of the SPCK tied him securely to the world of moral outreach, but he also had ties to the trading world. Newman began his life in Massachusetts and attended Harvard, with the idea of becoming a clergyman. After serving as a librarian at Harvard, he became a chaplain on a merchant ship and then a merchant in his own right, focusing on the Newfoundland fish trade. It was during this period of his life that he moved to London, became a member of the SPCK, and eventually, in 1708, became its secretary.[13] In this role, he often nurtured links between the religious society and commercial companies. He wrote to the East India Company requesting that religious books and men be sent to the east.[14] He told the company: "The E[ast] India, the African & South Sea Companies do now in a manner divide the World between 'em, I hope it is reserv'd to them to have the honour of propagating the best Religion to the remotest Countries." He then massaged the East India Company's ego: "The E[ast] India Company as their Territories are the largest & most distant so their Zeal in so good a Cause will be proportionable. They have hitherto been generously foremost in their Endeavours & I hope they will always have cause to rejoice in the success."[15] The companies sometimes reciprocated. When the Royal African Company was organizing the princes' journey, it also asked the SPCK to recommend a schoolmaster to be sent to Gambia by a different ship.[16] Thus, these very different institutions had worked together long before the princes came onto the stage.

How and when the SPCK learned about the princes is opaque. When Henry Newman laid out the princes' story, he recorded that Dr. Oldfield had taken pity on the two men and that, in a tragic case of passive voice, "Our Society were soon after this inform'd of the case of these princes."[17] He leaves who informed them unsaid. The society's minutes first mention the princes in late January 1721, but Newman had received an invitation to dine with the princes almost two months earlier.[18] Judging from past and future actions, it would not be surprising if Chandos had notified Newman, who then kept track of the men and monitored the interest level of the SPCK. At first it was relatively low. Besides their meetings with Newman, the princes first interacted with the society in early 1721, when it sent them two copies of the New Testament, copies of the Book of Common Prayer, and "Lewis's Exposition of the Catechism."[19] But besides sending the texts, the company showed little additional interest. Other ventures occupied its members time. They were backing the creation of a translation of the New Testament into Arabic to support Christians living within the Ottoman Empire. They were also assisting clergymen settled in East India Company factories and helping a Danish Lutheran mission at Tranquebar, now known as Tharangambadi, on the southeast coast of India. Money, books, and even a printing press landed there courtesy of the society.[20] The support for the mission at Tharangambadi was a bit of a departure for the society. Most of its international ventures involved maintaining Christian souls, not converting them. It certainly was not against such ventures, though. Newman wrote to a chaplain at Fort St. George, in what is now Chennai, India, that he rejoiced "to hear that the

Dry Bones of that Vast Paganism, begin to be blown upon by the Spirit of the Lord, and the pure light of the Gospel to shine among Heathens."[21] Conversion on a grand scale, however, always seemed outside the SPCK's purview. It sent books, not missionaries. Thus, it is not surprising that initially the society sent books to the princes and then forgot about them.

A slap on the wrist from the archbishop of Canterbury in August 1721 spurred the SPCK into action regarding the two men. When the princes complained to the archbishop's chaplain about Captain Hill, he in turn informed the archbishop. His Grace then took the SPCK to task.[22] Newman defended their actions: "Finding 'em as it were immured by those who had care of 'em & seldom permitted to visit our Places of Pub. Worship it was to no purpose to propose a solemn Instruction of them," but now that Captain Hill had dismissed their religious instructor the society intended to have the princes "more effectually instructed, and sent home in a maner suitable to the Honor of the Nation and the Religion we Profess."[23] And the society must have been pleased that John Sharrow was named the princes' new caretaker, as his relative Penelope Rowland had left both him and the society money. The society trusted the "near Relation of Good Mrs Rowland" to treat the princes well and look after their spiritual well-being.[24]

The following months saw the SPCK making up for its past neglect of the princes and determining how to send them home in a way that would "Honor the Nation" and the Anglican religion. In the beginning, this meant sharpening the princes' Christianity. First, in September the society followed its tried-and-true method—it sent books. Soon the princes received Bibles (although they already had them) and other religious texts.[25] Then they found themselves presented with dictionaries, English grammars, and spelling books.[26] The society had also decided to send them home to Africa with "a noble present of Books" that would keep them on the Christian path.[27] For four months the society fiddled with the book list, adding some, taking others away. In the end, most of the books were practical religious guides: observations on the scriptures and directions for reading them, multiple guides on the catechism, and works by Thomas Bray to promote religious understanding. Other books, like *The Whole Duty of Man*, were devotional texts meant to sustain the princes' faith and help them ruminate upon it. The society also included books meant to explain the Bible by explicating the peoples and events mentioned in it. This probably explains the inclusion of works by Flavius Josephus, an early Jewish historian who lived in the first century after Christ's death. The society wanted to give a sense of the longevity of the church, adding books like Laurence Echard's history of the early days of the Christian Church.[28] In the mind of the SPCK, these books would help the princes sustain, understand, and respect their faith.

But their teachings did not stop with religion: many of the texts were secular in tone. The society included a history of England and maps of the modern and sacred worlds.[29] The maps would have given the princes a chance to see where Mpfumo fit in the Western conceptions of the world. The society also included an almanac and John Comenius's picture book for the teaching of children.[30] The SPCK wanted the princes to embrace both the Anglican religion and English culture, and so it added books on husbandry, gardening, and cookery.[31] The society believed that European culture was a necessary foundation for Christianity.

The list of the books sent with the princes also reveals that the SPCK had begun to look beyond the princes to their people. It could not resist such an opportunity of "conveying the light of the Gospel to a Country at present abandoned to the grossest darkness & ignorance."[32] Some books it sent in pairs or as single copies for the use of the two princes or their instructor. But it added a dozen psalters, catechisms, expositions on the catechism, directions for reading holy scripture, guides for understanding baptism and the Lord's Day, and devotional texts. It also threw in twelve copies of books against swearing, uncleanliness, and drinking, although these could have been meant for the ship's crew.[33] It wanted these texts to guide the souls of Africans away from what they saw as "the grossest darkness" to the light. The prospective converts first had to be able to read them, however, so the society also stocked the ship with eight books on spelling and grammar, twelve primers, and four hundred pens.[34] Converting souls had always been hard for Protestants because their religion was so text based. True Protestants should not only accept the Lord into their hearts but should also be able to read about his works in the Bible. Education and conversion often went hand in hand. This is how Dr. Oldfield approached the education of the princes. He had "a Church man to go daily to teach 'em to Read," and then only "by proper degrees" was he "to instruct 'em in the Christian Religion."[35] Learning to read came before instruction in the faith.

Furthermore, the SPCK did not believe it could trust the princes with the conversion of their people. As one observer said, they "seem glad they know Religion, and are resolv'd to endeavour to convert their people at their return, but I fear for want of some European to accompany them they will fall short of their good purposes."[36] Such concerns prompted the society to begin to search for "Two Sober Mechanicks of Competent Knowledge in Religion" to send with the princes. These men, the society hoped, would "preserve and improve that Instruction" already given to the princes and help them "in recommending Christianity to their own Nation."[37] According to the records, the princes applauded this plan. Such men, they said, "should be kindly receiv'd," and they wrote a letter of thanks to a supporter of the endeavor.[38] In the eyes of the society's members, the ideal religious instructor would be settled in his religious ideas and "qualified to teach them to the Heathen in Africa." The SPCK wanted "piously well disposed persons" not only able to read and write but also with "a desire to Improve themselves by good Books which the Society may from time to time put into their hands."[39] Such men, however, proved hard to find.

The society spent months searching for qualified instructors to send with the princes.[40] They tried to tempt one Mr. Kauffman, "a Learned Pious Melancholy German," and a Mr. Smith, who was sober and knew a number of languages.[41] Kauffman balked from the beginning, insisting on having the "Liberty to return in the ship, if he d[id]n't like the Country."[42] Neither man decided to go. Another candidate, Joseph Adams, would have possessed a unique perspective on the princes' enslavement, for he had been recently ransomed from enslavement in Muslim North Africa.[43] At first he appeared keen to go, saying he "should be willing to go any where for the Service of the Christian Religion."[44] His friends and relations, however, soon convinced him to decline, in part because of "the commonness of Pirates upon that Coast makes it very hazardous."[45] This rejection caused one of the princes' supporters, Sir John Perceval, to lament that the society could not find an instructor, writing: "Some saying there is work enough at home for them, and others that they fear ye Pirates."[46] In the end, the only man tempted enough by the thirty-pound allowance and willing to face the pirates swarming along the coast was Marmaduke Penwell.

There are no known records detailing where Penwell came from or why he was willing to go on such a journey. He first appears in the SPCK's records in late January 1722 when the society formalized its request to the Royal African Company to send two instructors.[47] He seemed committed to the project, staying with it even after it became clear that there would be no second instructor. The recommendation the society received highlighted his "Sobriety & good Morals," but even before the ship left there were concerns about his qualifications. Newman thought he lacked "several parts of knowledge necessary to shine in the Station he goes." Newman did admit, however, that

Figure 14. This engraving shows a mature John Perceval in 1734, the year after he was made Earl of Egmont and ten years after he had promoted the princes. At this time, he was also the president of the Georgia Trustees, a group given permission to start the colony of Georgia, one of Perceval's projects after the princes' departure. John Faber Jr., *John Perceval, 1st Earl of Egmont*, 1734, National Portrait Gallery, London, NPG D1851. Reproduced by permission of the National Portrait Gallery, London, United Kingdom.

"if he had those parts of knowledge perhaps he would have thought himself above accepting the service."[48] Newman would later blatantly say, "He was the best we could get."[49]

One of Penwell's (and the princes') most determined supporters was Sir John Perceval, an Irish baronet and later first Earl of Egmont, who spent most of his time in London (fig. 14). If the Duke of Chandos never met a financial scheme he did not like, Perceval never encountered a scheme for moral reform he shied away from. He had only just become a residing member of the SPCK in March 1720, and his engagement with the princes was his first real foray into the society's projects.[50] He had, however, previously established a charity school on his lands in Ireland, which would, in his mind, lead the children of his Catholic tenants to the Protestant fold and teach them the virtues of industry, which he saw working hand in hand. After seven years, though, the school project was sputtering to a close. In October 1720, he declared that he was unwilling to continue to "offer pearls to Swine" and that he wanted the school closed. Perceval blamed the failure on "the bigotry of the Parents who being influenc'd by the Priests were unwilling their children should be educated protestants."[51] He decided to look for more willing souls.

He joined the Commission for Relieving Poor Proselytes, which worked to support those who had already turned away from Catholicism, and he found the princes.[52]

Perceval jumped into the princes' cause feet first. He mentioned them in late December 1721 when writing a letter to a relative. He told him, "I intend very shortly to have to dinner two Blacks who have been here about a year & speak English." He then recited their whole story. He had already spoken to them, and he filled his letter with tidbits the princes had told him—from the fact that "their people know nothing of God that made the World" to the idea that their religion "be the original of ancient Idolatry."[53] These men and their story obviously intrigued Perceval. He was sure to carefully copy two letters from them into his letter book, the only material we have that was composed by the two men.[54]

Perceval was also the only one to ever refer to the two men as "the two negroes."[55] And as we have just seen, he also called them "two Blacks." For the members of the SPCK the men's princely status did not matter, only their souls concerned them. Perceval even disparaged their royal status, stating to his relative that he called them princes "for so they are at home tho of little regard with us."[56] Other members of the SPCK concurred. Thomas Bray lamented that the princes' early supporters, "not imagining, I presume, what Sort of Princes these Barbarians, whether *African* or *American*, usually are" gave them "something of a Princely Education." Bray refused to address them as their highnesses when he visited them and thought such treatment spoiled them.[57] He, and other members of the SPCK, wanted the two men humble, and harping on their color and referring to them as "negroes" reflected their urge to see them as less than Europeans and in need of the "civilizing force" of Christianity.

Perceval worried about the commitment of the other members, however. By late January their stunted zeal was beginning to annoy him. Certain members of the society, he roared to Thomas Bray, believed that the SPCK was not "instituted to promote Christian knowledge otherwhere than in England," and they were using formalities to block the venture. A project, Perceval declared, that had as its goal "the Instruction of a Heathen Nation in Christianity" requested "by their chief People . . . deserv'd greater Epithets, & some Degree of zeal." He would pay all Penwell's salary if needed.[58] He even wrote to Newman asking for a list of the society's subscribers, "to find as many amongst them as [he] could influence." Newman assured him it was all bluster and he should not worry, which caused Perceval to admit that he was "apt to despond when my own views for doing a good are not readily approved."[59] In the end, he need not have worried, as the society unanimously agreed to send the two instructors, but Perceval's disproportionate tantrum does attest to his commitment to the venture.[60] It also points to the tremendous influence certain individuals could have. The Royal African Company would not have supported the princes had it not been for the Duke of Chandos, and the SPCK would not have picked up the princes' cause had it not been for Perceval. Powerful backers within these institutions mattered, as did the links between the different organizations.

Perceval was so intent on this project that he and Bray worked together to form a list of instructions for Penwell to follow during his travels. It began, as one would expect, with suggestions on how to instruct the princes on the trickier elements of the Christian religion: how Christ could be God and man, how the Trinity worked, and how to prove the Bible was the book of God. But they also wanted Penwell to gather information as well as to disperse it. First, unsurprisingly, Perceval and Bray wanted to know about the religious beliefs of the princes' people. The list, however, quickly turns into what we would see as anthropological inquiries: Perceval and Bray wanted to know "the Temper of the Inhabitants," their "recreations and occupations," the nature of the king's power and the extent of his dominions, "their method of living," their modes of warfare, their diseases, their weather, and, finally, their modes of navigation. The instructions end by telling Penwell to take one of the maps around with him: "Write down in the margent the names of Rivers, mountains, towns & Countries as you learn them pronounc'd by the Inhabitants."[61] For these men conversion was not simply the profession of a new faith, it necessitated a total cultural conversion. To Bray, "in Order to prepare the Nation of Delagoa to receive Religious Instruction, and to retain the same," the people needed to "leave off their savage way of living in Woods, and in Hunting Wild Beasts." Instead, they needed to "betake themselves to a Human and Sociable way of Living."[62] No communal property. Houses should be built. Plows put to work. Men should work the fields, women should stay in the home making bread, butter, and cheese, roasting meat, brewing beverages, spinning wool or linen, and weaving cloth.[63] Basically, for Christianity to take hold, Mpfumo had to become England. The questions Perceval and Bray sent Penwell to answer were to determine how far along the path to "civilization," and thus Christianity, those living around the bay were.

While the SPCK wanted know Mpfumo better so that it could evaluate the how many souls it might obtain, the Royal African Company wanted to gather information about the area to see what profit it could make. As Chandos declared to Hans Sloane, the secretary of the Royal Society, the voyage was an "opportunity to make what discoveries they can of ye Products of these Parts of the World." To make this happen the voyage needed men of science or at least some individuals, wrote Chandos, "whose capacity and knowledge may be usefull towards rendering successfull such an undertaking." This was why Chandos had contacted Sloane. In fact, his letter requesting help was delivered by Colin Hay, a hopeful candidate, who had the reputation of being "a sound Botanist" and one who could "understand the nature of plants and drugs pretty well." Chandos wanted Sloane to put Hay through his paces. He also asked Sloane if he would put together some instructions on how to tell what plants might be useful.[64] He next wrote to Sloane to ask if he could see his chart of Maputo Bay, as he wanted Leonard Ely, the other man employed by the Royal African Company to go with the ship, to copy it for the voyage.[65] The company had tasked Colin Hay and Leonard Ely with exploring the natural, and it hoped profitable, wonders of the area.[66]

The company gave the men specific instructions on how to accomplish this task: "[Make] the most diligent and thorough search you can into what the Countrey does produce as well in regard to Elephants teeth, woods, drugs, minerals, spices, &c." Medicinal herbs, in particular, interested the company. It instructed Ely and Hay to keep a keen eye out for "bitter wood, wherof the Natives make a draught for their cure when sick or indispos'd." This wood, the company suspected, was like "Jesuits bark," or modern-day quinine. Someone, perhaps the princes, had informed it that the wood went by the name of "quinquina" in Mpfumo, and the correlation appeared promising. More generally, Ely and Hay were to pay attention to the sicknesses that struck the Mpfumans and what they used as cures, especially if these involved herbs. They were to gather all the samples they could both of medicinal herbs and of other commodities. To help them along, the company gave them what it described as "a Box containing samples of several drugs, spices, minerals & c to guide you in your search after them." The company thought they could show these samples to those living around the bay to facilitate communication and cut down on confusion. The directors also wanted them to show the locals their map and to ask them a set of questions about what lay to the west, the direction of Monomotapa.[67] One never knew what new riches could be found. New commodities could mean a newly profitable Royal African Company.

The directors believed that the new commodities and trading links found in the princes' homeland could help sustain their new settlement at Cabinda, in what is now Angola, on the west coast of Africa. Ely and Hay should look out for nutmeg to see if it could "be propagated" at Cabinda.[68] More important, the directors hoped to connect Cabinda to the vast interior trade by developing links from the east. They still hoped to reach Monomotapa. To their minds, it should be easy. They believed that the major river that spilled into Maputo Bay reached that kingdom.[69] They told Ely and Hay to see if "it may not be possible by the friendship of the King of Monomatapa or any other Neighbouring Princes to open a communication over land or by navigatable rivers . . . to Cabenda."[70] They hoped that the company's fortunes in the west could be amplified from the east.

Unsurprisingly, the directors hoped that some of this new trade would involve gold—and not just from Monomotapa. Their excitement must have been palpable when the two princes told them that there were mines "not many days distant from their own Country" and that they just happened to go "by the name of Ophir."[71] This meant that miners had to be sent along, and the company employed a group of them from the mining center of St. Agnes in Cornwall under the watchful eye of their leader, Captain Paul.[72] The company wanted these men to test the soil for any signs that "mines or gold ore may be found."[73] The miners would also prove useful at Trindade, the small island in the Atlantic that Chandos wanted to inspect. The *Northampton* was to go there first, in the company of another ship, the *Dispatch*, with Captain Jeremiah Tinker in command. The miners were to see if they could find any signs of gold, silver, or other minerals on the island. If they found gold, their instructions demanded that they dismiss all other plans. Captain Tinker should fetch the governor of Cabinda and enough men from that factory to start a settlement. During that time, the directors said, Captain Sharrow should keep the miners "constantly Employ'd in raising of ore which Capt Tinker may bring home to us."[74] Once Tinker returned with the men from Cabinda they would discuss if the *Northampton* would continue on to the princes' homeland or not. Gold took precedence.

The company knew that these golden visions of Trindade would probably not become a reality, and they had a backup plan. Company officials wanted Sharrow, Ely, and Hay to find the best place on Trindade to establish a settlement and gave them a description of the island written by Edmund Halley twenty years before. They could use this settlement as a trading post to connect Africa to the Americas. Goods from Cabinda, especially enslaved bodies, could be brought to the island and then sold to the Portuguese, who would sail out from Brazil. The company knew, however, that more than

seven hundred miles might be a bit far for most Brazilian slave traders to
travel, and so they also directed the *Northampton* to stop off at Ilha Grande,
just off the Brazilian coast near Rio de Janeiro. They were to see, the company
said, "if the Governour cannot be prevailed with to permit sloops to come
from Cabenda to that island with Negroes or other commoditys."[75] If it could
not prosper through gold, it would try to prosper through enslaved bodies.

For the Royal African Company this was a voyage full of projects, however, these were projects fueled by desperation. Since the turn of the century
it had been floundering, and this seemed its last chance at survival. Financial
redemption lay within its grasp if it could only unearth, in some cases literally, a commodity other British colonies had failed to produce, be it nutmeg,
quinine, or gold. If they did not find such goods, perhaps this voyage would
open up the interior of Africa to trade or at least provide a lifeline for the new
settlement at Cabinda. Even if that lifeline did not come from eastern Africa,
there was the prospect of the riches of Trindade and trade with Brazil. This
was a fight for economic survival, and the company loaded all these hopes
within the wooden walls of the *Northampton*.

Those hopes rested on the shoulders of two men, Prince James and Prince
John, and they kept themselves busy supporting these imaginings. This was
necessary, since the activities of the two institutions depended on the active
participation of the two men. The SPCK was probably relieved to hear the
princes say that they hoped "they should not only never forget the Christian
Religion, but be Instrumental to propagate it among their Country Men."[76]
The papers of the Royal African Company echo this dependence on the two
men. During the voyage, the company instructed Sharrow, Hay, and Ely to be
"in conversation with the Princes" about possible commodities.[77] Then, upon
arrival, it was hoped that one or both of the princes would go with them when
they traveled to Monomotapa, "in order to introduce them to the Emperor
their Brother in Law, and the better to engage him to come into such Treaty
and Trade."[78] Whether these plans would succeed or fail depended upon the
princes' actions.

The language in the official records of the Royal African Company and
the SPCK emphasize the princes' participation. In the circular letter sent to
members of the SPCK about princes and in the draft of the petition the
society sent to the company asking for permission to send an instructor with
them, it is the princes who "expres'd an earnest Desire" for a religious instructor to accompany them home.[79] Similarly, the minutes of the Royal African
Company's Committee of Trade stated: "[The princes] desire the Company

will give Orders for their being sent home to their Brother the King of Delagoa on the South East Coast of Africa."[80] The records do not reveal if the princes truly did desire these things, but these institutions constructed the situation as such to strengthen their cases.

This dependence on the princes meant that they had a lot more time face to face with the governing bodies of the Royal African Company and the SPCK.[81] In fact, at one point the two institutions vied for their presence. At one meeting Sharrow apologized to the SPCK because he and the princes could only stay for about an hour—they had to attend a meeting with the Royal African Company as well.[82] To get more time with the princes, the SPCK hosted a dinner with the princes at Leg Tavern on Fleet Street after one of their meetings.[83] How loud the princes' voices were in these meetings is not always clear. As we have seen, when they visited the SPCK in October 1721, Sharrow spoke first and dominated the discussion. But about halfway through the visit the princes piped up when asked about the SPCK sending an instructor with them.[84] The society relied on Sharrow for information regarding business in London, but for business in Africa they looked to the princes. Only they would know if an instructor would be welcomed and if he would be allowed to leave. By January, when the princes again visited the SPCK, they did not even need Sharrow to accompany them for the first part of the meeting. He was held up by business with the Royal African Company, and so they came on their own.[85] When they took leave of both sets of men in February 1722, they had become familiar faces and knew that their words mattered.[86]

They also corresponded with their supporters. Two of their letters survive in Sir John Perceval's letter book. The letters themselves are formulaic. In the first, they inform Perceval: "[Dr. Bray has told us] of your good design in sending a person with us into our own Country" and "[we] beg leave humbly to return your Lordship our most hearty thanks for the same, being affected with Gratitude & a deep sense of your Lordship's Favours towards us."[87] The next, written about a week later, thanks Perceval for his response and his "Great Christianity." They then promise him: "[We shall use our] utmost endeavours to teach & instruct our Friends when we arrive in our own Country" and that they shall take care of Marmaduke Penwell. The letter concludes with a fervent promise to carry on a correspondence with him once the *Northampton* sails.[88] Perhaps Bray or their instructor breathed down their necks as they composed these letters or perhaps the princes had simply conquered the form of the complimentary letter. Maybe they knew the rules of British civility and were playing along. They certainly seem to have hit the right notes on most occasions while in London.

The princes knew that the Britons they encountered saw them as repositories of African knowledge, and they appear to have fulfilled this expectation. During one visit, Perceval settled down for a chat with the two of them about their religion, and an elaborate discussion followed. He related to a relative that the princes told him "their people know nothing of the God that made the World, tho they believe Spirits & another World." Instead, they informed him, they worshipped ancestors who "when living were esteem'd for their wisdom goodness or courage to whose graves they repair and pay a respect." If you strain your ears, the tone of this conversation lightly surfaces. The princes embraced the grandiose. It is likely that they used the phrase "God that made the World," perhaps picking it up from Britons trying to explain Christianity to them. And a slight impish sense of humor seems to arise when they discuss polygamy. They said that while their people would be open to other aspects of Christianity, "they had no hopes to make the old men leave their plurality of wives."[89] Interestingly, these accounts of the religious practices of Mpfumo do correlate with later accounts of their spiritual beliefs.[90]

The princes appear to be skilled conversationalists and to know what their interrogators wanted to hear. It is unlikely that they had ever heard of the celebrated Kingdom of Monomotapa or the rich mines of Ophir before they arrived in London. They did not know English well before they arrived in Jamaica, and it is unlikely that stories of Monomotapa and Ophir were discussed there. Suddenly, however, while in London they were sure that the emperor of Monomotapa was a relative and that the mines of Ophir were just down the road. This was the information the Royal African Company wanted to hear, and the princes seem to have known this. Chandos first declared that their brother was the emperor of Monomotapa, but four months later he admitted that their brother-in-law was the emperor.[91] It is possible that the princes first let Chandos believe that all his dreams had come true and that they were the brothers of the ruler of the rich kingdom he wished to find and then, when the questions got more complex and the voyage more real, they downgraded their brother's status while keeping the link. Perhaps they were simply trying to answer truthfully as Chandos trotted out such unfamiliar names with such hope and fervor. The princes also led the Royal African Company to believe that they were the key to the riches the British desired. The capital of Monomotapa was only "a Moon from their own Capitall," they had told the company.[92] And mines were "not many days distant from their own Country." Those mines "they say" go "by the name of Ophir."[93] Again, it is unclear if the princes were manipulating the company or if its members were simply hearing what they wanted to hear, but it is likely that the princes could tell which answers their listeners wanted to hear, and they probably did not try too hard to argue to the contrary.

But what did the princes want to hear from the British? What was *their* Monomotapa? All their actions imply, at this point, that they wanted to go home to Mpfumo. They made no attempt to craft an argument to stay. They could have. The British ego was large enough to embrace the argument that the princes' Christianity was safer in England and that they would not wish to leave such a wondrous land. Diego made this very argument to Henry Newman when he did not want to return to Barbados.[94] The princes probably knew, however, that the largesse of their patrons depended on their departure. Princes who stayed too long would no longer be princes. And, furthermore, it would be no wonder if they simply wanted to go home. As we shall see, however, as soon as they left port the actions of one prince would shatter these assumptions.

What about the two men's Christianity? How deep did their conversion go? To British eyes the princes seemed to embrace the faith. Newman told a correspondent, "[They] seem very much pleas'd with their being Christians," and Perceval said, "[They] seem glad they know Religion."[95] The repetition of "seem" betrays uncertainty, though; the British knew they could not see into their guests' souls. The princes were vocal in their support of the SPCK's plan to send an instructor with them. They promised to look after and listen to Marmaduke Penwell and to promote Christianity at home.[96] The later actions of one of the princes would suggest this was a promise he meant to break. The princes could have been pretending to convert while secretly holding on to their old faith because they knew that the appearance of conversion would make things easier. They might also have known that learning about Christianity meant that they would learn other things like reading and writing, and at least as far back as their days enslaved in Jamaica the two men knew that knowledge of one's enemies was power. It could also be that the trauma of the past years had truly caused them to reject their past beliefs and be open to new ones. It is also possible that their African faith, being centered on the adoration of those who "when living were esteem'd for their wisdom goodness or courage," was not too unlike Christianity. The hierarchy and formality of the Anglican Church would have been different: at home there were no trained priests or days reserved for religious practice, but to see Jesus as a past life marked by "wisdom, goodness or courage" would not be a hard sell.[97] What went on in the princes' hearts and minds will probably never be known.[98] What *is* known is that, in the eyes of their supporters, when they boarded the *Northampton*, they were Christians ready to bring to their people the word of God and the desire for a trade in gold.

The princes, then, were not simply pawns moved around by the Royal African Company and SPCK as they constructed castles in the air. Indeed, they helped those castles float. They honed the skills they knew the British valued. They conquered the English language, they learned to read and write, they dressed and ate appropriately, they cultivated connections to those with power, and they used their knowledge of Africa and their purported commitment to Christianity to get home. They employed these skills the best they could to subtly shift their trajectory in the direction they wanted. When they were unhappy, as they were with Captain Hill, they made their voices heard. They raised those same voices to those in charge of their future to the extent that the plans for their return to Mpfumo were not simply laid out by the members of the Royal African Company and the SPCK but were made in conversation with the princes. Once the *Northampton* sailed, however, the unity that had seemingly bound the two princes together since they decided to "see England" would begin to unravel in ways that casts doubt on these early objectives.[99]

CHAPTER 6

Falling Apart

Off Gravesend, Kent, England, 13 March 1722

Marmaduke Penwell was frantic. He desperately needed to find the Anglican devotional manual *The Whole Duty of Man*. Once he had located it, he quickly flipped through it to chapter ten. It covered the sin of murder, and he had narrowly missed witnessing such a crime a moment before: Prince James had just attempted to kill his brother. According to Penwell, James had no provocation. The two brothers had been reading in their cabin on board the ship, probably with Penwell, when James "drew his Sword & made a thrust at his brother designing to kill him, which he had done if his brother had not catched his Sword in his hand." All Prince James would say was that "they would have me kill my brother."[1] So Penwell sat him down and read to him about the "most loud crying sin" of murder. As the manual stated, its heinous nature was evident in "the first Act of this kind, that was committed": Cain's murder of his brother, Abel. Such a sin, he read, "leaves a stain even upon the Land where it is committed, such as is not washed out, but by the blood of the Murtherer."[2] Cain and Abel. Blood and sin. Something had gone terribly wrong on board the *Northampton*.

Four days later, on 17 March 1722, tragedy almost struck again. That evening Prince James "took up a knife off the table at Supper & offer'd to cut his throat: quickly after, he offer'd to Stab himself." Plaintively, he cried "he was full of pain & no body wou'd cure him." Seemingly, everyone jumped into action and subdued him. Penwell later spoke to the doctor who said it was probably gout.[3] It was obviously something more, and it was a portent of things to come.

Before this moment the records had always presented the two men as an undifferentiated pair. They were the "two Delagoa princes" or the "two African princes." There was no sense of separate personalities, separate desires, or separate pains. They moved as one, unified in thought and action. Clearly this was not the case. Some inner angst was eating away at Prince James, and it would increasingly corrode his relationship with his brother, the crew, and his supporters in London. The fracturing of these relationships echoed the larger disillusionment that would envelope the whole venture.

The crew and passengers of the *Northampton* began as a unified group, at least on paper. The list of the ship's the crew and passengers, held in Britain's National Archives, presents them as an organized and united whole. At the top is Captain John Sharrow, forty years of age. Marching, in a neat line, after him are his first and second mates, his surgeon, the gunner, the carpenter and his mate, the boatswain, Sharrow's thirteen-year-old servant, and eleven seamen ranging in age from the seventeen-year-old William Rydost to the forty-year-old Patrick Tomalty. Finally, bringing up the rear, are the cook, the cooper, and the twenty-year-old "Company Black," Syraleone Tomay.[4] They were, Sharrow assured the SPCK, "a Crew of very Sober Fellows." Furthermore, two of them had been on the *Mercury* with Captain White and, as Sharrow put it, "are seemingly honest Fellows and give a favorable Report of the Country."[5] This last fact, one imagines, made boarding the ship a bit surreal, and more than a bit uncomfortable, for Prince James and Prince John.

Below the names of the crew is a list of the passengers. Leonard Ely and Colin Hay come first, aged forty-five and thirty-five, respectively. These were the two men whom Chandos sent along "to make what discoveries they can of ye Products" found in Mpfumo.[6] The princes come next, listed on separate lines. Prince James, as the elder, comes first. His "quality" is recorded as "Prince of Delagoa" and his age as thirty. Prince John comes next. He too is a "Prince of Delagoa," and his age is recorded as twenty-five. Listed last on the manifest is Marmaduke Penwell, thirty-four years old and "tutor to ye Princes."[7] His place on the list reflected the faith the SPCK had in him. Newman pleaded with Captain Sharrow to take pity on poor Penwell: "[He] wants several parts of knowledge necessary to shine in the Station he goes."[8] Newman thought Sharrow, Hay, and Ely could help instruct him.

Newman and the Royal African Company pictured a happy crew of sober men who would "take particular care" of the princes and "treat [them] with all respect imaginable."[9] They would lend a helping hand to each other and make the voyage proceed as smooth as silk. This was not to be. Sharrow, Penwell, Prince James, and Prince John would all prove disappointments to the men in London, and the voyage itself would dissolve into violence as the true

Figure 15. The ship on the right has just left the Downs, a sheltered anchorage right off the English Channel, and dropped off its pilot, who had safely guided it to open waters. When the *Northampton* reached this point in its journey, Prince James's mental health was deteriorating. Charles Brooking, *Shipping in the English Channel*, c. 1755, Yale Center for British Art, Paul Mellon Collection, B1981.25.65. Reproduced by permission of Yale Center for British Art, New Haven, Connecticut.

colors of the voyagers began to surface. The plans forged in London were based on hopes linked together with scraps of information, much of it supplied by the princes, who had reasons to twist the truth a bit in order to go home. They were pushed by men like Chandos and Perceval who had a lot of power in their organizations but who perhaps had less knowledge about the areas they were interested in than they would acknowledge. Once the ship had left port, the cracks would become more apparent. The voyage home also serves as a lesson about how little we know about Prince James and Prince John. The vision provided by the British sources is one that mirrors the dreams and racism embraced by those who wrote about them. For their supporters, the princes were curiosities and tools, not complex individual men, and this hinders the telling of their story and counsels caution. It is only on the voyage home that the two men become nuanced and individualized, albeit in tragic ways.

The actions of Prince James started the voyage on figuratively stormy seas, and a literal storm would soon divert the *Northampton* as it sailed along the southern coast of England. On 19 March the ship had left the Downs along with the *Dispatch*, Captain Jeremiah Tinker in command (fig. 15). The *Dispatch* was another Royal African Company ship that was to accompany the *Northampton* on the first part of its journey. Five days later, both ships ran into trouble. As they made their way through the English Channel, along the coast between Portsmouth and Plymouth, the weather got rough and the winds shifted to the southwest.[10] As night fell, Captain Sharrow became worried and began looking for a safe haven. Most mariners would have made for the Isle of Wight, Portland Harbor near Weymouth, or Tor Bay, but Sharrow looked to Exmouth.[11] This was not a good idea. Even in the later nineteenth century sailors considered such an approach dangerous and felt "it should not on any account be depended upon as a safe refuge to make for in stormy weather." The channel into the river was "very narrow, with a long shallow bar of broken water, bounded on the north side by a ridge of dangerous rocks uncovering only at low water, and on the south-east by far-spreading treacherous sands."[12] Sharrow and his ship would find this out the hard way. There is no record of what the princes thought as the rocks grew closer. They had felt such fear before, and memories of the hurricane that had taken the life of Joshua Bowes and nearly their own must have flashed before their eyes. Perhaps Prince James even welcomed the impending disaster. They both must have wondered if this was truly how it all would end.

Exmouth, Devon, England, March 1722

It was not. The ship ended up on the rocks, but all on board survived.[13] The *Northampton* was gravely damaged, however, and would take months to repair. And the trust that had bound the voyagers together had begun to fray. John Sharrow and Marmaduke Penwell's relationship shattered on the rocks that night. As the ship teetered, Penwell decided to bring all the items provided by the SPCK ashore. What happened next is a bit of a mystery. According to Penwell, people took advantage of his need and overcharged him for taking the items ashore. Penwell then wrote to the society asking for funds to cover the cost.[14] Sharrow and others, however, quickly wrote letters to Henry Newman accusing Penwell of trying to take advantage of the society.[15] Newman shared the letters with Perceval and the society's treasurer, but they decided not to share the accusations with the rest of the members. Surely, they thought, his "Rash misrepresentation" was "done in the Fright while the Ship was upon the Rocks, Imagining that he was fallen among such Rapparees as Cornwall abounds with."[16] They should at least give him a chance to explain himself. In fact, Newman thought Penwell was "under some concern for the rash Account he gave me" because he had not responded to Newman's letter.[17] Newman subtly alluded to his concerns in his letter to Penwell, stating: "I am glad to understand from other hands that your Loss is like to be much less than you fear'd it might be upon the Accident that happen'd to the Northampton," and adding that he and the society would appreciate a detailed account of his expenses.[18] But, as Newman told Sharrow, what really bothered him was "that [Penwell's] Misrepresentation has Lessen'd Your Esteem for him."[19] One thread of trust and respect had already snapped.

The esteem the Royal African Company had for Sharrow was also under great strain. Sharrow's actions that stormy night had shocked the Committee of Shipping. It believed he "ought to have Bore away for Portland Road, or the Isle of Wight, this being the first instance of any Merchant ship that ventured to go over the Bar of Topsham."[20] Chandos brought this opinion to Sharrow's attention. After taking him to task for delaying his departure from the Downs, he launched into Sharrow, saying: "Putting into Topsham where hardly ever any ship ventur'd before hath given great offense to ye whole Court of Assistants" and "ye Danger you brought ye ship in hereby hath been so great that 'tis next to a Miracle she was preserv'd." Chandos said he hoped that in the future Sharrow would "regain ye good opinion of ye Gentlemen who employ you, for I cannot forbear acquainting you that they resent very much this Proceeding of yours."[21] This was not exactly a ringing endorsement. Ten days later, the secretary of the Royal African Company wrote Sharrow a letter bearing ill tidings: the Court of Assistants was not sympathetic to his complaints about an employee and the Committee of Shipping was seriously annoyed that he had not answered their last letter. The secretary ended by stating that he was certain Sharrow "would chuse not to have any disputes with the Committee of Shipping."[22] Never again would Sharrow be a popular figure at Africa House.

As these ties began to give way, new ones were forming. Once the ship was brought in for repairs, the SPCK and the Royal African Company began mobilizing their networks. The same day the company heard from Sharrow and Captain Tinker of the *Dispatch* about the accident, it swung into action. It ordered Sharrow to hire Mr. Mitchell of Exeter and John and Joshua Veal to repair the ship.[23] The company's secretary rapidly conveyed these instructions; pen sharpened, he wrote to Mitchell, Veal, Tinker, and Sharrow that night.[24] The SPCK officers met that day as well and read the letter from Marmaduke Penwell. They too instantly attacked the problem. They decided that they would advance Penwell ten pounds, that they would take it from the funds for the project, and that he should draw on Richard King of Topsham, a member of the society, for funds while in Exmouth.[25] Newman also sat up that night and wrote letters to King and Penwell and also to Perceval, to inform him of the accident.[26] Newman was confident about the society's abilities to handle the situation from afar. As he told Perceval: "The Society have several residing & Correspondent members in and about Exeter, who will be all pleas'd with an opportunity of shewing their respect to any body going abroad in the Service of the Society." And he instantly named not only King but also one Dr. Foulkes, who lived in Exeter near Exmouth, as men willing to assist.[27] King was the obvious choice, though, for he already had links to the voyagers. In fact, he had been at the meeting when the princes were introduced to the society.[28] Furthermore, Newman told King in a postscript, Sharrow was "a near Relation of Good Mrs Rowland who left us a Benefaction of 50L which came through your hands."[29] Society funds and perhaps personal ties already connected the princes, Sharrow, and King. These were tightly linked communities whose networks functioned at a distance.

These institutions, at least in the case of the SPCK, also expected more than monetary support for the voyagers. Newman was sure to tell Penwell, "[King is] a very worthy person" and "would be glad to see you and the Princes at his House." Meeting King was just the beginning, though: "He has many Friends at Exeter that can easily recommend you to those who will shew the Princes and you the Curiosities of that City, while the Ship is refitting."[30] These men were to be social connections and tour guides. King followed through on his promise and visited the princes, Sharrow, and Penwell.[31] Whether his friends showed them "the Curiosities" of Exeter, more than twenty miles upriver, was left unsaid, but over the next month the princes do seem to have made connections in Exmouth. But the ties between Sharrow, Penwell, Prince James, and Prince John continued to erode.

When the men arrived in Exmouth, Prince James was already persona non grata, and during their stay nothing altered. When the company's secretary wrote to Sharrow in Exmouth, he sent his greetings to both princes, but "especially Prince John."[32] Prince James was not endearing himself to those in Exmouth either. After the princes' arrival, Penwell later recounted, he "continued in an unaccountable bad humour." He and Penwell began to snipe back and forth. When Prince James refused to read, saying "he was not well," Penwell struck back, telling him "that he eat drunk & slept very heartily, which are very good signs of health." As the days passed, Prince James began to "swear & curse for every trifle, & gave his mind to drink to excess." Penwell, in turn, threatened to tell his patrons of his actions, which got James to half-heartedly pick up his books from time to time.[33] His relationships with the others were not much better. On 18 April Prince James tried to join Colin Hay and Captain Tinker on a walk. They refused to have anything to do with him. In response, Prince James tried to return to London. He walked eight miles to Sidmouth, a town up the coast, and managed to hire "a Man & two horses to carry him back to London." But a member of the crew thwarted his plans and dragged him back to Exmouth.[34] Meanwhile, Leonard Ely wrote to Chandos: "[Prince James] behaves himself in the same, outrageous manner He did when he was at Gravesend."[35]

What had changed Prince James from the "well behaved" prince of Perceval's memory is unclear.[36] Perhaps he never was well behaved. Perhaps seeing the ship brought back memories he did not wish to revisit or perhaps it simply made the voyage home real. Boarding a ship had never boded well for him. One voyage had led him to slavery. Another had resulted in the death of his patron and nearly his own. Neither the seas nor the Europeans who sailed upon them could be trusted. He was also a different man from the one who had left Mpfumo six years before. The rises and falls in his fortunes, the constant striving, the need to shape and reshape his sense of self in alien environments—all must have left a mark. It was this man who had to return home, not the young prince who had left it. Perhaps now he realized what going home meant. He was clearly distraught and dangerously depressed. He had decided to no longer play the game. He rejected reading, which was, in British eyes, the lifeline to Christianity. He drank and swore. He said what he wished and went where he desired. The British were losing control. As for Prince James, he was in pain, and no one was listening.

The theory held by the other voyagers at this point was that he had committed such crimes against his brother, the ruler back in Mpfumo, that he dared not return. It was Prince John who fed them this idea. The crimes were such that Chandos thought it "no wonder he [was] so fearfull to return unto his own Country." No one ever recorded what exactly those crimes were. Chandos, as always, managed to see the silver lining. As he told Ely, the ruler of Mpfumo would be doubly thrilled, for he would have his innocent brother returned along with the criminal one, whom he could bring to justice.[37] Prince John could simply have been creating a cover story for his brother's actions, but he could have picked one that cast a kinder light upon his sibling. Or maybe what he claimed was true.

By the end of April everyone involved with the voyage eyed Prince James warily. Chandos told Ely that they should all "be more upon ye Guard to prevent his doing any mischief either to Himself or any of his Companions."[38] The Royal African Company's secretary told Sharrow, "Use all fair means you can to reduce him to quietness and ease, having at the same time a regard to your selves and the safty and success of your voyage."[39] This was a far cry from Sharrow's original instructions regarding the princes, whom he was "to take particular care of during the voyage and treat with all respect imaginable."[40] It appears that the respect was gone, at least in the case of Prince James, and that "particular care" had taken on a new meaning. Prince James must have felt the glances of suspicion and seen his chances of returning to London dwindle. Everything came to a head on the night of May the first.

Late that night, around ten o'clock, Prince James and Prince John quarreled, about what is not recorded, but soon words became blows.[41] Then Captain Sharrow intervened. According to one account, Prince James struck him in the face, causing Sharrow to strike back.[42] At this point Penwell, who had been upstairs, rushed down and saw "Capt. Sharrow a beating Prince James." Sharrow then lashed out at Penwell. Turning, and radiating wrath, he called Penwell "a Presbiterean rogue" and threatened to treat him "like a Scoundrell" once they had left Exmouth and were on board ship. This was too much for Penwell, who slithered back upstairs to bed "for fear he shou'd be foul of me." Whether the beating continued we do not know, but the landlord told Penwell that half an hour later Prince James stormed off.[43] This was one lashing too many.

Prince James first stopped at the house of Sir John Colleton. This was an interesting choice. The Colletons certainly were prominent citizens of Exmouth. They were also prominent Barbadian planters and one of the first families of South Carolina. Sir John's grandfather had been one of the first Lords Proprietors of that colony.[44] Most of the family's wealth came from land worked by enslaved men and women. Sir John himself, while mainly a merchant settled in England, had also spent time in South Carolina. In fact, he introduced the magnolia plant to England.[45] While we might find it odd that Prince James first turned to a slave owner, it is not unlikely that Sir John, because of his familiarity with enslaved Africans, had engaged with the princes more than other residents. They were not as foreign to him. Unfortunately for Prince James, it was late, around eleven at night, and the housekeeper, the only one awake, refused to rouse the household on Prince James's account or to offer him lodging. She did break the slumber of one of the footmen, who told the prince he would accompany him home. Prince James refused the escort and trudged along, still searching for a welcoming hearth. Colleton's housekeeper sent the footman to Captain Sharrow instead, and according to Penwell, not the world's most reliable informant when it comes to Sharrow, the captain had replied "that he might go & hang himself for he wou'd not send after him."[46] Prince James then knocked on Colonel Reymond's door. Here too everyone was asleep except for a maid. She told him "she durst not let him in."[47] His options were shrinking.

While Prince James's late night search for shelter seethes with desperation, it also suggests that he had found a level of acceptance in this coastal town. He did not knock on doors seeking only the help of servants, he felt entitled to call upon their masters—at eleven o'clock at night. The servants knew who he was, and each tried to accommodate him to a degree. Colleton's housekeeper "beg'd" him to go home and offered to send the footman with him. Reymond's maid did not order him from the premises but rather told him that she "durst not let him in," a phrasing that suggests a wish to do just that.[48] It is possible that if Prince James had knocked on these doors a few hours earlier his story might have a different ending. But he did not.

Despair enfolded him at this point. Doors were closed to him. Anger waited at home. He was "full of pain & no body wou'd cure him."[49] He wandered a quarter of a mile farther until he came to a field with an apple tree, not far from his lodgings.[50] It was edging on midnight, and by this time his eyes would have adjusted to the thick darkness around him.[51] Perhaps he was drawn to the bright white blossoms that can bloom on the branches of apple trees in the spring. If so, it would have been a pleasant place. He sat by the tree and began to dismantle some of his European finery. He unrolled his stockings to reveal the garters tied below his knees.[52] These long lengths of woven silk would prove useful. He hung them around the branch of the apple tree and wrapped them around his neck, and thus cured his own pain and suffering.[53]

This is where Prince James's story ends, and it flummoxes the modern reader. Why, after enduring enslavement, surviving a hurricane, and fighting tooth and nail to get home, would he end his life now? We feel we understand why captives on board slave ships would starve themselves or throw themselves overboard. Ship captains and their surgeons discussed the suicide of the enslaved and wrote texts about ways to stop them.[54] When those enslaved on a plantation took their own life, we accept it. All the underpinnings of these men and women's lives had been undone, and they were not easily put back together. As one historian has stated: "A lack of social cohesion, linguistic and cultural differences, regimes of labor, corporal punishment, sexual battery, and physical pain combined to foster self-destructive impulses in newly arrived Africans."[55] Even Hans Sloane wrote of the enslaved in Jamaica: "[They] regard death but little, imagining they shall change their condition by that means from servile to free" and "for this reason often cut their own throats." He also reported that they believed their souls would return home.[56] For Sloane, and for us today, the suicide of the enslaved is often seen as a form of resistance, a form of freedom and release. Stories seem to signal defiance against the system. Take the death of an enslaved man in Jamaica who in 1739 stole a small trunk holding his master's "papers of Consequence," tore them up, threw them into the sea, and then "Cutt his belly open."[57] His destruction of self feels tied to the destruction of his master's important possessions. But it was also an act of desperation that cost him his life. The men and women who followed such a path might be free of slavery, but they were not alive to enjoy that escape.[58] To a degree, suicide of the enslaved is fathomable to us in a way the suicide of free individuals is often not. Prince James, however, was a free man on his way home when he committed suicide, which throws a wrench into our preconceived notions.

What exactly caused him so much pain and why he felt the need to end his own life are his stories to withhold. To our modern eyes he appears to be suffering from depression and perhaps other mental health issues. We could follow Emile Durkheim's theory and say it was a case of "egotistic suicide," that Prince James felt so detached from both British society and Mpfuman society he saw suicide as the only answer.[59] He had just begun fighting with his brother, his main tie to Mpfumo. He was shunned by Hay and Tinker and beaten by Sharrow. This is all speculation, however, and applying our modern ideas can be anachronistic. Perhaps the why is simply unanswerable and was so to James at the time. He just knew that "he was full of pain & no body wou'd cure him." But it does open a moment where we can consider what he had been through and the strains put upon his sense of self, even if those strains were disconnected from his actual suicide.

Whatever the impetus or reason, it was a drastic measure with drastic consequences for his soul in the eyes of contemporary observers. A European ethnographer, at the end of the nineteenth century, believed that the people around Maputo Bay thought that everyone became a spirit when they died, but those who died when pregnant or who committed suicide became "gods of bitterness." They were angry and feared spirits.[60] This would be an appalling fate to embrace. The Anglican ending was not much better. The Church of England saw suicide as an affront. It was a sin because it was a violation of God's sixth commandment not to kill. It was self-murder. Many of the catechisms published in the early part of the eighteenth century make this abundantly clear. In William Wake's catechism, in the section regarding the sixth commandant, the question "What is your opinion of Self-Murder?" is asked, and the response is unequivocal: "That it is as much Forbidden by this Commandment as any other."[61] Three copies of "Archbishop Wake's Comment on the Church Catechism" were on board the *Northampton*.[62] Another catechism held that "the killing of Man's self stands here condemn'd as the grossest of all murder."[63] Suicide was "a high usurpation of God's Prerogative, who has not put our Lives in our own power, but reserve'd to himself the disposal of them." God made us and he had the right to destroy us. Taking one's own life was a small rebellion against God, for it took away his prerogative and showed "a great Dissatisfaction in his present dealings, and an utter Distrust of his Goodness for the future."[64] The chapter that Penwell read to Prince James on the sin of murder after he attacked his brother supported the idea that life was God's to take away. Murder was "the usurping of God's proper Right and Authority. For it is God alone that hath Right to dispose of the Life of Man; 'twas he alone that gave it, and it is he alone that hath power to take it away."[65] Furthermore, it was a rejection of the community that supported and depended upon the victim.[66] Wives suffered, children suffered, creditors suffered, and patrons suffered. British observers could have read Prince James's suicide as a slap in the face, as a rejection both of their God and of them. In this way, it could have been Prince James's final rebellion. But if he had embraced the Christian faith, he would have knowingly damned himself, for these catechisms declare that "the self-murderer at once Kills his Body, and (as may be justly feared) Damns his Soul."[67] The church denied burial to those found guilty of suicide.

Catechisms, however, only show one side of the story. Arguments raged over suicide at this time in Europe. Increasingly, freethinkers were putting forth the idea that one's life was one's own to do with as one pleased. In fact,

Montesquieu's *Persian Letters*, translated into English the same year that Prince James died, included a letter criticizing the harsh measures taken against suicides and disputed arguments against the act.[68] The clergy did not take this lying down and published tracts supporting traditional ideas regarding the act of self-murder. It still, they argued, usurped man's duties to God and to the government.[69] Beyond the highflying intellectual arguments, however, it is also true that slowly but surely coroner's juries were increasingly declaring that those who committed suicide were non compos mentis, or "not of sound mind." This meant that their property would not be confiscated, and they would be allowed a Christian burial.[70] The attitude of some churchmen began softening as well. John Shaw, a rector in Wiltshire, made it clear in his catechism that suicide was "a Sin, and one of the greatest-Magnitude and deepest Dye," but he thought that when it resulted from "excessive Sorrow, Melancholy, Madness, Sickness or a Phrensy" the case should "be pitied and bemoaned, and without doubt God will extend his Bowels of Mercy and Compassion towards such."[71] Thus, many could have felt pity for Prince James.

Most of the recorded responses to Prince James's death did not, however, dwell on pity; rather, they argued that it was a case of madness. His violent behavior and previous threats of suicide meant that his actions were not a great surprise. The secretary of the Royal African Company told Sharrow that the Court of Assistants now knew about "the violent death of Prince James" and was "Sorry to hear it, tho it was what might be expected from his late behavior."[72] The same day, Henry Newman wrote to the archbishop of Canterbury, William Wake no less, explaining, "I believe your Grace has been informed of the disorder of his head wch he has discover'd at certain times wch makes this accident the less surprising to his friends."[73] This explanation implies that perhaps Prince James's resistance and troublesome behavior might have predated the voyage itself. By 1727, Thomas Bray rather callously declared, when describing the princes' story, that "one of these Wretches hang'd himself in an Orchard in the West of England . . . for what Reason we could never certainly Learn." Others blamed the fight with his brother or "a Phrenzy, with which it was suppos'd he was something affected."[74] The idea that he had a "disorder in the head" or was afflicted with "a Phrenzy" would have made him a good candidate for a verdict of non compos mentis, especially if the jury accepted his status as a prince, since this verdict was most often given to the elite.[75] It would also have helped that, in eighteenth-century eyes, he exhibited other signs of madness: he embraced his passions over reason, he exhibited violence toward a family member, and he showed a deep melancholy.[76] That melancholy, in the words of Robert Burton in *The Anatomy of Melancholy* years before, could have "deprived [him] of all reason, judgment, all, as a ship that is void of a pilot much needs impinge upon the next rock or sands, and suffer shipwreck."[77]

This appears to have been enough to have Prince James laid to rest in a consecrated grave. According the Penwell, he "was buried in Whitingham Church yard, 2 miles from Exmouth."[78] Penwell probably meant the church in Withecombe Raleigh, which is about the correct distance away. The church, which according to a nineteenth-century observer "was a rather small unpretending brick building," had been rebuilt in 1720. One of the main contributors to the new structure had been Sir John Colleton.[79] One wonders if a somewhat guilt-ridden Colleton subtly, or not so subtly, pressured church authorities to allow him burial there.

Prince John now became the focus of all hopes. Newman told King, "[Prince James is] out of the reach of our Prayers," but he hoped "that his Death may facilitate the good End the Society have in view of introducing Xtian Knowledge among his Country Men by means of the Surviving Brother."[80] It was not an easy time for Prince John. Penwell told Perceval, initially after his brother's death "[Prince John] did not appear to be sorry at all, but the next day I saw he was very much troubled & continued so when his brother was buried."[81] One wonders if Prince John's mind returned to the traditions of his African homeland. There they cut down the trees where suicides took place to deter repetition and to rid the community of the tainted wood—custom even forbade burning it.[82] The burial might have been comforting. At home, they too buried their dead, even those who committed suicide, but in Britain there was no sacrifice of an animal chosen "in proportion to the Ability of the deceased," nor any dancing in his honor around the grave.[83] What the nature of the discord between the two brothers was we will never know, but losing his brother after all they had survived must have been a shock, and it certainly changed Prince John's existence. No longer were there two African princes; now there was just Prince John. And he continued to conform to the expectations of those around him. Penwell reported that he seemed on course, and the Royal African Company told Sharrow: "Prince John's behavior recommends him very much to the Court."[84] While the SPCK stopped asking for donations for the "African Affair" after Prince James's death, others in the society, and many in the Royal African Company, still hoped that the voyage could turn itself around.[85] The death of Prince James did not have to be an omen of what was to come.

The *Northampton* sailed out of the river Ex on 17 May 1722 on its way to Falmouth to pick up the miners hired by Chandos. All was not well when it arrived. Chandos found himself writing letters to both Colin Hay and Leonard Ely in Falmouth, begging them to continue on the journey. Sharrow's dark temper, it appears, was directed not only at Prince James and Marmaduke Penwell. Chandos could tell that there was "no prefect good agreement" between Sharrow and the two men, and he told them: "[I am] concerned Capt. Sharrows temper should give you any grounds to apprehend you shall not be treated by him with that Respect you ought to be."[86] He did, however, state his hope, nay belief, that once they got to open waters and Sharrow opened his instructions he would see that they were his equals on this voyage.[87] Then, just to be sure, Chandos wrote to Sharrow reminding him that he, Ely, Hay, and Captain Tinker of the *Dispatch* were to confer about what was best for the company and that he should treat them with civility and respect.[88] Hay and Ely eventually agreed not to leave the voyage, but it was not a happy ship that left Falmouth on 4 June 1722.[89]

CHAPTER 7

Going Home

The Atlantic Ocean, Summer 1722

Prince John continued to read and write, to listen to Marmaduke Penwell drone on, and to not rock the boat, literally or figuratively.[1] It would be a long voyage home, and he kept a low profile. Most of the passengers and crew seemed happy to ignore him. No letters survive from the point the *Northampton* left Falmouth in June until it arrived at the Cape of Good Hope in late November, almost six months later. The only record of the voyage comes from the journal of Captain Paul, the leader of the miners, who came on board at Falmouth.[2] It is an account that totally leaves out Prince John. His name is never mentioned. It is as though both princes had taken their lives in Exmouth. Prince John's exclusion could reflect that, for Paul, his presence was unimportant. Paul was there for the precious metals and nothing else. He never mentioned Penwell either. For him this was not a benevolent voyage but rather a scouting trip for riches that could be found with or without the help of an African prince. Other sources survive, however, that record what happened once the *Northampton* reached Mpfumo. The Dutch had set up a trading post there while Prince John had been on his travels, and they kept two journals that recorded what happened on a day-to-day basis when the British arrived.[3] They kept a close watch on the *Northampton* and on Prince John.

Before the *Northampton* reached Mpfumo, though, it made multiple stops that would crush the hopes and dreams of the Royal African Company. After leaving England, it sailed to Madeira and then stopped at Trindade, the small speck of an island in the middle of the Atlantic where Chandos had hoped to find riches. It proceeded next to an island off the coast of Brazil, where the company sought to profit by setting up a trade in enslaved bodies with the Portuguese. Then, it stopped at the Cape of Good Hope, before arriving in

Mpfumo in January 1723. The instructions for the voyage dripped with optimism.[4] As the voyage moved on, however, their hopes would be shattered.
The men's information was old and incomplete, they faced European powers
who did not want to share, and they encountered African polities that were
stronger than both the Dutch and the British. They would use their sense of
racial superiority as a shield, but clearly they were the ones who were pawns
in a larger game when they arrived in Mpfumo.

Trindade, August 1722

It took the *Northampton* more than six weeks to sail from Madeira, where
they briefly stopped after Falmouth, to Trindade. When they arrived in mid-
August, it did not look promising.[5] Trindade is a volcanic island, and its
geography is not welcoming to visitors. Steep volcanic plugs punch their way
upward, and rocky shores warn against landing. The *Northampton* arrived
at night, and when the sun rose the men on board carefully began to look
around them. Waves crashed high upon the shores, and the small exploratory
boat they sent out found no place to land. They did, however, see a "Cleft
in the North west part of the Island a Black Vein like unto a mine." Hopes
no doubt rose. The next day Captain Sharrow, the miners' Captain Paul,
and some of the men decided to look closer. There seemed to be cause for
optimism. Paul reported in his journal: "It lookt as well like a Mine as ever
I saw." Getting a closer look was a challenge, though, "the place being so full
of Rocks, and the Sea always very great in towards the Land." But eventually,
"with very great Danger," they got ashore. This was only the first obstacle.
They could not for the life of them get near the possible mine. They tried to
climb up to it with no luck, and so then clamored to the top of the peak and
attempted to climb down to it, "but found that to be worse than the other"
route. Paul's only option was to look at the rocks that had dropped from the
vein. Even this was not easy, and all day he was "in very great danger for the
Rocks were so Rotten with the Sun that it was very dangerous treading on
'em." For his troubles, he came across some "spots of Isinglass and some black
glittering stones, but found nothing that would produce any sort of Mettle nor
any ways enclined to it." Yet he remained optimistic and thought: "This Point
is as hopefull a ground for Mines and for the feeding of Mines as ever I saw."
But he estimated it would take four or five men two or three months to even
get to the possible mine, and they did not have time for that.[6]

The men next turned their attention to the rest of the island. That was not exactly hospitable either. They could find no place to land the following day. They finally "got ashore in a little Sandy Bay," but it was a struggle, as it was so "full of Rocks" that on the approach "some of us were very like to be drowned." At least here they found some hogs, the descendants of pigs left by passing ships as an emergency food supply, and then, to get the lay of the land, they set it on fire. They burned a few acres and found a "good stream of water & a very good Landing place very Nigh the fresh water." As they sat on the smoke-choked rocky shore, they probably felt some sense of relief. They had found food, water, and a landing place, but they had not found valuable minerals. No gold. No silver. The men spent the next ten days sifting through the sand along the shore to see if it held any gold, watching where the water came down from the mountains and trying the soil around there in hopes of seeing hints of gold or silver washed down from the hills. They even hiked as far up the mountains as they could in hopes of seeing something promising, but all for naught. Paul reported to Chandos that they "could not find anything that was any way inclined to Mines. The N. West Point being the only place of any Hopes of Mines in the whole Island." Paul did think, however, that they could make the island habitable and then bring over some miners to work their way to the possible mine. It would only take a few years. This was not exactly the report Chandos had been hoping for. There was certainly no reason to send Captain Tinker and the *Dispatch* to Cabinda to fetch more men. Paul's last words on the island probably summed up Chandos's thoughts: "So much for Trinedada."[7]

Off Ilha Grande, Brazil, September 1722

The next shot in the dark was Brazil. The Royal African Company instructed the *Northampton* and the *Dispatch* to stop at Ilha Grande, an island just south of Rio de Janeiro, where they were to "consult and endeavour to form some scheme of trade for Negroes or any European commoditys to be carry'd on to that island."[8] The instructions called on them to talk to one Mr. Maynard and one Mr. Sherwyn about the scheme.[9] Forming ties with Brazil seemed like a good idea at the time. The gold of Minas Gerais, in southwestern Brazil, was drawing settlers like flies to honey, and the British were anxious to join in the profits through the selling of their own manufactured goods or, in the case of the Royal African Company, enslaved Africans.[10] The Portuguese usually required that the riches of Brazil be funneled through Lisbon before British traders could access them, but in Chandos's mind the company could now go straight to the source. He was not the only one with this idea; smuggling had already become rampant. This did not please the Portuguese government. According to treaties made in the later seventeenth century, the Portuguese were supposed to allow four British and four Dutch merchant families to live in each of their overseas ports. In reality, they tried to avoid complying with this stipulation, and in 1723 the British envoy to Lisbon would claim "that in all Brazil there is not above one British house established."[11] Thus any British ship that sailed into Brazilian waters would be eyed with suspicion, as the *Northampton* found to its detriment. The men were almost taken prisoner by the Brazilians, but happily eight French ships arrived and joined forces with them. Seemingly, the opportunities and connections promised by Captain Sharrow, who had raised the idea in London, had failed to materialize. On 10 October, the ships left the Brazilian shore.[12]

Cape of Good Hope, 28 November 1722

More than a month later, they arrived at the Dutch settlement at the Cape of Good Hope (fig. 16). But any hopes of a friendly reception were quickly squelched. After anchoring, Captain Sharrow went to see the governor, and things rapidly went downhill. The governor, according to Penwell, "order'd him to go on board his ship, & told him he shou'd not have so much as a hogshead of water."[13] Captain Paul elaborated: "The Governour would not have us so much as one Drop of Water, nor Provissions, nor Greens nor the least thing imaginable."[14] Dutch sources from the Cape support this. The officials recorded: "The Governor gave the provisional order that no one should be allowed to land, and that no refreshments were to be sent on board."[15] So why the cold shoulder? It appears, according to Dutch authorities, that the ship lacked the proper documentation: "The captain was without a Royal Commission, or authority from the East India Company to proceed to that spot."[16] It seems that Sharrow did not have the license promised by the East India Company, and the Dutch were not willing to take him at his word.

His final destination also worried the Dutch. The "spot" that Sharrow wanted to proceed to was Maputo Bay. Both Penwell and Paul told the Royal African Company that it was their destination that caused all the trouble. Things had changed in Maputo Bay since the princes had left. About a year

Figure 16. This engraving from 1736 shows a view similar to that seen by Prince John when the *Northampton* arrived at the Cape of Good Hope. The Dutch had started a settlement there in 1652, and they too were interested in Prince John's homeland. Print made by Gerard van der Gucht, *The Cape of Good Hope*, 1736, Yale Center for British Art, Paul Mellon Collection, B1978.43.271. Reproduced by permission of Yale Center for British Art, New Haven, Connecticut.

and a half previously, the Dutch had started their own trading post there. Penwell recorded that the governor told Sharrow that "he had no business at Delogoa, for the Dutch had settled a Factory there with great expense & the loss of 300 Mens lives, & they had 2 Ships there now."[17] This was an unexpected problem.

Like the British, the Dutch had long pondered setting up a trading post either in southeastern Africa or on Madagascar. They too hoped to make contact with Monomotapa and its gold mines or at least make a profit off the trade in ivory. The Dutch established their trading post in Mpfumo, the princes' homeland, in April 1721, and it struggled from the start. Relations with the local polities were rocky, and a year later, in April 1722, pirates attacked the settlement.[18] As records from the Cape reported, "They had sacked the station, taken what they liked, and destroyed almost what remained." The entry ended: "Affairs there are pretty considerably in a confused state."[19] It is no wonder the officials at the Cape were wary when a British ship sailed into port looking to go to Maputo Bay when their outpost there was at its weakest point.

There were, however, some friendly faces at the Cape. The commander of the East India ship the *Caesar* took the *Northampton* under his wing. He provided it with six sheep, half an ox, and some roots and greens. Sharrow must have given fervent thanks, as at this time their food supply was "very bad," and Penwell noted: "Where or when we shall get more is very uncertain."[20] The captain of the *Caesar* also carried letters home. He took two letters from Penwell for John Perceval and also carried official East India Company correspondence; one of the official letters was from Captain William Mackett, who had known the princes when they traveled on board the *Mercury*.[21] He too was at the Cape.

In the years since his voyage aboard the *Drake*, Mackett had moved up in the world and had become a captain for the East India Company. In February 1721, the company had given him command of the *Nightingale*, bound for Fort St. George in Madras.[22] The voyage did not go as planned. The ship was caught up in a tremendous storm off the Cape (formerly known as the Cape of Storms) in June 1722. The journal kept by Dutch officials called it "a sorrowful and disastrous day." In the afternoon things had begun to get rough, and by nightfall conditions were dire. Those on shore at the Cape began to hear the firing of guns, which meant the ships were drifting from their anchorages. They started to see vessels blown ashore, and wreckage started to wash up upon the beaches. The governor's council gathered to see what could be done, but the winds were too high and too strong, and "everything was, therefore, left to the gracious providence of God." All they could do was light a fire on the least rocky beach to guide the ships in.[23] In the morning, the sight of broken ships met their eyes. Most had made it to shore, but they had been ravaged to varying degrees. Six Dutch ships lay smashed upon the shore, along with the three British East India Company ships, the *Nightingale*, the *Addison*, and the *Chandos*. The *Nightingale* faired the best. She was found "lying on her side with her mainmast overboard, and one man drowned." The *Chandos* had been smashed against the rocks and lost two men, and the *Addison* "was broken to pieces" with all but ten men lost. In the end, more than six hundred men perished in the storm.[24] Luckily for Mackett's future with the company, most of his nonperishable cargo was recovered.[25] But the *Nightingale's* days were over, and Mackett and the other survivors spent an extended period at the Cape sorting out the details and looking for a way home. They would not leave for more than a year, on 13 July 1723.[26]

Tensions immediately flared up between Prince John and Captain Mackett. Penwell reported: "A Commander of a ship that was lost here July last past knew Prince John." Mackett, Penwell continued, had raged at Prince John and called him a "villain." He declared that Prince John had trespassed on the Royal African Company's good will "in telling them that he was a Prince & brought Elephant teeth and Ambergreece from Delogoa, for it was false." Toogood too "knew better," but "he had a mind to make a hand of them."[27] Penwell did not record Prince John's reply.

These were strong and surprising claims. The East India Company had sometimes let an element of doubt creep into their discussions of the princes' identity, often stating that they were "said to be princes," but no one had blatantly attacked the princes' royal credentials like this since the planters in Jamaica.[28] Interestingly, when the East India Company was deciding whether to send the princes back, it considered Mackett as a possible commander of the voyage.[29] Perhaps the doubt it sometimes spouted came from his whispers. Mackett's outburst does cast doubt on the status of the princes, but what happened when Prince John returned to Mpfumo supports his claims to high status. Penwell downplayed the allegation when he wrote home to Perceval. It came in the middle of the letter, and he prefaced it with the information that Prince John was "very well & much improved in his learning."[30] No more was directly said about the incident.

Whatever the truth of Mackett's accusation, the *Northampton*'s few short days at the Cape shredded the threadbare confidence that much of the crew had in the voyage. The Dutch had planted a flag where Captain Sharrow wished to trade, and the prince, who was to assure the men's welcome, might not be a prince. As Penwell told Perceval, the "Ships company" was well, "but in a great consternation about our Voyage." They pondered cutting their losses and not proceeding to Maputo Bay. It might be easier, and more profitable, they thought, to simply turn around, stop for provisions on the western coast, and then "take in Slaves for the West Indies" farther north.[31] According to Penwell, they decided on this easy option. Prince John was "very much troubled at this disappointment" but assured Penwell that he "always said that he would return with the ship from Delagoa to England."[32] The ship left the Cape on the first of December, but somewhere on the high seas minds changed, for, in the end, the ship made for Maputo Bay.[33]

The *Northampton*'s forays to Trindade, Ilha Grande, and the Cape of Good Hope had revealed to the men on board the instability of British knowledge.

In London it was simple to build castles in the air. Rumors about Trindade were easy to take seriously. It seemed straightforward to start up trade with the Brazilians, especially since the British had contacts there. The Cape was an unscheduled stop, but their visit there showed the deep lack of knowledge that the Royal African Company had about Dutch actions. The captain did not have the right documentation and had no idea that a Dutch factory had been started at Maputo Bay more than a year earlier. Information, especially regarding foreign powers in distant places, moved slowly. When the *Northampton* arrived at these locations, it was clear that the lack of British ties in these areas and the absence of recent and detailed information about them had misled minds in London. It was easy to dream big with tantalizing scraps of information within the safety of four walls as a warm fire crackled and brandy flowed. The experience in Mpfumo would amplify this sense of disconnect. Not only had distance made the hard look easy, not only did the men lack accurate information, but now they had to do business, not with other Europeans, but with people who in London seemed inferior to themselves but who in Africa held all the power.

Mpfumo, Southeastern Africa, 7 January 1723

One wonders if Prince John came on deck and watched as the *Northampton* crept into Maputo Bay.[34] It was night, and so darkness might have obscured the familiar "red clife" that stood near Mpfumo, but after the ship anchored he would have seen that much had changed.[35] For one thing, the Dutch had set up their trading post, and they were less than overjoyed to see a foreign ship in the harbor. According to the British, the Dutch fired one musket shot as a salute when the *Northampton* came into view. The British ship gave no answer. The Dutch fired two more shots, this time "loaden with shot" and insisted that the captain come ashore. This time Captain Sharrow responded, and he, along with Ely and Hay, met with the Dutch.[36] This British triumvirate advancing upon the fort was a show of force—not that the Dutch could do much damage at this point. As the Britons found, their settlement was "in a very weak Condition."[37] The attack by the pirates in April had left the fort in shambles. They had plundered their supplies, taken two ships, and a number of men.[38] But even more dire in the long run, they had shown the limits of Dutch power. The people around the bay did not fear the Europeans.

They itched to reach for their spears at any sign of disrespect, and the Dutch believed that the local people had begun to believe that guns could not harm them. The Dutch feared they would soon have to prove otherwise.[39]

The tensions between the Europeans and Africans had increased recently, but such strains were not new at the Dutch settlement. After a short honeymoon period, relations between the groups had soured. By the time the Dutch had been there for six months the settlement's commander decided that the local people were "venal," "treacherous," and "barbarous."[40] Ivory supplies were low, and food was scarce. The Dutch constantly stumbled into local rivalries. When they made a deal with the leader of Mpfumo, Prince John's relative, they were not aware that he was under the thumb of Mateke, a vassal of the leader of Magaia. Soon Mateke was complaining about the favor shown to Mpfumo. The squabbles quickly became serious when several of Mateke's men led an attack on the vegetable gardens attached to the Dutch fort. The Mpfumans helped repel the attack, and the Dutch then agreed to an alliance with Mpfumo.[41] The Dutch soon learned, however, that even the leader of Mpfumo was not their constant friend. In the late summer of 1721, the Mpfuman laborers who worked the land for the Dutch simply stopped showing up. The absence of these workers, mainly women and children, threatened the food supply at the fort. The Mpfumans held up their hands, telling the Dutch that Mateke had forbidden them to work until he got a larger share of the profits. After employing both the carrot and the stick to convince them to come back to work, the Dutch went to talk to Mateke. It turned out that he had never ordered the work stoppage, but he *had* demanded more tribute from the Mpfumans, which in turn had caused their leader to order a work stoppage until the Dutch offered to pay the laborers more. The Dutch had no choice but to give in and agree to the higher wages.[42] Thus, even before the pirates wreaked havoc, the local African leaders knew they were the ones in charge.

Initially, Prince John's return threatened the Dutch presence in Mpfumo. The Dutch identified him as the nephew of the leader of Mpfumo, and rumors reached them that he wanted his uncle to kick out the Dutch. Tensions ran high that first week. The Dutch gave all their men grenades to throw at the Mpfumans in case they attacked, and they fretted over the fact that they had only twelve functional muskets. All of this desperate preparation, a Dutch official lamented, "was caused by a black named Naphumbo, who came with the ship Noord Hapton."[43] Since the British could not easily establish trade due to the Dutch presence, Naphumbo or Prince John (this might be John's

African name, although his uncle is given the same name) "persuaded his Uncle . . . Naphumbo (to whom this land belongs) to give this post to the English, and drive [the Dutch] out."[44] Supposedly, John's uncle, Naphumbo (also written Maphumbo), went to his overlord Mateke to complain that the Dutch were not allowing him to trade with the British and that the Dutch should be wiped out.[45] The next day both Maphumbo and Mateke's people attempted to soothe Dutch fears, although Maphumbo's representative took some things from the Dutch, making a not so subtle point about who was in charge. That same day, Sharrow denied talking to either Maphumbo or Mateke and said that he would help the Dutch if the Africans attacked.[46] After this moment the threat simply simmered rather than boiled, but the Dutch continued to worry about this new power player in the region. It appears that Prince John was true to his promise to help the British with their endeavors once they arrived in Maputo Bay.[47]

For about a month, the British traded with abandon, much to the disgust of the Dutch. As the miner's Captain Paul wrote, "[It] proved very lucky for us, for their Weakness caused Liberty for trading."[48] The *Northampton* anchored far up the river out of reach of the Dutch fort and set about trading. On 16 January the crew traded with Prince John and his uncle at the beach, and three days later the Dutch reported that the British had given Maphumbo gifts and traded with him daily.[49] By the end of January, they were trading with multiple groups: Mpfumo, Magaia, Matola, Manisse, and others.[50] Then, in early February, they took to trading upriver, away from prying Dutch eyes.[51] They found the people "very civile" and thought their trade "returned very well."[52] The Dutch revealed to their superiors that the British offered better bargains than they did and thus had received almost the same amount of ivory in a single month as the Dutch had gathered in two years.[53]

According to the Dutch, the British were offering "corals and linens" and getting not only ambergris and ivory but also "pumpkins, pineapples, watermelons, etc."[54] It seems the British did not follow the advice of one adviser who recommended that they bring brass in the shape of collars and bracelets, beads, coarse cloth, and some bars of tin. He also had some creative ideas. He remarked that the residents "ware a straw of about 8 or 9 inches long into which with a piece of cloth they draw their P[enis]," and this observation sparked an epiphany: "These if made of brass in the shape of a case-knife handle, but longer and thicker about will sell well amongst them." Furthermore, they could sell the cloth to be used "for their P[enis] cases." These would come in long rectangular pieces fringed at the ends, "like a Muslin

Neck cloth," and "strung with white, yellow or purple beads." These "would please them ye better."[55] It seems that those who stocked the *Northampton* decided on more simple and dependable goods.

This same observer gives a sense of the dangerous nature of this trade. Doing business in the bay, he said, "is always done at the Mussells of your musketts." The traders should first approach the leaders and present them with a small gift like "a collar or a few Beads." Then they should throw a carpet across the ground, lay their goods upon it, and wait for the king to sit and trade. But, he implied, things were tenser outside these more ceremonial moments. Most trade was done near the ship or with the longboat close at hand. One trader should bring goods to the shore to show to prospective buyers and carry the ivory back, but the rest of the men should "sitt on board all ready by their arms upon the least occasion." If the locals wanted to come on board, that was acceptable, but they should not "trust too many of them at a time."[56] On the whole, the advice given the crew of the *Northampton* should have made them wary. The local people, the observer noted, were "very decietfull and treacherous," and he ended with a warning that they needed "to be watchfull and keep a good guard, especially in time of Trading."[57] As we shall see, the men on board the *Northampton* did not always heed such advice.

During this time, Marmaduke Penwell was collecting information on the peoples around the bay. He had the questions that John Perceval and Thomas Bray had prepared for him about the area.[58] In their idealized world, they imagined that Penwell would come ashore, two notebooks in hand, one to record his observations and the other to record important words in the Africans' language (the pages should be divided into columns, and each letter of the alphabet should have a few pages dedicated to it). With these books in his pockets, he would stride up to the ruler and declare that he had arrived to continue to help the ruler's long-lost relative and also "out of love to his & his peoples Souls to teach them how to Save them by knowing the true God." A God whose commands were "written by his own orders in a book," a book he had in his possession and, if they wanted, he could read it to them. Penwell's power was to be in his connection to Prince John and in the Bible.[59] Prince John and Penwell appear to have parted ways once the ship anchored in Mpfumo. Penwell had lost his prince, and no one seems to have asked to hear the words of the Bible. He was left with his notebooks. The first, his dictionary of Mpfuman words, does not survive, although it made it home to Britain, but Perceval did keep a copy of Penwell's observations.[60]

Penwell did not hold out much hope for the conversion of Mpfumo. Almost everything he says about the area and its people is negative. The amount of vitriol he directed at the people he described is nearly comic. When asked about their religion he responded, "They have no shew of religion," nor do they "acknowledge" a God or have "any notions concerning him." According to Penwell, even the concept of the devil was lost on them, as was the basic concept of the soul. Their everyday existence did not receive any more praise. They were drunken, revengeful, lazy, and dull. When asked if they were "Just or Fraudulent," Penwell answered: "No greater Thieves in the Universe." His frustration and bitterness ooze from the page. When asked about their wars, he answered: "Their method of making War is not to be known nor even guess'd at their Country being such a confusd heap of Rubbish."[61] In his eyes, it was obvious that the British should not waste their time on the people of the bay.

Yet despite all this anger and disappointment, Penwell did at least make a good-faith effort to answer the queries Perceval sent to him. He left the ship and talked to those around him. Some of the information probably came from other Europeans at the bay, since the language barriers were not as vast. During one conversation, a Dutchman revealed that he thought the soil would be "very fruitfull if the Inhabitants knew how to manage it."[62] And it was "a Portuguese" who told Penwell that Tembe was the greatest power along the bay, so it appears that the Portuguese had not entirely abandoned the region.[63] At times, however, Penwell insinuated that it was from the locals themselves that he got his information. When discussing their facial scarification practices, he recorded: "They say it makes their Faces handsomer." When answering a question regarding snakes, he wrote: "They say they have Serpents but I saw none."[64] Obviously some communication was going on. Penwell's detailed information on their food preparation and the inside of their houses implies that he entered their abodes, watched meals being prepared, and perhaps ate some of them.[65]

Sifting through Penwell's statements, we can get a vision of life around the bay, even if it is through a glass darkly. The landscape was flat and rather treeless, except for an "abundance of fruit trees." Dotting it were clusters of three to six beehive-shaped houses that, in Mpfumo alone, housed about three hundred people. Poles only four and half feet high formed the skeleton of these dwellings, and interwoven reeds covered them. They were low lying and dark but also warm, with a fire burning in the center and reed mats to rest upon. But most of the work happened outside the house. If it was the right time of year, the women would sow corn (maize), which they surrounded with an "indifferent Fence" to keep their cattle out. They employed their iron hoes to break up the sandy soil and create "little Hills like Mole Hills" to plant the corn. There were no true boundaries to the land, which astounded Penwell, but they worked a piece of land for a while and then moved on, letting the livestock, which included cattle, sheep, goats, and a few horses and pigs, wander in common pasturage. The women were the main agricultural workers, and the main employment Penwell saw the men engaging in was iron and copper work, which they did without heating the metals, instead beating the cold metal on a hard rock. They made lances for warfare and collars for trade.[66]

Penwell also got a sense of what they ate. A form of polenta, boiled corn meal, was the base of their meal, but they also consumed different forms of fruit. The crew of the *Northampton* tried some of the fruit. Much of it they found "not wholesome," including one that was "round as a Ball but very large with a hard Shell upon it, when Ripe is full of something like Honey." They liked "another sort" much better, even if it was a bit sour. They "used it in Punch like Tamarin." Broiled fish and poultry could also brighten the monotony of the cornmeal. The locals built weirs to catch herring at low tide and also feasted on bream, eel, shrimp, and turtle. And the poultry was "very large and good." After the meal, the people of the bay would perhaps engage in singing and dancing, which Penwell thought was their only recreation.[67]

He also observed their power structure and provided a strikingly detailed, if brief, depiction of their ruler. Every village had a ruler, who in times of need looked to the leader above him. At the top was the uncle of the two princes, whom the British called "Capt. Moffooma." Penwell thought he was "about thirty years of Age" and stood "about five feet 9 inches high." He was "a Strait well limb'd strong man." But this strength worried Penwell, who found him "proud Cruel and deceitfull."[68] Penwell did learn that although Mpfumo was "a large Country & well peopled" it was not nearly the most powerful; that title went to Tembe, whose leader was "the Powerfullest Captain of any around Delagoa." In fact, Penwell stated that the ruler with the least amount of power was the leader of Mpfumo.[69]

It turned out, however, that the British had reason to worry about the ruler of Mpfumo. First came the rumors. Captain Paul wanted to lead an expedition into the mountains to search for mines, but Captain Sharrow, Ely, and Hay urged him not to go. They had an account that the leader of Mpfumo "intended to take the Ship and plunder her." Then on 19 February the rumors became reality. Six of the men, including Paul and Sharrow, had taken the longboat to trade with the leader of Matola, whom they saw as "the best dealer in that Country." Sharrow and three men went ashore to spend the night, while Paul and the other man stayed with the boat. As midnight approached, so did the warriors of Matola. They took Sharrow and his three men prisoner. Paul and his companion slept on, unaware, until morning. They had a rude awakening. As the African warriors surrounded them, Paul made a desperate attempt to save his trade goods, but they ran at him, their lances pointed straight at his breast. The danger seemed so great that he resigned his soul to God, but luckily no one struck home, and they left him unharmed. Instead, he recorded in his journal, "[They took] all the Goods that were in the Boast and all our Cloaths." The two men were marched to town and found Sharrow fuming in one of the rulers' houses.[70] Some of the men were taken to the leader of Mpfumo. The Africans then tried to take the ship, but the crew, sensing their intention, picked up their weapons, and the Africans "fled head over heels off board, one party jumping from above down into the water, swimming straight to land."[71]

What had happened to change the attitude of the leaders of Mpfumo and Matola toward the British is unclear. Dutch records indicate that a little over two weeks previously, the leader of Mpfumo and other high-status men had been guests on the *Northampton*, with fiddle music played all day to entertain them.[72] The only hint given is that the princes' uncle and Mateke later told the Dutch they should let them kill the British because they "had taken their uncle and other people away from here."[73] Could Sharrow have decided to kidnap some of those he traded with? Or was this a reference to the earlier voyage of Prince John, Prince James, and their attendants? Perhaps it was a reference to other British ships who stole people from the bay. The leader of Matola would later claim that the British owed him because "one of his friends" had been "shot dead by the captain of the pirates" and that pirate had been English: "You are also English, *ergo* one nation."[74] What is clear is that the "very civil" people Paul had encountered before had now been angered enough not only to cut off trading relations but also to threaten to cut short the lives of the British sailors. Prince John is not mentioned, but it appears his loyalties had shifted.

The men were held captive for four days. During this time, the rulers of Matola and Mpfumo attempted to turn the Dutch against the British. They first asked the Dutch to help them take the ship, but the Dutch refused. Then "Maphumbo said that [the Dutch were] obligated to it because [they] live[d] in his country."[75] The people of the bay were asserting their sovereignty. The Dutch were here on sufferance. This was African land. The Dutch replied that the Africans had not helped them when the pirates attacked and that they could not condone the deaths.[76] The leaders of Matola and Mpfumo then looked to ransom the men, asking the crew on the ship to supply them with coral rings and pewter.[77] Interestingly enough, Paul, with his mind always on minerals, noted that his captors: "make some Collers with the Copper they had from the Mountains & they put amongst it some of our Pewter which made it look the whiter," which suggests where this desire for pewter came from.[78] The British decided to risk rescuing the men. On 23 February, ten or twelve men were given muskets or pistols, and they made their way upriver. They "went ashore before or at daybreak," marched into town, found Sharrow, armed him, and made their way back to the ship.[79] No resistance seems to have been given by Matola or Mpfumo. The next day was a Sunday. Unsurprisingly, the passengers and crew, in Paul's words, "had prayers and gave Thanks to Almighty God for our Deliverance." By 27 February 1723, they were gone: "Every one very glad that we were got off so well as we were"—alive, that is.[80]

The British and the Dutch had learned a hard lesson in the unfriendly environs of Maputo Bay. The Dutch factory would limp along for another seven years. Ivory supplies dwindled. A trade in enslaved Africans never took off.[81] At the Cape of Good Hope, the men employed by the Dutch East India Company saw the Maputo region as a place you were sent to die. Disease ended the lives of most, and wolves, they heard, dug up the bodies, requiring the company to send special coffins.[82] The climate, the scarcity of ivory and other goods, and the aggressive actions of the local powers ended the hopes of the Dutch, just as they had those aboard the *Northampton*. The Europeans learned that here their power, even their guns, did not amount to much. Here they were but pawns in a larger game of African power being played by the rulers around the bay. In the late eighteenth century, first the British, then the Austrians, and finally the Portuguese would return, drawing the powers of the bay back into European economies and squabbles.[83] In 1723, however, it was the Africans who ruled the bay. Prince John probably smiled as he saw the *Northampton* raise anchor and move toward open water. He knew now what side he was on.

Epilogue

The *Northampton* limped home to London laden with disenchantment. It made a dilatory stop at what is now Camps Bay, near present-day Cape Town. Captain Paul "tried the Sands" but found no gold. Then, following their instructions, the ship anchored at Cabinda, the new Royal African Company settlement in Angola. Paul once more "tried the sands" and broke "several Rocks on the Sea Shore" but, again, found nothing.[1] The trading post itself was on its last legs. The company had encountered hostility from the Portuguese who were settled in the area and from the Africans themselves. Later that year, the Portuguese, supported by the local Africans, would destroy the company settlement.[2] The *Northampton* stayed here for about a month until it set sail on 15 May 1723.[3] Its next stop would be the British Isles.

Meanwhile, their well-wishers in London had given up on them. They had heard nothing of the ship since the letters delivered from the Cape of Good Hope, which reached London in late February 1723, just about the time Sharrow and Paul had freed themselves from captivity. Already, though, the news from the Cape had sounded the death knell of their good expectations. After receiving the letters, both Chandos and another company supporter lamented the "ill success of the Northampton voyage." Chandos wrote: "A fatality hangs over this poor Company and prevents their succeeding in any of their undertakings." He and his correspondent, he felt, should have gone themselves; they could have made the venture work.[4] Henry Newman and John Perceval felt equally disenchanted. Perceval noted the "disappointment [of] our Delagoa Mission," but he comforted himself that Prince John "for whom we were so carefull has behaved himself well."[5] After receiving Perceval's letter, Newman told the members of the SPCK "to put an end to their Expectations from the Delagoa Mission which like many other good designs was well intended, tho the Success has not answer'd the wishes of those that promoted it."[6]

It was six months before they heard of the *Northampton* again. The governor of Cabinda sent a letter that mentioned the ship. When the letter arrived in late August, the Royal African Company was all aflutter. It was, Chandos told the commander at Cabinda in a letter, "a very agreeable Piece of News, for we had almost given this ship over for lost." The curt nature of the letter, however, frustrated the company. Chandos lambasted the commander, writing: "You likewise just mention the Differences in the Northampton, but you don't explain anything what you mean by it, how these differences arose, whom you judge to be in the wrong." Furthermore, the commander did not say "what's become of the Black Prince." Chandos ended by stating, "Surely you must think us very indifferent whether we hear anything of these concerns or not!"[7] A week later, as August drew to a close, the *Northampton* finally dropped anchor in Kinsale, Ireland, and these questions would begin to have answers.[8]

The last months of 1723 saw the Royal African Company and the SPCK slowly wrap up their involvement in the voyage. The ship came up the river to London on 16 September 1723, and members of the company and the SPCK were waiting.[9] The society focused its attention on Marmaduke Penwell. He visited its headquarters on 24 September and related the story of the voyage. He also kept a journal, he told them, which John Perceval had now, but as soon as he finished it, it would be passed on to the society. He had also brought back the chest of books and mathematical instruments.[10] Little in congratulation or condemnation colored the society's response. Penwell was paid, and there was a small buzz surrounding his journal.[11] The society finally got to read it in mid-October.[12] The journal then began to make the rounds. A copy of the words Penwell had learned in Mpfumo was sent to one SPCK member, and Newman wrote to Richard King, the princes' supporter in Exmouth, to see if he wished to have a copy of the journal.[13] He did.[14] The journal was still in circulation sixteen years later when Newman sent a copy to the bishop of London.[15]

The society was obviously displeased with how the voyage had turned out. Thomas Bray, one of the princes' main supporters, used it as an example in a book he wrote of what not to do when attempting to convert people. He thought that the instructions he and Perceval had laid out for Prince James and Prince John would be more useful in the American colonies, where conditions were more promising. In Africa, he argued, prospective converts had "no Restraint from living in a Wild and Savage Manner," but in America they had the colonists to help restrain their inclinations—whether they wanted it or not.[16] He noted that Penwell's account "was all the Fruit we reap'd after great expense, and the most prudent Measures we could Devise, in order to accomplish the good Work."[17] Besides continuing to support the Danish mission in Tranquebar, what is now Tharangambadi, the SPCK left the work of conversion to their sister institution, the Society for the Propagation of the Gospel in Foreign Parts, which focused on the Americas.

John Perceval soldiered on. In his mind, he might have failed to save the souls of Prince James and Prince John, but there were others. He had joined the Commission for Relieving Poor Proselytes, a body formed to support those who converted from Catholicism to Protestantism. But these converts, it turns out, would prove just as disappointing as the princes. In the same letter in which Newman told Perceval of Prince James's suicide, he also mentioned the case of John Barrett. This seemingly saintly individual had told the commissioners that he had converted from Catholicism, and Perceval, Newman, and Bray worked hard to find him employment. They were horrified at an assassination attempt on his life and tried to get his manuscript on "priestcraft" published. After failing to find him a position in Britain, the men tried to send him to America as a missionary, but he never arrived. It turned out the man was, in Perceval's words, "a notorious cheat." He had never been a Catholic and had returned to his home in the north of England rather than sail to the Americas to help convert lost souls.[18]

As this disappointment surfaced, Perceval was also supporting the brainchild of his friend George Berkeley, who wished to establish a college in the West Indies to educate the sons of planters who would go home with "good morals and good learning, a thing (God knows!) much wanted." Furthermore, the same college would train a number of indigenous Americans, who would "become the fittest Missionaries for spreading Religion morality & civil life among their Countrymen."[19] Bermuda, Berkeley decided, was the perfect location. Part of the funding for this project was to come from the legacy left by a Dutchman, Abel Tassin, Sieur D'Allone, who had left funds for the establishment of schools for the enslaved. All Berkeley had to do was add enslaved individuals to his list of converts. He was happy to, but due to doubts about the project's feasibility (most agreed that Bermuda was not a good choice) and internal wrangling over funds, the college never materialized.[20]

In fact, the only project that Perceval became involved in that succeeded, and saying it succeeded is a bit of stretch, was the establishment of the colony of Georgia. Perceval was one of the Georgia Trustees, and their goal was to begin a colony for the poor of Great Britain where they could live in idyllic simplicity on small plots of land without the temptations of enslaved labor or alcohol. The colony became a reality, but so did the enslaved men and women and the alcohol.[21] These ventures do show, however, that Perceval was not utterly disillusioned by his experience with the princes, but his focus would change and become centered more on troubled British souls.

If the SPCK and Perceval had to settle for Penwell's journal as their "fruits" from the voyage, the Royal African Company arguably got more: the cargo. On board the *Northampton* was a collection of ivory, redwood, copper bars, and ambergris.[22] But the company had lost the dreams of wealth and expansion that had fueled the voyage. It placed most of the blame on Captain Sharrow's shoulders. In February 1724 a stinging condemnation came from the Committee of Shipping, which criticized "the unreasonableness of Captain Sharrow's accounts in the Northampton, as also severall other mismanagements and misbehaviours during the voyage to Delagoa and back."[23] The company dismissed him from its service.[24] He tried to work his way back into Chandos's favor, but the duke rebuffed him in a devastating letter sent by his secretary: "His Grace" had received Sharrow's letter and book, the secretary wrote, but "his time is too much taken up to afford him Leisure enough to peruse it." Furthermore, the issue Sharrow brought up in the letter was for the Committee of Shipping to determine, not Chandos. Sharrow should not give himself "the trouble of calling at His Grace's House" about the issue, as "My Lord orders me to let you know that he has neither Friendship for nor Acquaintance enough with you to endeavour it when it proves to be disagreeable to the rest of the Gentlemen [on the Committee of Shipping]."[25] So much for Sharrow's future with the Royal African Company.

The others who returned had better luck to a degree. The company paid Captain Paul and offered both Leonard Ely and Colin Hay new positions.[26] Ely was to become the new governor at Cabinda, a position he eventually turned down, leading to his dismissal from the company.[27] Hay, the company decided, would become the new chief merchant at Sierra Leone.[28] In April 1724 he set sail for the western coast of Africa on board the *Northampton* once again.[29]

There is another man who, though not recorded on the list of passengers on that voyage, made it to Sierra Leone as well: Marmaduke Penwell. The former instructor hired for his "Sobriety and good Morals" had decided that his future lay with Royal African Company.[30] When exactly he first arrived in Sierra Leone is unclear, but he was there by October 1725. He surfaces in the records because Sierra Leone was in trouble. Captain William Gower of the *Clarendon* had dropped anchor there and found "all things in confusion." Colin Hay was dead, and there was no obvious person to put in charge. In the end, Gower sighed that he had "pitch'd upon" Marmaduke Penwell, "who had been some time in the Company service."[31] But his faith in the man was shaky. Echoing the sentiments of the SPCK years previously that he was "the best [the SPCK] could get," Gower thought "he was the fittest person then to succeed" but would "not be a proper person to be continued."[32] Penwell was in charge at Sierra Leone for more than a year until his replacement, Walter Charles, arrived in December 1726. Charles was not pleased with the state of the settlement. He found "the fort in a most miserable condition," those enslaved by the company for labor in Africa had run away, private traders had taken over the warehouses, and Penwell had let on that "he had received the Company's orders to sell all off."[33] It took only three more days for Charles to report that he had "discovered great mismanagments."[34] As the months wore on, the charges against Penwell grew. By April, Charles informed the company of "Penwell's insincerity and incapacity" and stated that "the Company will be great Loosers by him."[35] It appears that Penwell was working hand in glove with the private traders in the region. The company wanted Charles to prepare a full account of Penwell's "several frauds and embezzlements" before sending him home to face its wrath.[36] The company would never have the chance, for on 9 July 1727 Penwell "Escaped in the Night with 3 Others."[37]

He and the three who had escaped with him probably went to live with the private traders residing along the river, with whom they had done business.[38] Charles had complained to the company of the Europeans who had "taken the liberty to settle themselves so near our settlements without any legal authority and in open defiance of our Rights and privileges." The "destructive practices of those vagabonds and Banditti" had to be stopped.[39] These traders worked together with a number of gromettos, African wage laborers, and together they could be a dangerous combination for the Royal African Company men.[40] There was at least one account of "the murther of a white man by Sample's Gromettos."[41] Sample was one of the interlopers causing so much trouble. But the leader of this faction was José Lopez, a Portuguese African, who did business with the company, borrowed from it, and competed with it.[42] These were the men who now controlled the area, and Penwell cast his lot with them. He chose the winning side. In 1728, Lopez and his supporters, including those who had worked for and been enslaved by the Royal African Company, attacked the fort and sent the British scurrying. The company never returned.[43]

It was a blow to company prestige. Not only did the company lose its settlement in Sierra Leone, but, as a company official complained, its detractors in London would not soon let it forget that "an undisciplined Herd of Negros" had destroyed the settlement.[44] Perhaps Penwell took away more from his relationship with the princes than he let on, perhaps he learned the value of intercultural cooperation. It is unknown if he participated in the attack, however. The last word on his fate comes from Henry Newman, who seems unaware of his disgrace. When sending Penwell's journal to the bishop of London in early 1740, he simply stated that "his behavior in this Voyage recommended him afterward to the service of the African Company in which he dy'd."[45] He leaves the other details unsaid.

The failure of the princes' voyage, of the factory at Cabinda, and of the settlement at Sierra Leone ended the last realistic attempt to revive the flagging Royal African Company. In 1723 its exports had risen to £102,560 from the meager £69,449 it had brought in two years before, but two years later that number fell to £3,917.[46] By 1730 the company depended on a government subsidy to maintain and defend its forts. A statute was passed in 1750 to dissolve the company and reform it as the Company of Merchants Trading to Africa.[47] The trade in enslaved people was now left to the free traders who would push it to its greatest extent in the coming fifty years. The company had, however, rid itself of the memory of the princes' voyage long before. In September 1725, just as Penwell was about to take over at Sierra Leone, the company ordered a servant to rummage through "the Cloaths and necessarys . . . which belonged to the two Black Princes" to find items for "the Negro which came home by the Bonetta Brigantine."[48]

And what of the surviving "black prince"? He appears to have become a person of status in his community. By 1726 the Dutch found that business with the polities around the bay was faltering. Ivory and enslaved Africans only trickled in. The people of the bay were suspicious of the slave trade and, in the words of the Dutch at the Cape, "[believed] that our slave trade is done with no other purpose than to fatten them up and eat them."[49] The Dutch took quick and direct action when they became aware of this. The officials at the fort in Maputo Bay sent three high-ranking African representatives to the Cape to show them that the Dutch did not eat those they enslaved but rather employed them. One of these high-ranking Africans was Prince John. They arrived on the *Spieringshoek*, which laid anchor on 21 August. The Dutch at the Cape were not entirely pleased about Prince John's arrival. His facility with English and his ties to that country worried them, especially since a British ship, the *Stanhope*, was to arrive in the next few days and John could divulge the dire state of things in Maputo Bay to them. The Dutch decided to keep the emissaries in town, away from prying British eyes, and to wine and dine them in the hopes that, as the Dutch records have it, "[they] may be more and more entwined with our friendship."[50] After London, one wonders if the clothing, food, and entertainment impressed Prince John at all. Did he flash back to his time in London? Was he reminded of the brother he had lost? We know that he was aware that the Europeans did not literally eat the enslaved, but he did know that they figuratively did—among them his brother, his former attendants, and almost all the Africans he met after leaving home. The records are silent on John's opinions about whether Mpfumans should join the slave trade, but the trade in enslaved bodies certainly did not pick up after this visit to the Cape. But the fact that he was part of this delegation suggests that he had found a place of authority among his people after coming home.

The people of the bay had begun to shut down European trade in the area. They turned away Africans coming from the interior to trade with the Dutch, and those who did make it through to the Dutch often found themselves robbed on their way home.[51] The polities around the bay were also almost constantly at war with one another during this period. For a brief shining moment in 1728, Prince John's Mpfumo held the upper hand, until being almost decimated the next year.[52] For the Dutch these wars were a disaster. They found it increasingly difficult to remain neutral. Their trading post was faltering. By 1730 the Dutch threw up their hands in defeat and disbanded the settlement.[53] Between 1730 and the late 1770s Maputo Bay remained an open port. Eventually Portuguese interest in the region would be rekindled. After kicking out an Austrian trading company in 1781, the Portuguese set up a trading post. Their power would slowly grow until the settlement around the bay became the capital of the Portuguese colony of Mozambique, a designation it would keep when that nation gained its independence in 1975.[54]

With the value of hindsight, the voyage of the *Northampton* appears bound to fail. But there was a reason Chandos and the Royal African Company acted on these schemes. They were desperate. They were men in charge of a trading company at the dawn of free trade. The problem of private traders or interlopers dogged all the big companies during this period and caused them to consider changing course. The East India Company too was looking for new answers. Before drawing inward to shut down interlopers, it almost opened itself up to Atlantic possibilities. But in looking for alternatives, these companies began to consider schemes that held too many unknowns to be feasible. The East India Company was less apt to act on these projects than the Royal African Company; it was less desperate. But it considered them. In this world, inept leaders like Sharrow and adventurers like Penwell stood a chance. While this moment in the 1720s opened the door for unlikely schemes and shady characters, it also points to a time when the shape and nature of the British Empire could have altered. This moment could have changed the geographic makeup of the empire or at least its trading routes. Southeastern Africa and South America could have moved into the British sphere of influence. This would have been a different world.

But it was not to be. The British were not powerful enough to exploit these openings to wealth and power. Africa was still very much in African hands. The British presence on the western coast was always at the mercy of African rulers, not the European traders. On the east coast they had even less control. They were just one pawn among many. Over the next century or so the people of the bay would toy with different European powers as they came and went: the British, the Dutch, the Austrians, and the Portuguese. Until the Portuguese, none would maintain a foothold there.

Furthermore, the dreams many Britons had of global expansion had slavery at their heart or at least intersected with it. Captain White of the *Mercury* came to southeast Africa because he wanted to purchase enslaved men, women, and children in Madagascar. The East India Company might have wanted to find gold in southeast Africa, but it was more interested in the possibility of entering the transatlantic slave trade and expanding upon the trade in enslaved bodies in the Indian Ocean. The Royal African Company was looking for gold and other trade goods in southeast and central Africa, but only because the company was not as competitive in the slave trade as it had once been. Slavery was one of the most powerful economic motors at the time.

Other wronged African princes would surface in London, indicating growing British involvement in the slave trade. In 1733 Ayuba Suleiman Diallo would be feted in Britain and return to his home in modern-day Senegal a year later. The tensions between the British and the French there would plague him on his return, although he would remain friendly with the British until his death, in 1773.[55] In 1748, William Unsah Sessarakoo would arrive in London. He would return to what is now Ghana two years later, and he and his father, the ruler of the area, would use his British ties to their advantage, but it was clear that no deep emotional tie existed. In fact, he came to blows with one Englishman after Sessarakoo discovered that he was receiving watered-down brandy like other African slave traders.[56] In 1773 two African princes from Calabar (modern-day Nigeria), who had been kidnapped into slavery, came to Bristol and won their freedom. After their return home, they requested missionaries, but Christianity did not take root.[57] These four princes embraced and used their ties with Great Britain after their return home because their world on the western coast was more embedded with the British due to the slave trade. Prince John, however, could throw off his British ties on his return. British influence, he found, was of little use.

The journeys of Prince John and Prince James show the limits of global power and global inclusion. British ships sailed to all corners of the world, and British societies and companies looked to these far corners for new opportunities, secure in their knowledge and power. But visits do not equate to power, and assumed knowledge often masks ignorance. In the eighteenth century, the British were not strong enough to dominate countries far from home, and their pathways of information were slow and often misleading. The British were also not willing to include those they saw as different. Prince John and Prince James met with their supporters, ate with them, and prayed with them. But their patrons never saw them as equals. The princes too could not cross the cultural divide. Prince James appears to have attempted to merge his African and British identities, but the two halves of his whole failed to cohere, and this perhaps destroyed him. Prince John maintained a facade to please the British but discarded it.

These ships of fools, whether the *Mercury*, the *Northampton*, or the institutions and individuals who supported their voyages, were bound to crash on rocky shoals, but the wind that blew their sails taut and set them on course tells us much about the vision of the globe possessed by the British and by the Mpfumans. For both, the early decades of the eighteenth century were times of change and struggle, times when supporting an inadvisable journey offered hope. These dreams were not innocent: they were about slavery, profit, and power. Dark dreams indeed. They do, however, gesture to a fracture point where the map of British power and trade might have altered and where a different form of globalization might have taken root. And to a future where Mpfuman power dominated the bay and established ties with the British. It did not come to pass, but it could have. It also reminds us of the cost of these dreams and the lives lost: the vicious inclusion of the enslaved Africans such plans required; the Malagasy unwillingly brought aboard the *Mercury*, who were sold into slavery in Jamaica and were not freed; the lost story of the princes' attendants; and Prince James's broken body laid to rest in a British grave far from home. His death was an escape, a denial of British power, and a scream of despair.

NOTES

The following abbreviations appear in the notes.

BL   British Library, London, U.K.
Bod   Bodleian Library, Oxford, U.K.
Cam   Cambridge University Library, Manuscript Department
DNA   Nationaal Archief, The Hague, Netherlands
HEH   Huntington Library, San Marino, Calif.
IOR   India Office Records
LMA   London Metropolitan Archives, London, U.K.
SPCK   Society for Promoting Christian Knowledge
TNA   The National Archives, Kew, U.K.

Prologue

1. Selecting what terms to use to designate the princes' homeland was a complex task. When referring to their polity, I use Mpfumo. However, when referencing the larger bay and the polities around it, I use the modern Maputo Bay. This allows me to avoid using the terms, like Delagoa, imposed on them by Europeans. The term Delagoa will of course be used in quotations from the period. There are multiple different spellings of the surrounding polities as well, and I have attempted to choose the spellings accepted today by scholars. The name Maputo also comes with a fraught backstory. During the struggle for independence the term KaMpfumo was often used to refer to the capital rather than the Portuguese Lourenço Marques, but when independence came, Maputo was chosen to mark a fresh start away from the feudal resonances that clung to KaMpfumo. The Maputo River marked the border with South Africa, and during the push for independence, the motto "from the Rovuma to the Maputo" was often used to mark the farthest northern and southern limits of the new nation. Tiago Castela and Maria Paula Meneses, "Naming the Urban in Twentieth-Century Mozambique: Towards Spatial Histories of Aspiration and Violence" in *Urban Planning in Lusophone African Countries*, ed. Carlos Nunes Silva (London: Routledge, 2015), 215–18. https://doi-org.libproxy1.usc.edu/10.4324/9781315548760.

2. Until the 1750s stockings were usually "drawn up over the breeches above the knee and then turned down in a flat roll over the garter which was fastened below the knee but generally hidden by the stocking." The garter itself was usually made of woven silk some with designs woven into them. C. Willett Cunnington and Phillis Cunnington, *Handbook of English Costume in the Eighteenth Century* (London: Faber and Faber, 1957), 83.

3. Here I am engaging a small piece of "critical fabulation" through the use of "restrained imagination." The archive that tells the princes' story often excludes details about them, treating them as objects. Rather than telling the story of the lead-up to Prince James's death through archival eyes, I wanted to do it through his, to center the story on him. Many of the details I mention are visible in the sources. Marmaduke Penwell writes that Prince James left his lodging at 10 P.M. and that he "hanged himself in his garters." Henry Newman says a bit more, stating, "He went out about eleven a clock & was found next morning hanging by his garters on an apple tree." The Royal African Company minutes state that Prince James "had hanged himself with his own Garters in a field near adjoining to their lodgings." A later account by Thomas Bray holds that he "hang'd himself in an Orchard in the West of England." Newman and Penwell also mention that it was after a fight with his brother and a beating by the ship's captain, hence the mention of fists and anger. Marmaduke Penwell to John Perceval, 21 May 1722, BL Add. MS 47029, f. 122v; Henry Newman to John Perceval, 8 May 1722, BL Add. MS 47029, f. 121v; 9 May 1722, Minutes of Court of Assistants, TNA T 70/91, f. 138; Thomas Bray, *Missionalia: Or, A Collection of Missionary Pieces Relating to the Conversion of the Heathen; Both the African Negroes and American Indians* (London: Printed by W. Roberts in the Year 1727), 45. *Eighteenth Century Collections Online* (accessed February 9, 2024). https://link-gale-com.libproxy1.usc.edu/apps /doc/CW0117415598/ECCO?u=usocal_main&sid=bookmark-ECCO&xid=89c0052b&pg=1. For "critical fabulation" see Saidiya Hartman, "Venus in Two Acts," *small axe* 12, no. 2 (June 2008): 11, and also Tiya Miles, *All That She Carried: The Journey of Ashley's Sack, A Black Family Keepsake* (New York: Random House, 2021), 17–18. On the need for imaginative reconstruction within limits also see Wendy Warren, "'The Cause of Her Grief': The Rape of a Slave in Early New England," *Journal of American History* 93, no. 4 (March 2007): 1049; Natalie Zemon Davis, *The Return of Martin Guerre* (Cambridge, Mass.: Harvard University Press, 1983), viii, 5.

4. 21 January 1723, Day Register, 23 June 1722 to 31 May 1723, DNA VOC Archives, 1.04.02, Part 1/E.5.b, 4367, f. 328. Translated by Julie van den Hout.

5. 24 January 1723, Day Register, 18 January 1723 to 31 May 1723, DNA VOC Archives 1.04.02, Part 1/E.5.b, 4367, f. 589. Translated by Jason Perlman.

6. 3 March 1723, Day Register, 23 June 1722 to 31 May 1723, DNA VOC Archives 1.04.02, Part 1/E.5.b, 4367, f. 338v. Translated by Julie van den Hout.

7. 7 March 1723, Day Register, 23 June 1722 to 31 May 1723, DNA VOC Archives 1.04.02, Part 1/E.5.b, 4367, f. 340v-341. Translated by Julie van den Hout.

8. "The Memorial of Mr. Toogood in behalf of the two Princes of Delagoa to the Honourable Court of Directors of the East India Company," BL IOR E/1/11, f. 326.

9. A. K. Smith, "The Struggle for Control of Southern Mozambique, 1720–1835" (Ph.D. diss., UCLA, 1970), 28–34.

10. Some historians have traced parts of the princes' story or told truncated versions of it. See Elizabeth A. Eldredge, *Kingdoms and Chiefdoms of Southeastern Africa: Oral Traditions and History, 1400–1830* (Rochester: University of Rochester Press, 2015), 120–26; Zachary McLeod Hutchins, *Before Equiano: A Prehistory of the North American Slave Narrative* (Chapel Hill: University of North Carolina Press, 2022), 104–14; William Pettigrew, *Freedom's Debt: The Royal African Company and the Politics of the Atlantic Slave Trade, 1672–1752* (Chapel Hill: University of North Carolina Press, 2013), 169; Robert C.-H. Shell, "The Twinning of Maputo and Cape Town: The Early Mozambican Slave Trade to the Slave Lodge, 1677–1732" in *History, Memory and Identity*, ed. Vijayalakshmi Teelock and Edward A. Alpers (Reduit, Moka: University of Mauritius and Nelson Mandela Centre for African Culture, 2001), 178–88; Brent Sirota,

The Christian Monitors: The Church of England and the Age of Benevolence, 1680–1730 (New Haven: Yale University Press, 2014), 240–42; A. K. Smith, "The Struggle for Control of Southern Mozambique, 1720–1835" (Ph.D. diss., UCLA, 1970), 58–61.

11. The records hold different spellings of their names. In the newspaper account of their baptism, they are James Shandois and John Togood. "News," *London Journal*, 24 June 1721, 4. *Seventeenth and Eighteenth Century Burney Newspapers Collection* (accessed 1 May 2024). https://link-gale-com.libproxy1.usc.edu/apps/doc/Z2001382378/BBCN?u=usocal_main&sid =bookmark-BBCN&xid=e86feb94. In the parish records they are James Shandayes and John Twogood. London Metropolitan Archive, St. Mary the Virgin, Twickenham, Composite register, 1720–1761, DRO/174/A/01/006. In the letters they wrote they signed themselves James Chandos and John Towgood Maffoom. James Chandos and John Towgood Maffoom to John Perceval, 24 January 1721, 1 February 1721/2, BL Add. MS 47029, f. 97, 101v. Later the Society for Promoting Christian Knowledge would refer to them as James Maquillan Muffoom and John Chaung Muffoom. Minutes of the Society for Promoting Christian Knowledge (SPCK), 5 October 1721, Cam SPCK MS A1/9, f. 195; Minutes of the Standing Committee, 6 February 1722, 27 March 1722, Cam SPCK MS A5/4, f. 87, 97. When Prince John returns to Mpfumo, the Dutch once call him Naphumbo, which may be his African name, but they call his uncle, the king, by the same name, so it is unclear if this is what he was called among the Mpfumans. 24 January 1723, Day Register, 18 January 1723 to 31 May 1723, DNA, VOC Archives 1.04.02, Part 1/E.5.b, 4367, f. 589. Translated by Jason Perlman.

12. The early history of the area that is now called Maputo has not drawn much scholarly interest. The most detailed study, and the one most scholars depend on, is Alan Smith's dissertation from 1970, which is based mostly on the records of the Dutch East India Company, although papers from the Portuguese also surface. After contacting scholars of the region, I have not been able to find any reference to oral histories or archaeological accounts that cover Mpfumo itself during this period. There is an account of the area originally published in 1912 by Henri Junod, a missionary and ethnographer, who lived in Mozambique from 1880 to 1896, but this holds as much, if not more, bias than the eighteenth-century documents. A. K. Smith, "The Struggle for Control of Southern Mozambique, 1720–1835," (Ph.D. diss., UCLA, 1970); Henri A. Junod, *The Life of a South African Tribe*, 2nd Edition, Revised and Enlarged, vol. 1-2 (London: Macmillan, 1927).

13. The memorial, which is the most detailed account of the princes' early travels, can be found in a volume of received correspondence kept by the East India Company. "The Memorial of Mr. Toogood in behalf of the two Princes of Delagoa to the Honourable Court of Directors of the East India Company," BL IOR E/1/11, f. 326. The story of the princes, and the plans of the East India Company regarding them, can also be found in the minutes of the Court of Assistants, the minutes, reports, and memoranda of the Committee of Correspondence, factory letters, and home miscellaneous papers. See British Library, India Office Records, B, D, E, G, and H from the years 1713 to 1730.

14. Robert Drury, *Madagascar: Or Robert Drury's Journal* (London, 1729), 431.

15. For their time in Jamaica see: "News," *Weekly Journal or British Gazetteer*, 3 December 1720, 3. *Seventeenth and Eighteenth Century Burney Newspapers Collection* (accessed 9 February 2024). https://link-gale-com.libproxy2.usc.edu/apps/doc/Z2001586992/BBCN?u=usocal_main &sid=bookmark-BBCN&xid=8bd27aae.

16. They surface most prominently in the letters of John Perceval, who would become the Earl of Egmont, and James Brydges, the first Duke of Chandos. Perceval's letters are held in the

British Library, and references to the princes can be found in his letter books. Brydges's letters are held at the Huntington Library, and references can be found in his letter books. British Library, Add MSS 47029-30. Huntington Library, ST 57.17-22.

17. The Royal African Company's papers are held in the British National Archives in Kew, and the most detailed references to the princes can be found in the minute books of the Court of Assistants: T70/90-92. The papers for the Society for Promoting Christian Knowledge are held in the Cambridge University Library, Manuscript Department, and references to the princes can be found in the general minutes and the minutes of the Standing Committee as well as the correspondence of the society. Cambridge University Library, Manuscript Department, SPCK MSS, A1/9-10, A5/4, D4/11-13.

18. There are many surviving records from the Dutch East India Company's factory at Maputo held in the Dutch National Archives (VOC Archives 1.04.02, Part 1/E.5). Of most use to this project were two day registers kept by two different people at the settlement that recorded the day-to-day happenings at the factory. See Day Register, 18 January 1723 to 31 May 1723, DNA VOC Archives 1.04.02, Part 1/E.5.b, 4367, and Day Register, 23 June 1722 to 31 May 1723, DNA, VOC Archives, 1.04.02, Part 1/E.5.b, 4367.

19. For speculation on Prince James's suicide see Marmaduke Penwell to John Perceval, 21 May 1722, BL Add. MS 47029, f. 122v; Henry Newman to John Perceval, 8 May 1722, BL Add. MS 47029, f. 121v; Minutes of Court of Assistants, 9 May 1722, Royal African Company Papers (RAC), TNA T 70/91, f. 138; Bray, *Missionalia*, 45. *Eighteenth Century Collections Online* (accessed 9 February 2024). https://link-gale-com.libproxy1.usc.edu/apps/doc/CW0117415598 /ECCO?u=usocal_main&sid=bookmark-ECCO&xid=89c0052b&pg=1.

20. For information on John's actions observed by the Dutch see: Day Register, 23 June 1722 to 31 May 1723, DNA, VOC Archives, 1.04.02, Part 1/E.5.b, 4367, f. 328-41; Day Register, 18 January 1723 to 31 May 1723, DNA, VOC Archives 1.04.02, Part 1/E.5.b, 4367, f. 589.

21. For their letters see: James Chandos and John Towgood Maffoom to John Perceval, 24 January 1721, 1 February 1721/2, BL Add. MS 47029, f. 97, 101v.

22. Hartman, 2-3.

23. While not an exhaustive list in any fashion, for attempts to interrogate the archives created by enslavers, which often silences or twists the stories of the enslaved, and to make those stories more legible from the eighteenth century see: Trevor Burnard and Sophie White, eds., *Slave Narratives in British and French America, 1700-1848* (New York: Routledge, 2020); Marisa Fuentes, *Dispossessed Lives: Enslaved Women, Violence, and the Archive* (Philadelphia: University of Pennsylvania Press, 2016), Lisa A. Lindsay and John Wood Sweet, eds., *Biography and the Black Atlantic* (Philadelphia: University of Pennsylvania Press, 2014), Simon P. Newman, *Freedom Seekers: Escaping from Slavery in Restoration London* (London: University of London Press, 2022), James Sweet, *Domingos Álvares, African Healing, and the Intellectual History of the Atlantic World* (Chapel Hill: University North Carolina Press, 2011), Wendy Warren, "The Cause of Her Grief": The Rape of a Slave in Early New England," *Journal of American History* 93, no. 4 (March 2007): 1031-49, Sophie White, *Voices of the Enslaved: Love, Labor, and Longing in French Louisiana* (Chapel Hill: University of North Carolina Press, 2019). Also see the special issue of the *History of the Present* published in the fall of 2016. Brian Connolly and Marisa Fuentes, eds., Special Issue of *History of the Present* 6, no. 2 (Fall 2016): 105-215.

24. Jennifer L. Morgan makes the point that questioning what is stated in the archive, and making that questioning evident in the work, reveals the instability of the archive. Jennifer L.

Morgan, "Accounting for 'The Most Excruciating Torment': Gender, Slavery, and Trans-Atlantic Passages," *History of the Present* 6, no. 2 (Fall 2016): 201–2.

25. Most scholarship on the trading companies focuses on a single company. See Philip J. Stern, *The Company-State: Corporate Sovereignty and the Early Modern Foundations of the British Empire in India* (Oxford: Oxford University Press, 2011), Emily Erikson, *Between Monopoly and Free Trade: The English East India Company, 1600–1757* (Princeton: Princeton University Press, 2014), K. G. Davies, *The Royal African Company* (London: Longmans, 1960), William Pettigrew, *Freedom's Debt: The Royal African Company and the Politics of the Atlantic Slave Trade, 1672–1752* (Chapel Hill: University of North Carolina Press, 2013). For those looking at how these institutions overlapped and intersected see Jonathan Eacott, *Selling Empire: India in the Making of Britain and America, 1600–1830* (Chapel Hill: University of North Carolina Press, 2016), William A. Pettigrew and David Veevers, eds., *The Corporation as a Protagonist in Global History, c. 1550–1750* (Leiden: Brill, 2019), William A. Pettigrew, *Global Trade and the Shaping of English Freedom* (Oxford: Oxford University Press, 2023), Philip J. Stern, *Empire, Incorporated: The Corporations that Built British Colonialism* (Cambridge, Mass.: Harvard University Press, 2023).

26. Eacott, 72–99; Pettigrew, *Freedom's Debt*, chaps. 1 to 4.

27. Slave Voyages database says that 263,963 enslaved Africans were taken aboard British ships between 1551 and 1700. Then it holds that 273,705 enslaved people were taken abroad British ships between 1701 and 1720. Slave Voyages Database, https://www.slavevoyages.org (accessed 8 June 2024).

28. Philip Curtin estimates that the majority of those enslaved by the English in 1713 embarked from Benin and the Gold Coast, with those being the top two locations again in 1724. Slave Voyages Database gives similar answers, noting that most English ships embarked with enslaved Africans from the Gold Coast (4,387) and the Bight of Benin (2,512), with 1,244 embarking from Senegambia and the offshore Atlantic and 4,469 coming from other African locations. Slave Voyages Database, https://www.slavevoyages.org (accessed 14 January 2024). Philip Curtin, *The Atlantic Slave Trade: A Census* (Madison: University of Wisconsin Press, 1969), 129.

29. Between 1514 and 1866 Slave Voyages Database for transatlantic voyages lists only fifty-one voyages to Madagascar by British ships: none until 1664 and then eight between 1664 and 1679, twenty-two between 1680 and 1689, two in the 1690s, only one between 1700 and 1716, thirteen between 1717 and 1721, four between 1727 and 1758, and none after that year. Slave Voyages Database, http://www.slavevoyages.org (accessed 1 June 2015). For detail on some of these voyages see Robert C. Ritchie, *Captain Kidd and the War Against the Pirates* (Cambridge, Mass.: Harvard University Press, 1989).

30. Between 1650 and 1750 the British loaded 1,131,436 enslaved people onto ships; of those 12,793 embarked from East Africa or the Indian Ocean islands. Slave Voyages Database, https://www.slavevoyages.org (accessed 14 January 2024).

31. For European engagement with Madagascar see James C. Armstrong, "Madagascar and the Slave Trade in the Seventeenth Century," *Omaly sy Anio*, 17–19 (1984): 211–33; R. J. Barendse, "Slaving on the Madagascar Coast 1640–1700," in *Cultures of Madagascar: Ebb and Flow of Influences*, ed. Sandra Evers and Marc Spindler (Leiden: International Institute for Asian Studies, 1995), 137–55; Arne Bialuschewski, "Pirates, Slavers, and the Indigenous Population in Madagascar c. 1690–1715," *International Journal of African Historical Studies* 38, no. 3

(2005); Jane Hooper, *Feeding Globalization: Madagascar and the Provisioning Trade, 1600–1800* (Athens: Ohio University Press, 2017); Virginia Bever Platt, "The East India Company and the Madagascar Slave Trade," *William and Mary Quarterly*, 3rd series, 26, no. 4 (Oct. 1969); Solofo Randrianja and Stephen Ellis, *Madagascar: A Short History* (Chicago: University of Chicago Press, 2009), chap. 4; Robert C. Ritchie, *Captain Kidd and the War Against the Pirates* (Cambridge, Mass.: Harvard University Press, 1986).

32. See Randy Sparks, *Where the Negroes Are Masters: An African Port in the Era of the Slave Trade* (Cambridge, Mass.: Harvard University Press, 2014); Randy Sparks, *The Two Princes of Calabar: An Eighteenth-Century Atlantic Odyssey* (Cambridge, Mass.: Harvard University Press, 2004).

33. For British interest in Africans, especially princes, and foreign visitors see Kate Fullagar, *The Savage Visit: New World People and Popular Imperial Culture in Britain, 1710–1795* (Berkeley: University of California Press, 2012); Catherine Molineux, *Faces of Perfect Ebony: Encountering Atlantic Slavery in Imperial Britain* (Cambridge, Mass.: Harvard University Press, 2012).

34. For the need to look at overlaps between the Atlantic and Indian Oceans see Alison Games, Philip J. Stern, Paul W. Mapp, and Peter A. Coclanis, "Beyond the Atlantic," *William and Mary Quarterly* 63, no. 4 (2006): 675–742.

35. James Walvin, *Black and White: The Negro and English Society, 1555–1945* (London: Allen Lane, Penguin Press, 1973), 17; Peter D. Fraser, "Slaves or Free People? The Status of Africans in England, 1550–1750," in *From Strangers to Citizens: The Integration of Immigrant Communities in Britain, Ireland and Colonial America, 1550–1750*, ed. Randolph Vigne and Charles Littleton (Brighton, U.K.: Sussex Academic Press, 2001), 255–56.

Chapter 1

1. The ship *Mercury* was two hundred tons. Dispatch Books, 15 March 1715/6, BL IOR E/3/98, 429v.

2. "Directions for the Bay of Delagoa and the River therein, with some Memorandums concerning the Trade of that Place," TNA T70/1185, f. 18.

3. While there is no scholarship on slavery in Mpfumo in particular, Africanists and those studying slavery in the Indian Ocean world stress that these societies were deeply hierarchical and everyone was usually part of complex webs of dependency. They push against the Western binary of slavery or freedom and rather look to a spectrum of dependency. Igor Kopytoff and Suzanne Miers, "African 'Slavery' as an Institution of Marginality," in Suzanne Miers and Igor Kopytoff, eds., *Slavery in Africa: Historical and Anthropological Perspectives* (Madison: University of Wisconsin Press, 1977), 17, 30–31; Gwyn Campbell, "Introduction: Slavery and Other Forms of Unfree Labour in the Indian Ocean World," in *The Structure of Slavery in Indian Ocean Africa and Asia*, ed. Gwyn Campbell (London: Frank Cass, 2004), xxi.

4. The links between Atlantic and Indian Ocean trade have been pointed to by a number of scholars, including Alison Games, *The Web of Empire: English Cosmopolitans in an Age of Expansion, 1560–1660*; R. J. Barendse, "Slaving on the Madagascar Coast 1640–1700," in *Cultures of Madagascar: Ebb and Flow of Influences*, ed. Sandra Evers and Marc Spindler (Leiden: International Institute for Asian Studies, 1995), 137–55; Jane Hooper and David Eltis, "The Indian Ocean in Transatlantic Slavery," *Slavery and Abolition* 34, no. 3 (2013): 363, DOI: 10.1080/0144039X.2012.734112, 363; Jonathan Eacott, *Selling Empire: India in the Making of Britain and America, 1600–1830* (Chapel Hill: University of North Carolina Press, 2016).

5. Elizabeth A. Eldredge, *Kingdoms and Chiefdoms of Southeastern Africa: Oral Traditions and History, 1400–1830* (Rochester: University of Rochester Press, 2015), 120–26. She bases her information on Alan K. Smith's dissertation. A. K. Smith, "The Struggle for Control of Southern Mozambique, 1720–1835," (Ph.D. diss., UCLA, 1970), 23. Modern scholars and English and Dutch documents from the period spell the names of these polities differently. Finding the "correct" spelling is difficult, since there is not an established or accepted orthography for the Tsonga/Ronga terms. Mpfumo is also spelled Mfumo, Maffooma, and Masooma. Manisse is also Mainisse, Maijnisse, Menisse, and Manhiça. Magaia is also called Mabjaia, Lebombo, or Lebumbo (the name of the ruler who came over the Lebombo Mountains and conquered Magaia). Matola is also called Matolo, Matollo, Mattole, Matole, Matsolo, and Mattoll. Tembe is also sometime spelled Tembo. For modern scholars see Eldredge, 121, and Smith, 23. For eighteenth-century accounts see "Mr Penwells Account of Delagoa given me by himself," BL Add. MS 27990, f. 68. "Capt Pauls Journal of his Voyage to Delagoa Anno. 1722," HEH ST 9, ff. 70–71. Day Register, 23 June 1722 to 31 May 1723, DNA, VOC Archives 1.04.02, Part 1/E.5.b, 4367, f. 324v–341v, translated by Julie van den Hout; 3 March 1723, Day Register, 18 January 1723 to 31 May 1723, DNA, VOC Archives 1.04.02, Part 1/E.5.b, 4367, f. 588–93, translated by Jason Perlman.

6. Smith, 8, 27.

7. Smith, 28–31.

8. Smith, 33–34, 58.

9. Malyn Newitt, *A History of Mozambique* (Bloomington: Indiana University Press, 1995), 149–50.

10. D. W. Hedges, "Trade and Politics in Southern Mozambique and Zululand in the Eighteenth and Early Nineteenth Centuries" (Ph.D. diss., London School of Oriental and African Studies, 1978), 68–72. The Central Cattle Pattern has been a source of debate, with much of the critique focused on the fact that it puts continuity before change. Thomas N. Huffman, "The Central Cattle Pattern and Interpreting the Past," *Southern African Humanities* 13, no. 1 (2001): 19–35; Shaw Badenhorst, "The Central Cattle Pattern During the Iron Age of Southern Africa: A Critique of Its Spatial Features," *South African Archaeological Bulletin* 64, no. 190 (December 2009): 148–55; Thomas N. Huffman, "Debating the Central Cattle Pattern: A Reply to Badenhorst," *South African Archaeological Bulletin* 65, no. 192 (December 2010): 164–74; Raevin Jimenez, "'Slow Revolution' in Southern Africa: Household Biosocial Reproduction and Regional Entanglements in the History of Cattle Keeping Among Nguni-Speakers, Ninth to Thirteenth Century CE," *Journal of African History* 61, no. 2 (July 2020): 155–78.

11. Gerhard Liesegang, "New Light on Venda Traditions: Mahumane's Account of 1730," *Africa in History* 4 (1977): 166; Newitt, *A History of Mozambique*, 149–50.

12. Simon Hall states that these traders were from the Singo state. Simon Hall, "Farming Communities of the Second Millennium: Internal Frontiers, Identity, Continuity and Change," in *The Cambridge History of South Africa*, ed. Carolyn Hamilton, Bernard K. Mbenga, and Robert Ross (Cambridge: Cambridge University Press, 2009), 137. doi:10.1017/CHOL9780521517942.004; H. M. Friede and R. H. Steel, "Tin Mining and Smelting in the Transvaal During the Iron Age," *Journal of Southern African Institute for Mining and Metallurgy* 74 (1976): 461; N. J. Van Warmelo, ed., *The Copper Miners of Musina and the Early History of the Zoutpansberg*, Ethnological Publications, vol. VIII (Pretoria: Department of Native Affairs, Union of South Africa, Government Printer, 1940). "Capt Pauls Journal of his Voyage to Delagoa Anno. 1722," HEH ST 9, ff. 69–70; "Notes on this history, physical features and

products of Delagoa," Thomas Bowrey Papers, LMA CLC/427/MS24176/001/0036 [Microfilm: MS24177/001].

13. Newitt, *A History of Mozambique*, 155.

14. Newitt, *A History of Mozambique*, 151.

15. Michael Pearson, *The Indian Ocean* (London: Routledge, 2003), 23. Pearson states that Delagoa Bay was the southernmost border of the Swahili coast. Michael N. Pearson, *Port Cities and Intruders: The Swahili Coast, India, and Portugal in the Early Modern Era* (Baltimore: Johns Hopkins University Press, 1998), 19; Newitt, *A History of Mozambique*, 147.

16. Shula Marks and Richard Gray, "Southern Africa and Madagascar," in *The Cambridge History of Africa, Volume 4, c. 1600–c. 1790*, ed. Richard Gray (Cambridge: Cambridge University Press, 1975), 392.

17. Newitt, *A History of Mozambique*, 152.

18. Newitt, *A History of Mozambique*, 154. Pearson discusses the difficulty of determining where ivory came from. Pearson, *Port Cities and Intruders*, 86–87.

19. Pearson, *Port Cities and Intruders*, 104.

20. Pearson, *Port Cities and Intruders*, 113.

21. Newitt, *A History of Mozambique*, 153–55.

22. Newitt, *A History of Mozambique*, 152–55; Smith, 35–38.

23. Smith, 39; Newitt, *A History of Mozambique*, 157.

24. Smith, 44–45.

25. Newitt, *A History of Mozambique*, 156.

26. Smith, 44–45.

27. Smith, 40. The Portuguese were also getting cheaper ivory from the north. Newitt, *A History of Mozambique*, 155.

28. The ship the *John Galley* did stop in Maputo around 1702, and its captain would ask the East India Company for a license to go again in 1713, but he would be denied because he could not provide security against pirates. See Thomas Bowrey Papers for reference to the 1702 journey, LMA CLC/427/MS24176/014/1253 [microfilm: MS24177/004] and papers of the East India Company's Committee of Correspondence for the second proposal. BL IOR/D/93 f. 451. Thomas Bowrey would remain interested in the area in the early eighteenth century. He kept notes on the area and even tried to interest Prussia in setting up a colony there or in other areas of East Africa. See LMA CLC/427/MS24176/001/0036-37, 39, 40, 42, 43, 44, 45 [microfilm MS 24177/001] for his notes on the area and LMA CLC/427/MS03041/004 for correspondence about the proposed Prussian colony.

29. Newitt, *A History of Mozambique*, 157.

30. George McCall Theal, *History and Ethnography of Africa South of the Zambesi*, vol. 2 (London: Swan Sonnenschein, 1910; Cambridge: Cambridge University Press, 2010), 464. George McCall Theal was a historian, employed by the government of the Cape Colony, whose work at the turn of the century has been seen as supporting a positive view of colonialism and whose collection of works from European sources is described as helping to solidify that viewpoint and to deny the importance (or even existence) of African history before the arrival of Europeans. Carolyn Hamilton, Bernard Mbenga, and Robert Ross, "The Production of Pre-industrial South African History," in *The Cambridge History of South Africa*, vol. 1, ed. Carolyn Hamilton, Bernard K. Mbenga, and Robert Ross (Cambridge: Cambridge University Press, 2009), 21–22.

31. "Notes on this history, physical features and products of Delagoa," Thomas Bowrey Papers, LMA CLC/427/MS24176/001/0036 [Microfilm: MS24177/001].

32. "A Vocabulary of the Delagoa Language," Thomas Bowrey Papers, LMA CLC/427/ MS24176/001/0043 [Microfilm: MS24177/001].

33. "Directions for the Bay of Delagoa and the River therein, with some Memorandums concerning the Trade of that Place," TNA T70/1185, f. 19.

34. Christopher Kemp, *Floating Gold: A Natural (and Unnatural) History of Ambergris* (Chicago: University of Chicago Press, 2012), 6–7, 11–13; William Lewis, ed., *The Chemical Works of Caspar Neumann, M.D.*, vol. 1, 2nd ed. (London, 1773), 375.

35. "Directions for the Bay of Delagoa and the River therein, with some Memorandums concerning the Trade of that Place," TNA T70/1185, f. 18v.

36. Hamilton, 6.

37. "Directions for the Bay of Delagoa and the River therein, with some Memorandums concerning the Trade of that Place," TNA T70/1185, f. 18v.

38. Recent scholarship has also argued that prestige goods were of less importance to southern African economies than previously believed. Abigail J. Moffett and Shadrick Chirikure, "Exocita in Context: Reconfiguring Prestige, Power and Wealth in the Southern African Iron Age," *Journal of World Prehistory* 29, no. 4 (December 2016): 337–82.

39. "The Memorial of Mr. Toogood in behalf of the two Princes of Delagoa to the Honourable Court of Directors of the East India Company," BL IOR E/1/11, f. 326.

40. Piet Westra and James C. Armstrong, eds., *Slave Trade with Madagascar: The Journals of the Cape Slaver Leijdsman, 1715* (Cape Town: Africana, 2006), 103.

41. Randy Sparks, *The Two Princes of Calabar: An Eighteenth-Century Atlantic Odyssey* (Cambridge, Mass.: Harvard University Press, 2004), 14.

42. Aphra Behn, *Oroonoko* (London: Penguin Books, 2003), 37.

43. Newitt, *A History of Mozambique*, 157.

44. Captain Assou of Whydah would invite European traders to his house to dine in splendor. Robert Harms, *The Diligent: A Voyage Through the Worlds of the Slave Trade* (New York: Basic Books, 2002), 206–7.

45. "The Memorial of Mr. Toogood in behalf of the two Princes of Delagoa to the Honourable Court of Directors of the East India Company," BL IOR E/1/11, f. 326.

46. "The Memorial of Mr. Toogood in behalf of the two Princes of Delagoa to the Honourable Court of Directors of the East India Company," BL IOR E/1/11, f. 326.

47. Henri A. Junod, *The Life of a South African Tribe*, 2nd Edition, Revised and Enlarged, vol. 1 (London: Macmillan, 1927), 410–13.

48. The exact relationship that the princes had with the ruler of Mpfumo changes according to the documents; sometimes he is their brother and sometimes their uncle. This relative would have held much sway over their lives. Power around the bay was organized through different *sibongo*, or clans, that shared a patrilineal ancestor. The line that was thought to have the most direct connection to the founding ancestor was the most senior ruler. These rulers controlled the means of exchange and reproduction. Hedges, 67–68.

49. On their return trip in 1722 the Royal African Company recorded the ages of Prince James and Prince John as thirty and twenty-five years, respectively. It is improbable that this is their exact age, since it is unlikely that they kept track of their age using European measures, but to record such an age it must have been believable to the observers. TNA T70/1439, f. 46.

50. Hedges, 68.

51. Kopytoff and Miers, 17.

52. The importance of African rulers for European trade in sub-Saharan Africa stretches back to early Portuguese incursions in the fifteenth century. To legitimize the trade in enslaved Africans the Portuguese looked to African rulers as the ones who enslaved others, which eased the intellectual strain of justifying enslavement. Herman L. Bennett, *African Kings and Black Slaves: Sovereignty and Dispossession in the Early Modern Atlantic* (Philadelphia: University of Pennsylvania Press, 2018), 102–3.

53. David Northrup, *Africa's Discovery of Europe*, 3rd ed. (Oxford: Oxford University Press, 2014), 118–22.

54. Sparks, *Two Princes of Calabar*, 41, 45–47; Randy Sparks, *Where the Negroes Are Masters: An African Port in the Era of the Slave Trade* (Cambridge, Mass.: Harvard University Press, 2014), 44–52.

55. Randy Sparks, "Gold Coast Merchant Families, Pawing, and the Eighteenth-Century British Slave Trade," *William and Mary Quarterly* 70, no. 2, Special Issue: *Centering Families in Atlantic Histories* (April 2013): 334.

56. Jeremy Black, *The British Abroad: The Grand Tour in the Eighteenth Century* (New York: St. Martin's Press, 1992), 7–8, 221–22.

57. Unfinished Autobiography of John Perceval, BL Add. MS 47072, f. 103v.

58. Unfinished Autobiography of John Perceval, BL Add. MS 47072, f. 103v.

59. "The Memorial of Mr. Toogood in behalf of the two Princes of Delagoa to the Honourable Court of Directors of the East India Company," BL IOR E/1/11, f. 326; John Perceval to Charles Dering, December 1721, BL Add. MS 47029, f. 93v; James Brydges to Capt. N. Hereford, 23 May 1721, HEH ST 57.19, f. 73.

60. Sparks, "Gold Coast Merchant Families," 319–28.

61. Day Register, 18 January 1723 to 31 May 1723, DNA, VOC Archives 1.04.02, Part 1/E.5.b, 4367, f. 592. Translated by Jason Perlman.

62. In Toogood's memorial he mentioned that the princes took a number of attendants with them. BL IOR E/1/11, f. 326. Robert Drury's journal noted eight or nine Mpfumans on the ship, so there were probably six or seven attendants. Robert Drury, *Madagascar: Or Robert Drury's Journal* (London, 1729), 431.

63. Scholars hold that slavery did not deeply penetrate the Swahili coast to the north until the nineteenth century, although "modes of dependency and servitude in Swahili culture" could use further study. Thomas Vernet, "Slave Trade and Slavery on the Swahili Coast (1500–1750)," in *Slavery, Islam and Diaspora*, ed. Behnaz A. Mirzai, Ismael Musah Montana, Paul E. Lovejoy (Trenton, N.J.: Africa World Press, 2009), 51–52; Pearson, *Port Cities and Intruders*, 94.

64. Robert C.-H. Shell, "The Twinning of Maputo and Cape Town: The Early Mozambican Slave Trade to the Slave Lodge, 1677–1732," in *History, Memory and Identity*, ed. Vijayalakshmi Teelock and Edward A. Alpers (Reduit, Moka: University of Mauritius and Nelson Mandela Centre for African Culture, 2001), 182–83; Eldredge, 23–24.

65. Minutes of the Court of Directors, 6 January 1713/4, BL IOR/B/52, f. 592, and Instructions to Captain Alexander Reid, Commander of the Arabella, 22 January 1713/4, Dispatch Books, BL IOR/E/3/98, 131–31v; Thomas Bowrey Papers, LMA CLC/427/MS03041/003(ii). For more on Thomas Bowrey see Arne Bialuschewski, "Thomas Bowrey's Madagascar Manuscript of 1708," *History in Africa* 34 (2007): 31–42.

66. Arne Bialuschewski holds that the pirates in Madagascar had close ties to Maputo and would trade for ivory and to a small extent enslaved Africans. Arne Bialuschewski, "Pirates, Malata, and the Betsimisaraka Confederation on the East Coast of Madagascar in the First Half of the Eighteenth Century" in *Creole Societies in the Portuguese Colonial Empire*, ed. Philip J. Havik and Malyn Newitt (Cambridge: Cambridge Scholars, 2015), 197.

67. Philip Curtin's numbers for the period show that 99,400 enslaved Africans were exported by the English between 1690 and 1700. Between 1701 and 1710, the number rises to 119,600 and between 1711 and 1720 to 140,900. These numbers are not very different from those given by the Slave Voyages Database in 2023. The database gives 76,856 enslaved Africans taken by the British between 1691 and 1700; 129,415 taken between 1701 and 1710; and 143,751 between 1711 and 1720. Philip Curtin, *The Atlantic Slave Trade: A Census* (Madison: University of Wisconsin Press, 1969), 150; Slave Voyages Database, https://www.slavevoyages.org (accessed 27 July 2023).

68. Trevor Burnard and Kenneth Morgan, "The Dynamics of the Slave Market and Slave Purchasing Patterns in Jamaica, 1655–1788," *William and Mary Quarterly* 58, no. 1 (January 2001): 221.

69. Solofo Randrianja and Stephen Ellis, *Madagascar: A Short History* (Chicago: University of Chicago Press, 2009), 85; Stephen Ellis, "Tom and Toakafo: The Betsimisaraka Kingdom and State Formation in Madagascar, 1715–1750," *Journal of African History* 48, no. 3 (2007): 443–44. For the early slave trade in Madagascar also see James C. Armstrong, "Madagascar and the Slave Trade in the Seventeenth Century," *Omaly sy Anio* 17–19 (1984): 211–33.

70. Ellis, 443.

71. Armstrong, 216; Randrianja and Ellis, 106.

72. Westra and Armstrong, 11–13.

73. Richard Allen, *European Slave Trading in the Indian Ocean, 1500–1850* (Athens: Ohio University Press, 2014), 29–30; Barendse, 142. Around the time that the *Mercury* sailed it appears that the demand for enslaved bodies in Bengkulu, known to the English as Bencoolen, was growing. In November of 1713 the East India Company made plans to send the *Arabella* to Bencoolen with around 120 enslaved Malagasy. See BL IOR B/52, f. 526, 592; BL IOR E/3/93, ff. 128v, 130v–31v, 379. Interestingly, some of those enslaved in Bengkulu attempted to escape the English, and after their recapture the East India Company officials stated that those enslaved should now know: "They are not likely to get back into their own Countrey nor to be shelter'd in any place round about you." BL IOR E/3/93, f. 379.

74. Slave Voyages Database lists only fifty-one voyages to Madagascar by British ships between 1514 and 1866, none until 1664, then eight between 1664 and 1679, twenty-two between 1680 and 1680, two in the 1690s, only one between 1700 and 1716, thirteen between 1717 and 1721, four between 1727 and 1758, and none after that year. Slave Voyages Database, http://www .slavevoyages.org (accessed 1 June 2015). Virginia Platt also notes these two peaks, tying them to the changing policies of the East India Company. Virginia Bever Platt, "The East India Company and the Madagascar Slave Trade," *William and Mary Quarterly*, third series, 26, no. 4 (October 1969): 548–77. Jane Hooper concurs with these peaks. Jane Hooper, *Feeding Globalization: Madagascar and the Provisioning Trade, 1600–1800* (Athens: Ohio University Press, 2017), 131.

75. By the 1690s the East India Company was increasingly concerned about unlicensed ships going to Madagascar and bringing provisions for the pirates settled there because those pirates were interfering with company trade. At the same time, the government was pushing to

redefine the rights of the company. Its monopoly was lost in 1694, although a "New Company" was formed in 1698 that eventually made peace with the "Old Company" in 1709, creating the new "United Company of Merchants of England Trading to the East Indies." Platt, 551–52. For information on this first push see Jacob Judd, "Frederick Philipse and the Madagascar Trade," *New-York Historical Society Quarterly* 55, no. 4 (1971): 357, 367–68.

76. One dispatch to the officials on St. Helena from the company notes, "It is written Blacks are much wanted." East India Company Dispatch Books, BL IOR/E/3/98, f. 144v.

77. This is not the first time they had imported enslaved West Africans. In the 1660s to the 1680s the East India Company requested that a number of ships send enslaved West Africans to Bantam and St. Helena. Allen, 28.

78. Minutes of the Court of Directors, 16 October 1713, BL IOR B/52, f. 511. Also see BL IOR B/52, f. 515, and Dispatch Books, 16 October 1713, BL IOR E/3/98, f. 57.

79. Dispatch Books, 4 February 1713/4, BL IOR E/3,98, ff. 262, 268v.

80. In a dispatch sent to St. Helena in February 1717, the East India Company chided its officials in St. Helena because Captain White had told them that the officials did not take good care of the enslaved Africans they had brought them from the west coast. BL IOR E/3/99, f. 247v.

81. Court of Directors' Minutes, 13 July 1715, BL IOR B/53, f. 396. Platt too notes this request. Platt, 554.

82. Court of Directors' Minutes, 3 August 1715, BL IOR B/53, f. 406.

83. Papers of the Committee of Lawsuits, Home Miscellaneous, BL IOR H/23, f. 127.

84. Court of Directors' Minutes, 26 October 1715, BL IOR B/53, f. 468.

85. Papers of the Committee of Lawsuits, Home Miscellaneous, BL IOR H/23, f. 127.

86. Papers of the Committee of Lawsuits, Home Miscellaneous, BL IOR H/23, f. 127.

87. Papers of the Committee of Lawsuits, Home Miscellaneous, BL IOR H/23, f. 128.

88. In 1721 the Privy Council made it illegal for the company to trade with American smugglers. Philip J. Stern, *The Company-State: Corporate Sovereignty and the Early Modern Foundations of the British Empire in India* (Oxford: Oxford University Press, 2011), 194.

89. Papers of the Committee of Lawsuits, Home Miscellaneous, BL IOR H/23, f. 126.

90. For the complex legal status of the enslaved in England during this period see Holly Brewer, "Creating a Common Law of Slavery for England and Its New World Empire," *Law and History Review* 39, no. 4 (2021): 789–826.

91. Papers of the Committee of Lawsuits, Home Miscellaneous, BL IOR H/23, f. 128. Whether the enslaved were the same legally as other commodities traded by the company impacted what it could claim when ships traded illegally for enslaved peoples in its waters. Platt shows that usually the enslaved were seized like other parts of the cargo. Platt, 575–76.

92. BL IOR B/53, f. 513. William Heysham and his family had built their wealth through the slave trade and the exploitation of enslaved labor. Originally from Lancaster, the elder Heyshams made their fortunes in Barbados, lived in London, and profited off the slave trade. They were staunchly independent traders who had helped see to it that the Royal African Company lost first its monopoly and then, by 1712, its charter. William Pettigrew, *Freedom's Debt: The Royal African Company and the Politics of the Atlantic Slave Trade, 1672–1752* (Chapel Hill: University of North Carolina Press, 2013), 61–62, 123–25. Robert Heysham also corresponded with Adolph Philipse, who had traded with Madagascar in 1698. Judd, 367–68.

93. BL IOR E/1/7, f. 65, 148, 185.

94. BL IOR B/53, f. 607. Fryer and Knipe had a diverse trading portfolio, but they were joint owners of the slave ship the *Hamilton,* which had just delivered more than three hundred

enslaved Africans from Whydah and Jacquin to Kingston, Jamaica. The Slave Voyages Database, voyage 20642, *Hamilton* (1714), http://slavevoyages.org (accessed 16 January 2024).

95. BL IOR B/53, f. 608.

96. These are the ships noted in a dispatch to the officials in St. Helena as having a license to trade there and to bring them enslaved laborers. BL IOR/E/98, f. 429v.

97. BL IOR E/1/6, f. 275.

98. Court of Directors' Minutes, 7 March 1715/16, BL IOR B/53, f. 594.

99. Dispatch Books, BL IOR/E/3/9, f. 144v.

100. Philip Stern, "Politics and Ideology in the Early East India Company-State: The Case of St Helena, 1673–1709," *Journal of Imperial and Commonwealth History* 35, no. 1 (March 2007): 3–4.

101. Tony Cross, *St Helena, Including Ascension Island and Tristan da Cunha* (Newton Abbot: David and Charles, 1980), 16–25.

102. In 1717, The East India Company alerted their factors at St. Helena that seven ships, including the *Drake* and the *Mercury*, had licenses and would be stopping in St. Helena to supply them with enslaved Malagasy according to their contract. They said to expect at least twenty enslaved men, women, and children. BL IOR/E/99, f. 250v.

103. BL IOR B/53, f. 597.

104. BL IOR B/53, f. 597.

105. BL IOR B/53, f. 597.

106. BL IOR E/3/99, f. 250v.

107. Dispatch Books, 14 March 1715/6, BL IOR/E/3/98, f. 427; 22 February 1716/7, E/3/99 f. 247v.

108. Dispatch Books, 22 February 1716/7, E/3/99, f. 247v.

109. In their instructions to the officials in Bengkulu, the company mentioned "the Nais or Coast or other Indian Slaves" they used as labor. Dispatch Books, 14 March 1715/6, BL IOR/E/3/98, f. 128v.

110. Allen, 29. Enslaved labor had come from the Indian subcontinent since 1622, when enslaved peoples were requested from the Coromandel Coast. Allen, 27, 29.

111. Allen, 24. This was true for all European nations in the Indian Ocean. Barendse, 142–43.

112. Dispatch Books, 14 March 1715/6, BL IOR/E/3/98, f. 129. Enslaved people from South Asia were often called "East Asian blacks" or "East Asian negroes" in newspaper advertisements, so the overlap crossed oceans. Simon P. Newman, "Freedom-Seeking Slaves in England and Scotland, 1700–1780," *English Historical Review* 134, no. 570 (October 2019): 1149.

113. Allen, 32.

114. Dispatch Books, 14 March 1715/6, BL IOR/E/3/98, f. 129; Barendse, 142.

115. Dispatch Books, 21 March 1717/8, BL IOR E/3/99, f. 247v.

116. Drury, 445.

117. Captain William Mackett was an established slave trader. Between 1708 and 1712 he had embarked on three slave trading voyages that followed the usual route from London to West Africa to the Caribbean. The number of souls he carried across the Atlantic per voyage grew from 237 to 410 to 487, with mortality ranging from 15 to 25 percent. Another ship traveling under the license, the *Henry*, commanded by John Harvey, would arrive later. For the size of the *Drake* see BL IOR E/3/98, 429v. For Mackett's earlier voyages see the Slave Voyages Database: *Thomas and John* (1708) voyage id: 24126; *Houlditch* (1710) voyage id: 15204; *Mercury*

Gally (1712) voyage id: 21503, Slave Voyages Database, https://www.slavevoyages.org/voyages /TWWwmw7m (accessed 16 January 2024). For the size of the *Henry* see BL IOR E/3/98, 429v. Francis Sitwell, a wealthy slave trader who owned the ships, left Harvey a legacy in his will. Will of Francis Sitwell, TNA, Prob 11/653, ff. 35v–36. Sitwell did business with the likes of "King" Carter of Virginia. Louis B. Wright, *Letters of Robert Carter, 1720–1727: The Commercial Interests of a Virginian Gentleman* (San Marino: Huntington Library, 1940), 40–43, 52–53. Interestingly, these letters regard the voyage of the slave ship *Mercury* in 1719–1720. This was most probably the voyage on which White perished. He had again sailed to Madagascar but this time he died, and the new captain took the enslaved Africans to the Chesapeake rather than the Caribbean. *Mercury* (1720), voyage id: 75866, Slave Voyages Database, https://www .slavevoyages.org/voyages/lYLNSKDk (accessed 1 May 2024).

118. Starting in 1872 scholars debated whether Drury actually wrote the text, and many attributed it to Daniel Defoe. These claims have been dismissed, and the work is seen as a reliable text for information on Madagascar in the early eighteenth century. Mike Parker Pearson, "Reassessing 'Robert Drury's Journal' as a Historical Source for Southern Madagascar," *History in Africa* 23 (1996): 233–56.

119. Drury, 431.

120. They might, however, have known more. Arne Bialuschewski holds that the pirates in Madagascar had close ties to Maputo and would trade for ivory and to a small extent enslaved Africans. Bialuschewski, "Pirates, Malata, and the Betsimisaraka Confederation," 197.

121. Hooper, 135–38.

122. Hooper, 133.

123. Hooper, 138.

124. Drury, 432.

125. Drury, 439. The slow nature of the trade is emphasized by Jane Hooper. See Hooper, 138, and Hooper and Eltis, 363.

126. Drury, 440.

127. Hooper, 68–73.

128. Hooper, 132.

129. Hooper, 65–66, 141.

130. Drury, 124.

131. Hooper dates this demand to 1695. Hooper, 71.

132. Drury, 415.

133. There is a debate in the scholarship over whether the trade with Europeans led to more guns and thus more warfare and over whether they enslaved war captives or if more societies were willing to sell their enslaved due to unstable conditions caused by war. Barendse, 147–48, and Hooper, 140–43.

134. Drury, 424, 430.

135. Hooper, 69.

136. Hooper, 71–72.

137. Barendse, 147.

138. Arne Bialuschewski, "Pirates, Slavers, and the Indigenous Population in Madagascar c. 1690–1715," *International Journal of African Historical Studies* 38, no. 3 (2005): 407.

139. TNA CO 33/15, ff. 5v, 11, 68v; *Mercury* (1720), voyage id: 75866, Slave Voyages Database, https://www.slavevoyages.org/voyages/lYLNSKDk (accessed 16 January 2024).

140. Alexander X. Byrd, *Captives and Voyagers: Black Migrants Across the Eighteenth-Century British Atlantic World* (Baton Rouge: Louisiana State University Press, 2008), 33–36; Harms, 308.

141. Byrd, 36; Harms, 308–9.

142. Byrd, 37; Harms, 296–98.

Chapter 2

1. Charles Leslie, *A new and exact account of Jamaica*, 3rd ed. (Edinburgh, 1740), 14–15. *Eighteenth Century Collections Online*, link.gale.com/apps/doc/CW0100240843/ECCO?u=usocal_main&sid=bookmark-ECCO&xid=a19d21de&pg=1 (accessed 9 February 2024).

2. "News," *Weekly Journal or British Gazetteer*, 3 December 1720, 3, *Seventeenth and Eighteenth Century Burney Newspapers Collection* (accessed 9 February 2024). https://link-gale-com.libproxy2.usc.edu/apps/doc/Z2001586992/BBCN?u=usocal_main&sid=bookmark-BBCN&xid=8bd27aae. The newspaper article, which recounts the men's time in Jamaica, notes that "the Planters of the Island came on board to purchase, as usual." This practice is also noted in Stephanie Smallwood, *Saltwater Slavery: A Middle Passage from Africa to American Diaspora* (Cambridge, Mass.: Harvard University Press, 2007), 159–62, and Alexander X. Byrd, *Captives and Voyagers: Black Migrants Across the Eighteenth-Century British Atlantic World* (Baton Rouge: Louisiana State University Press, 2008), 60.

3. "News," *Weekly Journal or British Gazetteer*, 3 December 1720, 3, *Seventeenth and Eighteenth Century Burney Newspapers Collection* (accessed 9 February 2024). https://link-gale-com.libproxy2.usc.edu/apps/doc/Z2001586992/BBCN?u=usocal_main&sid=bookmark-BBCN&xid=8bd27aae.

4. "News," *Weekly Journal or British Gazetteer*, 3 December 1720, 3, *Seventeenth and Eighteenth Century Burney Newspapers Collection* (accessed 9 February 2024). https://link-gale-com.libproxy2.usc.edu/apps/doc/Z2001586992/BBCN?u=usocal_main&sid=bookmark-BBCN&xid=8bd27aae.

5. "News," *Weekly Journal or British Gazetteer*, 3 December 1720, 3, *Seventeenth and Eighteenth Century Burney Newspapers Collection* (accessed 9 February 2024). https://link-gale-com.libproxy2.usc.edu/apps/doc/Z2001586992/BBCN?u=usocal_main&sid=bookmark-BBCN&xid=8bd27aae. A pistole was worth about seven eighths of a pound, so the princes were sold for about thirty-four pounds, which is a hefty sum, since most enslaved Africans sold in the Caribbean between 1715 and 1719 sold for an average of £18.39. John J. McCusker, *Money and Exchange in Europe and America, 1600–1775: A Handbook* (Chapel Hill: University of North Carolina Press, 1978), 11; David Eltis, Frank D. Lewis, and David Richardson, "Slave Prices, the African Slave Trade, and Productivity in the Caribbean, 1674–1807," *Economic History Review* 58, no. 4 (2005): 679.

6. Robert Drury, *Madagascar: Or Robert Drury's Journal* (London, 1729), 451. Drury recorded: "Our Ship return'd, which was not till about the Middle of *September*, and then without Capt *White*; he being dead and bury'd at *Don Mascareen*: His business there was to sell some Slaves to the *French*, and buy more for the West India Cargo; but there happen'd to be no Demand for any." George Christiall was promoted to captain, and this voyage surfaces in the Slave Voyages Database. *Mercury* (1720), Slave Voyages Database, voyage id: 75866, https://www.slavevoyages.org/voyages/lYLNSKDk (accessed 16 January 2024). A will that might be White's can be found in the National Archives. TNA Prob 11/570, ff. 56–56v.

7. Trevor Burnard and Kenneth Morgan, "The Dynamics of the Slave Market and Slave Purchasing Patterns in Jamaica, 1655–1788," *William and Mary Quarterly* 58, no. 1 (January 2001): 215; Veront M. Satchell, *Hope Transformed: A Historical Sketch of the Hope Landscape, St. Andrew, Jamaica, 1660–1960* (Jamaica: University of the West Indies Press, 2012), 126–27.

8. Drury, who was on board the *Drake* in Jamaica, noted in his journal: "Here came in the *Mercury*, Capt. White from Madagascar, but we were ready to sail with a Fleet under Convoy of the *Winchelsea*, a forty Gun Ship. We departed Jamaica the 5th of July, beating thorow the windward Passage." Drury, 440.

9. Eltis, Lewis, and Richardson, 679.

10. White himself applied for the license for the *Mercury*, but the ship was probably owned by Francis Sitwell and others. The Slave Voyages Database lists four ships where Sitwell is noted as the owner. Two of them, the *Mercury Gally* and the *Drake*, were captained by William Mackett. The third is for the voyage of the *Mercury* in 1720, the voyage during which White perished. Sitwell was also tied to the voyage where White delivered enslaved West Africans to St. Helena. *Success* (1699), voyage id: 20170; *Mercury Gally* (1712), voyage id: 21503; *Drake* (1719), voyage id: 76515; *Mercury* (1720), voyage id: 75866, Slave Voyages Database, https://www.slavevoyages .org/voyages/TWWwmw7m (accessed 16 January 2024). Dispatch Books, 4 February 1713/4, BL IOR E/3/98, ff. 262, 268v.

11. Drury, 444.

12. Drury, 445.

13. Resolutions of the Council of Policy of Cape of Good Hope, 22 August 1726, Cape Town Archives Repository, South Africa, Reference code: C. 75, pp. 159–61. Translated by Jason Perlman. Day Register, 18 January 1723 to 31 May 1723, DNA, VOC Archives 1.04.02, Part 1/E.5.b, 4367, f. 588. Translated by Jason Perlman. Day Register, 23 June 1722 to 31 May 1723, DNA, VOC Archives 1.04.02, Part 1/E.5.b, 4367, f. 328. Translated by Julie van den Hout.

14. The story is on page 3 and notes that it was sent in by one "R. P." who declares "the Truth will at any Time be averr'd" by him. At the end, it is stated that the story was published in Jamaica by Robert Baldwin, who was the printer of the *Jamaican Courant*, although few issues of this newspaper survive. "News," *Weekly Journal or British Gazetteer*, 3 December 1720, 3, *Seventeenth and Eighteenth Century Burney Newspapers Collection* (accessed 9 February 2024). https://link-gale-com.libproxy2.usc.edu/apps/doc/Z2001586992/BBCN?u=usocal_main&sid= bookmark-BBCN&xid=8bd27aae.

15. "News," *Weekly Journal or British Gazetteer*, 3 December 1720, 3, *Seventeenth and Eighteenth Century Burney Newspapers Collection* (accessed 9 February 2024). https://link-gale-com .libproxy2.usc.edu/apps/doc/Z2001586992/BBCN?u=usocal_main&sid=bookmark-BBCN& xid=8bd27aae.

16. For the discussions about the slave trade in London see Abigail L. Swingen, *Competing Visions of Empire: Labor, Slavery, and the Origins of the British Atlantic Empire* (New Haven: Yale University Press, 2015), and William Pettigrew, *Freedom's Debt: The Royal African Company and the Politics of the Atlantic Slave Trade, 1672–1752* (Chapel Hill: University of North Carolina Press, 2013).

17. Brooke N. Newman, *Dark Inheritance: Blood, Race, and Sex in Colonial Jamaica* (New Haven: Yale University Press, 2018), 17; Christine Walker, *Jamaica Ladies: Female Slaveholders and the Creation of Britain's Atlantic Empire* (Chapel Hill: University of North Caroline Press, 2020), 4.

18. It was the South Sea Company that was put in charge of the asiento, and it moved its office from Barbados to Jamaica in 1719. Walker, *Jamaica Ladies*, 95.

19. Trevor Burnard, *Planters, Merchants, and Slaves: Plantation Societies in British America, 1650–1820* (Chicago: University of Chicago Press, 2015), 174. In 1683 and 1684 the Jamaican Assembly passed laws defining the enslaved as commodities and increasing punishments for resistance. Then, in 1713, it passed laws drawing a stricter divide between servants and the enslaved. Walker, *Jamaica Ladies,* 57–61, 12.

20. Walker, *Jamaica Ladies,* 14, 265, 287–89.

21. A census from 1730 records that 70 percent of the enslaved resided on plantations. Walker, *Jamaican Ladies,* 118. Trevor Burnard states that large plantations with more than 150 enslaved workers did not become common until the turn of the eighteenth century and that between 1710 and 1730 "the percentage of slave owners who owned more than 150 slaves doubled." Trevor Burnard, "Et in Arcadia Ego: West Indian Planters in Glory, 1674–1784," *Atlantic Studies* 9, issue 1, no. 2 (2012): 23; Burnard, *Planters, Merchants, and Slaves,* 178.

22. Walker, *Jamaica Ladies,* 124.

23. "A List of Negroes on Mesopotamia Estate taken 10th July 1762," West Indies Inventories of Slaves etc., 1754–1819, Bod MS. Clar Dep b. 37/2. For a detailed look at the history of the Mesopotamia plantation and its enslaved population see Richard Dunn, *A Tale of Two Plantations: Slave Life and Labor in Jamaica and Virginia* (Cambridge, Mass.: Harvard University Press, 2014).

24. For women as buyers see Burnard and Morgan, 228; Christine Walker, "Pursuing Her Profits: Women in Jamaica, Atlantic Slavery and a Globalizing Market, 1700–1760," *Gender and History* 2, no. 3 (November 2014): 491–95.

25. D. W. Hedges, "Trade and Politics in Southern Mozambique and Zululand in the Eighteenth and Early Nineteenth Centuries" (Ph.D. diss., London School of Oriental and African Studies, 1978), 69.

26. For more on pens see Verene A. Shepherd, "Trade and Exchange in Jamaica in the Period of Slavery," in *The Slavery Reader,* ed. Gad J. Heuman and James Walvin (London: Routledge, 2003), 161–74.

27. Trevor Burnard states that enslaved persons in urban spaces were frequently better clothed and fed and could often be more independent. Marisa Fuentes points out that urban enslavement was no less violent than plantation slavery, though, and that the violence and terror surfaced in different ways, especially for enslaved women. Trevor Burnard and John Garrigus, *The Plantation Machine: Atlantic Capitalism in French Saint-Domingue and British Jamaica* (Philadelphia: University of Pennsylvania Press, 2016), 60; Marisa Fuentes, *Dispossessed Lives: Enslaved Women, Violence, and the Archive* (Philadelphia: University of Pennsylvania Press, 2016), 8.

28. "News," *Weekly Journal or British Gazetteer,* 3 December 1720, 3, *Seventeenth and Eighteenth Century Burney Newspapers Collection* (accessed 9 February 2024). https://link-gale-com .libproxy2.usc.edu/apps/doc/Z2001586992/BBCN?u=usocal_main&sid=bookmark-BBCN& xid=8bd27aae.

29. Igor Kopytoff and Suzanne Miers, "African 'Slavery' as an Institution of Marginality," in *Slavery in Africa: Historical and Anthropological Perspectives,* ed. Suzanne Miers and Igor Kopytoff (Madison: University of Wisconsin Press, 1977), 17, 19, 30.

30. Robert Jordan and Harold Love, eds., *The Works of Thomas Southerne,* vol. 2 (Oxford: Clarendon Press, 1988), 91.

31. Jordan and Love, 124.

32. Jordan and Love, 156. The mention of the licking of feet echoes Drury's account in Madagascar when he often mentions the licking of feet or knees as a sign of submission. Drury 79, 82, 96, 313, 455.

33. Walker, *Jamaican Ladies*, 118.

34. Newman, *A Dark Inheritance*, 17.

35. Leslie, 327.

36. Leslie, 321–22. Also see 41–22.

37. Leslie, 322.

38. Leslie, 41–42.

39. Burnard, *Planters, Merchants, and Slaves*, 162.

40. Carla Gardina Pestana, *The English Conquest of Jamaica: Oliver Cromwell's Bid for Empire* (Cambridge, Mass.: Harvard University Press, 2017), 207–8.

41. Mavis C. Campbell, *The Maroons of Jamaica, 1655–1796: A History of Resistance, Collaboration and Betrayal* (Granby, Mass.: Bergin and Garvey, 1988), 46–52. For more on the wars with the maroons see Vincent Brown, *Tacky's Revolt: The Story of an Atlantic Slave War* (Cambridge, Mass.: Harvard University Press, 2019), 109–17. For tensions during this period see Trevor Burnard, *Jamaica in the Age of Revolution* (Philadelphia: University of Pennsylvania Press, 2020), 110–11.

42. Edward Rugemer, *Slave Law and the Politics of Resistance in the Early Atlantic World* (Cambridge, Mass.: Harvard University Press, 2018), 71.

43. *Journals of the Assembly of Jamaica, Volume 2, March 1, 1710–Feb 9, 1731* (Assembly of Jamaica, 1795), in *Slavery and Anti-Slavery: A Transnational Archive* (accessed 14 July 2016), 269; Campbell, *The Maroons of Jamaica*, 53. Both Rugemer and Livesay emphasize the importance that the maroons, and the conflicts with them, had on early Jamaican attitudes on how to manage enslaved populations and free people of color. Rugemer, 125–130; Daniel Livesay, *Children of Uncertain Fortune: Mixed Race Jamaicans in Britain and the Atlantic Family, 1733–1833* (Chapel Hill: University of North Carolina Press, 2018), 32–35.

44. *Journal of the Assembly of Jamaica*, 326–30.

45. Newman, *A Dark Inheritance*, 17.

46. Swingen, 161–66.

47. *Journal of the Jamaican Assembly*, 260.

48. *Journal of the Jamaican Assembly*, 335.

49. Rugemer states: "In Jamaica in 1681, perhaps for the first time, the assembly used 'white' as a racial descriptor that designated a particular relation of power." Rugemer, 46.

50. Susan Dwyer Amussen, *Caribbean Exchanges: Slavery and the Transformation of English Society, 1640–1700* (Chapel Hill: University of North Carolina Press, 2007), 141–42; Newman, *A Dark Inheritance*, 31–59.

51. Rugemer, 35–36, 38–41, 47–51, 68–71.

52. Daniel Livesay, *Children of Uncertain Fortune: Mixed Race Jamaicans in Britain and the Atlantic Family, 1733–1833* (Chapel Hill: University of North Carolina Press, 2018), 25–27; Rugemer, 39.

53. Walker, *Jamaican Ladies*, 13, 60; Livesay, *Children of Uncertain Fortune*, 41.

54. Livesay, *Children of Uncertain Fortune*, 32.

55. Livesay, *Children of Uncertain Fortune*, 31.

56. Livesay, *Children of Uncertain Fortune*, 31.

57. Livesay, *Children of Uncertain Fortune*, 32.

58. Vincent Carretta, "Who Was Francis Williams?" *Early American Literature* 38, no. 2 (2003): 221.

59. Samuel J. Hurwitz and Edith F. Hurwitz, "A Token of Freedom: Private Bill Legislation for Free Negroes in Eighteenth-Century Jamaica," *William and Mary Quarterly*, 3rd series, 24, no. 3 (1967): 423–26.

60. Amussen, 142.

61. Hurwitz, 432–36.

62. Daniel Livesay, "The Decline of Jamaica's Interracial Households and the Fall of the Planter Class, 1733–1823," *Atlantic Studies: Global Currents* 9, no. 1 (2012): 109–10.

63. Carretta, 221–22. For British approval of this act see TNA CO 137/12, ff. 130, 180.

64. TNA CO 137/12, f. 130; Newman, *A Dark Inheritance*, 65.

65. Unknown, *Francis Williams*, c. 1745, Victoria and Albert Museum, P. 83-1928.

66. Carretta, 216–21.

67. Carretta, 222–23.

68. Carretta, 223.

69. Newman, *A Dark Inheritance*, 65. Such restrictions would increase again in the 1730s and after Tacky's Revolt in 1760. Livesay, 110–13; Brooke Newman, "Contesting 'Black' Liberty and Subjecthood in the Anglophone Caribbean, 1730s–1780s." *Slavery and Abolition* 32, no. 2 (2011): 169–83.

70. Jack P. Greene, *Settler Jamaica in the 1750s: A Social Portrait* (Charlottesville: University of Virginia Press, 2016), 144.

71. For more on Spanish Town see James Robertson, "Where the Country Meets the Town: Spanish Town, Jamaica, and the Urban Roles of an Inland West Indian Town," *Journal of Caribbean History* 45, no. 1 (2011): 47–74; James C. Robertson, "Re-imagining Public Space: Jamaica's Main Square 1534–2000," *Caribbean Quarterly* 55, no. 2 (June 2009): 113–32; James C. Robertson, "Late Seventeenth-Century Spanish Town, Jamaica: Building an English City on Spanish Foundations," *Early American Studies* 6, no. 2 (Fall 2008): 346–90; James Robertson, "Giving Directions in Spanish Town, Jamaica," *Journal of Urban History* 35, no. 5 (July 2009): 718–42.

72. Walker, *Jamaican Ladies*, 137.

73. Burnard, *Planters, Merchants, and Slaves*, 172–73; Walker, *Jamaican Ladies*, 250.

74. Burnard and Garrigus, 77; Walker, *Jamaican Ladies*, 290.

75. Thomas Bray, *Missionalia: Or, a collection of missionary pieces relating to the conversion of the heathen; both the African negroes and American Indians* (London: Printed by W. Roberts in the Year 1727), 20. *Eighteenth Century Collections Online* (accessed 9 February 2024). https://link-gale-com.libproxy1.usc.edu/apps/doc/CW0117415598/ECCO?u=usocal_main& sid=bookmark-ECCO&xid=89c0052b&pg=1. While Bray's account is probably the least trustworthy, since it was written years afterward, it is interesting that he mentions the crew of the ship as a source of information on the princes' case. Julius S. Scott does argue that there were often links between the enslaved and sailors in the Caribbean. Julius S. Scott, *The Common Wind: Afro-American Currents in the Age of the Haitian Revolution* (London: Verso, 2018), 39–44.

76. John Perceval to Charles Dering, December 1721, BL Add. MSS 47029, f. 93v.

77. The earliest reference to Bowes is from 1716. In that year, he sent a letter to Thomas Onslow, a British member of Parliament who had married a Jamaican heiress, to tell of the "present unhappy Circumstances" of Jamaica. Thomas Onslow to William Popple, 24 October 1716, TNA CO 137/12, f. 34. Thomas Onslow was married to Elizabeth Knight, the daughter of James Knight, who had hired Bowes.

78. Burnard, "Et in Arcadia Ego," 29. We do know that he practiced law in Jamaica. In 1716 James Knight retained his services. TNA CO 137/12, f. 92.

79. These two friends, Richard Brereton and John Marcon, both appear in the *Register of Admissions* for Middle Temple. Brereton was admitted in 1702 and Marcon in 1703. Both were called to the bar in 1709. *Register of Admissions to the Honourable Society of the Middle Temple: From the Fifteenth Century to the Year 1944*, vol. 1 (London: Butterworth & Company, 1949), 252–53. Accessible online by the Honourable Society of the Middle Temple: https://www .middletemple.org.uk/archive/archive-information-access/sources-resources/digitised-records /registers-admissions.

80. Marriage of Joshua Bowes to Mary Chapman, 13 December 1712, St. Giles Cripplegate, LMA Composite register, 1711–1719/20, P69/GIS/A/002/MS06419, Item 014. For their ages see the marriage allegation of Mary Chapman, *Marriage Bonds and Allegations*. London, England, LMA, DL/A/D/003/MS10091/048. Bowes mentions his sisters-in-law, Elizabeth and Sarah Chapman, in his will, so we can be assured this is the right marriage. Will of Joshua Bowes, TNA Prob 11/576, ff. 97–99.

81. Will of Joshua Bowes, TNA Prob 11/576, ff. 97–99.

82. Will of Joshua Bowes, TNA Prob 11/576, ff. 97–99.

83. A Jamaican newspaper contains a story about one more enslaved man he owned who is not mentioned in his will. *Jamaican Courant*, 11 February 1718, 2. This issue of the *Jamaican Courant* can be found in TNA CO 137/13, 138–39.

84. Will of Joshua Bowes, TNA Prob 11/576, ff. 97–99.

85. Walker, *Jamaican Ladies*, 265–69

86. Walker, *Jamaican Ladies*, 259. Walker comes to this number through a sample of 503 wills made between 1674 and 1765.

87. Walker, *Jamaican Ladies*, 265.

88. Will of Joshua Bowes, TNA Prob 11/576, ff. 97–99.

89. Walker, *Jamaican Ladies*, 279–80.

90. Devisees of Bowes against Charlton, Exec of Bowes, 7 July 1739, Chancery Court Records, vol. 10, Jamaica Archives, Spanish Town. Thanks to Christine Walker for this reference.

91. Will of Joshua Bowes, TNA Prob 11/576, ff. 97–99.

92. Walker, *Jamaican Ladies*, 270.

93. "News," *Weekly Journal or British Gazetteer*, 3 December 1720, 3, *Seventeenth and Eighteenth Century Burney Newspapers Collection* (accessed 9 February 2024). https://link-gale-com .libproxy2.usc.edu/apps/doc/Z2001586992/BBCN?u=usocal_main&sid=bookmark-BBCN& xid=8bd27aae.

94. "News," *Weekly Journal or British Gazetteer*, 3 December 1720, 3, *Seventeenth and Eighteenth Century Burney Newspapers Collection* (accessed 9 February 2024). https://link-gale-com .libproxy2.usc.edu/apps/doc/Z2001586992/BBCN?u=usocal_main&sid=bookmark-BBCN& xid=8bd27aae.

95. In 1750, as part of the Acts of Parliament for Regulating the Slave Trade, such regulation on illegal enslavement was put in place. Randy Sparks, *Where the Negroes Are Masters: An African Port in the Era of the Slave Trade* (Cambridge, Mass.: Harvard University Press, 2014), 46.

96. The belief that African sovereigns should not be enslaved and that the legality of the process of enslavement mattered goes back to the beginning of the African slave trade. In 1476 Queen Isabel of Castile ordered that an enslaved Niumi king be freed due to a preoccupation with the established sovereignty of these lords and their connections to trade. Herman L.

Bennett, *African Kings and Black Slaves: Sovereignty and Dispossession in the Early Modern Atlantic* (Philadelphia: University of Pennsylvania Press, 2018), 124. The general sense that the English were more interested in criticizing the process of enslavement rather than questioning its existence went back at least to the middle of the seventeenth century. Michael Guasco, *Slaves and Englishmen: Human Bondage in the Early Modern Atlantic World* (Philadelphia: University of Pennsylvania Press, 2014), 158, 215.

97. "The Memorial of Mr. Toogood in behalf of the two Princes of Delagoa to the Honourable Court of Directors of the East India Company," BL IOR E/1/11, f. 326. Another account stated that White had acted "contrary to his faith." "News," *London Journal* [1720], 5 November 1720–12 November 1720, no. 68, 4, *Seventeenth and Eighteenth Century Burney Newspapers Collection* (accessed 9 February 2024). https://link-gale-com.libproxy2.usc.edu/apps/doc/Z2001382109/BBCN?u=usocal_main&sid=bookmark-BBCN&xid=15a90c25.

98. Jordan and Love, 118.

99. "News," *Weekly Journal or British Gazetteer,* 3 December 1720, 3, *Seventeenth and Eighteenth Century Burney Newspapers Collection* (accessed 9 February 2024). https://link-gale-com.libproxy2.usc.edu/apps/doc/Z2001586992/BBCN?u=usocal_main&sid=bookmark-BBCN&xid=8bd27aae.

100. The London bound ships that traveled with this fleet were the *Lewis*, the *Dragon*, and the *Asia*. It is most probable that the princes traveled on the *Lewis* since, in the hurricane, the *Asia* lost all men on board and the *Dragon* had all men saved. The *Lewis* only had five men saved. Since the princes survived and Bowes perished, the *Lewis* seems the best candidate. "News," *Weekly Packet*, 6 August 1720–13 August 1720, no. 424, 4, *Seventeenth and Eighteenth Century Burney Newspapers Collection* (accessed 9 February 2024). https://link-gale-com.libproxy2.usc.edu/apps/doc/Z2001604774/BBCN?u=usocal_main&sid=bookmark-BBCN&xid=d0279cad; "News," *Daily Courant*, 7 January 1721, no. 5995, 2, *Seventeenth and Eighteenth Century Burney Newspapers Collection* (accessed 9 February 2024). https://link-gale-com.libproxy2.usc.edu/apps/doc/Z2000199531/BBCN?u=usocal_main&sid=bookmark-BBCN&xid=1e6de57f.

101. June was early for a hurricane, although the terrible hurricane season of 1780 began with one that struck Puerto Rico and Santo Domingo in June. Satchell, 22; Stuart Schwartz, *Sea of Storms: A History of Hurricanes in the Greater Caribbean from Columbus to Katrina* (Princeton: Princeton University Press, 2015), 93.

102. "News," *Weekly Packet*, 6 August 1720–13 August 1720, no. 424, 4, *Seventeenth and Eighteenth Century Burney Newspapers Collection* (accessed 9 February 2024). https://link-gale-com.libproxy2.usc.edu/apps/doc/Z2001604774/BBCN?u=usocal_main&sid=bookmark-BBCN&xid=d0279cad.

103. Leslie, 43.

104. "News," *London Journal* [1720], 17 September 1720–24 September 1720, no. 61, 3, *Seventeenth and Eighteenth Century Burney Newspapers Collection* (accessed 9 February 2024). https://link-gale-com.libproxy2.usc.edu/apps/doc/Z2001382065/BBCN?u=usocal_main&sid=bookmark-BBCN&xid=4ba62afc. The newspaper account of their story states that Bowes and two of the princes drowned in the hurricane and that two others made it to London. "News," *Weekly Journal or British Gazetteer*, 3 December 1720, 3, *Seventeenth and Eighteenth Century Burney Newspapers Collection* (accessed 9 February 2024). https://link-gale-com.libproxy2.usc.edu/apps/doc/Z2001586992/BBCN?u=usocal_main&sid=bookmark-BBCN&xid=8bd27aae.

105. "News," *Weekly Journal or Saturday's Post*, 3 September 1720, no. 92, 4, *Seventeenth and Eighteenth Century Burney Newspapers Collection* (accessed 10 February 2024). https://link

-gale-com.libproxy1.usc.edu/apps/doc/Z2001594683/BBCN?u=usocal_main&sid=bookmark -BBCN&xid=e792d0fa; "News," *London Journal* [1720], 17 September 1720–24 September 1720, no. 61, 3, *Seventeenth and Eighteenth Century Burney Newspapers Collection* (accessed 10 February 2024), https://link-gale-com.libproxy2.usc.edu/apps/doc/Z2001382065/BBCN?u= usocal_main&sid=bookmark-BBCN&xid=4ba62afc.

106. "News," *London Journal* [1720], 10 September 1720–17 September 1720, no. 60, 3 *Seventeenth and Eighteenth Century Burney Newspapers Collection* (accessed 9 February 2024) https://link-gale-com.libproxy2.usc.edu/apps/doc/Z2001382063/BBCN?u=usocal_main&sid= bookmark-BBCN&xid=97de2891.

107. "News," *Weekly Journal or Saturday's Post*, 3 September 1720, no. 92, 4, *Seventeenth and Eighteenth Century Burney Newspapers Collection* (accessed 9 February 2024). https://link -gale-com.libproxy2.usc.edu/apps/doc/Z2001594683/BBCN?u=usocal_main&sid=bookmark -BBCN&xid=e792d0fa.

108. "News." *London Journal* [1720], 17 September 1720–24 September 1720, no. 61, 3, *Seventeenth and Eighteenth Century Burney Newspapers Collection* (accessed 9 February 2024). https://link-gale-com.libproxy2.usc.edu/apps/doc/Z2001382065/BBCN?u=usocal_main&sid= bookmark-BBCN&xid=4ba62afc.

109. "News," *London Journal* [1720], 17 September 1720–24 September 1720, no. 61, 3, *Seventeenth and Eighteenth Century Burney Newspapers Collection* (accessed 9 February 2024). https://link-gale-com.libproxy2.usc.edu/apps/doc/Z2001382065/BBCN?u=usocal_main&sid= bookmark-BBCN&xid=4ba62afc.

110. "News," *Daily Courant*, 7 January 1721, no. 5995, 2, *Seventeenth and Eighteenth Century Burney Newspapers Collection* (accessed 9 February 2024). https://link-gale-com.libproxy2 .usc.edu/apps/doc/Z2000199531/BBCN?u=usocal_main&sid=bookmark-BBCN&xid= 1e6de57f. The reference to the third prince is not supported in any other reports, but it does add to the mystery of how many men began the voyage with White.

111. "News," *Weekly Journal or British Gazetteer*, 3 December 1720, 3, *Seventeenth and Eighteenth Century Burney Newspapers Collection* (accessed 9 February 2024). https://link -gale-com.libproxy2.usc.edu/apps/doc/Z2001586992/BBCN?u=usocal_main&sid=bookmark -BBCN&xid=8bd27aae.

Chapter 3

1. John Strype, *A Survey of Cities of London and Westminster*, vol. 1, book 2 (1720), 150. For more on the Spread Eagle Inn see Kenneth Rogers, *Signs and Taverns Round About Old London Bridge: Including Gracechurch Street, Fenchurch Street and Leadenhall Streets* (London: Homeland Association, 1937), 109–11; Philip Jones, ed., *The Fire Court: Calendar to the Judgments and Decrees of the Court of Judicature Appointed to Determine Differences Between Landlords and Tenants as to Rebuilding After the Great Fire*, vol. 2 (London: William Clowes and Sons, 1970), 166.

2. Monday brought coaches from Colchester, Epsom, Portsmouth, and sometimes Canterbury. The middle of the week would be slower, with only the daily Epsom coach, and, depending on the time of year, the Canterbury coach stopping in. On Fridays the inn bustled as coaches set forth in all directions: to the northeast went the Colchester and Coxhall coaches, to the southwest trotted the Portsmouth and Epsom coaches, and the Hatfield coach rumbled toward the northwest. John Strype, *Survey of the Cities of London and Westminster*, vol. 2, appendix, 139–43. Henry Newman to the Rev. Dr. Wilkins, 18 August 1721, CAM SPCK MS D4/11, f. 19.

3. Henry Newman to the Rev. Dr. Wilkins, 18 August 1721, CAM SPCK MS D4/11, f. 19.

4. "News," *Daily Courant*, 7 January 1721, no. 5995, 2, *Seventeenth and Eighteenth Century Burney Newspapers Collection* (accessed 9 February 2024). https://link-gale-com.libproxy1 .usc.edu/apps/doc/Z2000199531/BBCN?u=usocal_main&sid=bookmark-BBCN&xid= 1e6de57f.

5. In the memorials sent to the East India Company and some letters he is Toogood. In a number of letters and the newspaper article detailing who survived the hurricane he is Towgood. In the description for one of the memorials sent to the East India Company he is Twogood. The records for the Royal Mines of Jamaica list him as "Colonel John Towgood." "The Memorial of Mr. Toogood in behalf of the two Princes of Delagoa to the Honourable Court of Directors of the East India Company," BL IOR E/1/11, f. 326; Henry Newman to John Toogood, 3 December 1720, Cam SPCK MS D4/33, f. 15; Henry Newman to the Marquis du Quene, 2 June 1721, Cam SPCK MS D4/33, f. 30; "News," *Daily Courant*, 7 January 1721, no. 5995, 2, *Seventeenth and Eighteenth Century Burney Newspapers Collection* (accessed 9 February 2024). https://link -gale-com.libproxy1.usc.edu/apps/doc/Z2000199531/BBCN?u=usocal_main&sid=bookmark -BBCN&xid=1e6de57f; Henry Newman to the Rev. Dr. Wilkins, 18 August 1721, Cam SPCK MS D4/11, ff. 18–20. Marmaduke Penwell to John Perceval, 30 November 1722, BL Add. MS 47029, f. 155. James Brydges to Mr. [Maurice] Pughe, 1 November 1720, HEH ST 57.18, f. 173; "The Memorial of Coll. Twogood of Jamaica in behalf of the two Princes of Delagoa," BL IOR E/1/11, f. 378v; Account Book of Royal Mines of Jamaica, BL Add. MS 43498, f. 13. Toogood did have ties to Jamaica, though. One Thomas Rose, who had a plantation there, left him money in his will. Will of Thomas Rose, TNA Prob 11/600, f. 204.

6. BL Add. MS 43498, f. 12, 13; BL Add. MS 22639, f. 13.

7. BL Add. MS 22639, f. 5; BL Add. MS 43499, f. 1.

8. James Brydges to Sir Nicholas Lawes, 23 September 1720, HEH ST 57.17, f. 181–82. Chandos was late answering Lawes's original letter because it had been lost in the same hurricane that the princes had survived. Chandos notes, "I received the Honor of your of the 28th May the Original of which never came to my Hands & I presume it was sent by one of Jamaica ships & lost in the Hurrican in which so many of that Fleet unfortunately perisht."

9. For the South Sea Company see John Carswell, *The South Sea Bubble*, rev. ed. (Phoenix Mill, U.K.: Alan Sutton, 1993); P. G. M Dickson, *The Financial Revolution in England* (New York: St. Martin's Press, 1967); Helen Paul, *The South Sea Bubble: An Economic History of Its Origins and Consequences* (London: Routledge, 2011); John Sperling, *The South Sea Company: An Historical Essay and Bibliographical Finding List* (Boston: Baker Library, 1962); Carl Wennerlind, *Casualties of Credit: The English Financial Revolution, 1620–1720* (Cambridge, Mass.: Harvard University Press, 2011), 197–234.

10. For the South Sea Company's push to become part of the banking industry see Richard Kleer, "The Folly of Particulars: The Political Economy of the South Sea Bubble," *Financial History Review* 19, no. 2 (August 2012): 175–97, Proquest, DOI:10.1017/S0968565012000078.

11. "Memorial of Mr. Toogood," BL IOR E/1/11, ff. 326–28.

12. "Memorial of Mr. Toogood," BL IOR E/1/11, f. 326.

13. Abigail Swingen, "Calico Madams and South Sea Cheats: Global Trade, Finance, and Popular Protest in Early Hanoverian England," *Journal of British Studies* 63, no. 1 (2024): 2, 3–10. https://doi.org/10.1017/jbr.2023.74.

14. Jonathan Eacott, *Selling Empire: India in the Making of Britain and America, 1600–1830* (Chapel Hill: University of North Carolina Press, 2016), 72–101.

15. Chloe Wigston Smith, "Calico Madams: Servants, Consumption, and the Calico Crisis," *Eighteenth-Century Life*, 31 no. 2 (2007): 29–55.

16. *Old Bailey Proceedings Online* (www.oldbaileyonline.org, version 6.0, 17 April 2011), 8 July 1719, trial of John Larmony and Mary Mattoon (t17190708-57); "News," *Post Boy*, 13–16 June 1719, issue 4663, 1. *Seventeenth and Eighteenth Century Burney Newspapers Collection* (accessed 1 May 2024). https://link-gale-com.libproxy2.usc.edu/apps/doc/Z2001406557/BBCN ?u=usocal_main&sid=bookmark-BBCN&xid=fb7f4b3a.

17. *Old Bailey Proceedings Online* (www.oldbaileyonline.org, version 6.0, 17 April 2011), 8 July 1719, trial of Joseph Green (t17190708-58).

18. *Old Bailey Proceedings Online* (www.oldbaileyonline.org, version 6.0, 17 April 2011), 8 July 1719, trial of Henry Stacy (t17190708-59).

19. "News," *Weekly Packet*, 6–13 June 1719, issue 362, 3. *Seventeenth and Eighteenth Century Burney Newspapers Collection* (accessed 1 May 2024). https://link-gale-com.libproxy2.usc .edu/apps/doc/Z2001604611/BBCN?u=usocal_main&sid=bookmark-BBCN&xid=156359a8.

20. *Old Bailey Proceedings Online* (www.oldbaileyonline.org, version 6.0, 17 April 2011), 8 July 1719, trial of John Humphreys (t17190708-56).

21. "News," *Weekly Journal or British Gazetteer*, 13 June 13 1719, 6, *Seventeenth and Eighteenth Century Burney Newspapers Collection* (accessed 9 February 2024). https://link-gale-com .libproxy1.usc.edu/apps/doc/Z2001586435/BBCN?u=usocal_main&sid=bookmark-BBCN& xid=8cd1e26f.

22. *Old Bailey Proceedings Online* (www.oldbaileyonline.org, version 6.0, 17 April 2011), 8 July 1719, trial of John Humphreys (t17190708-56).

23. "News." *Post Boy*, 11 June 1719–13 June 1719, no. 4662, 1, *Seventeenth and Eighteenth Century Burney Newspapers Collection* (accessed 9 February 2024). https://link-gale-com .libproxy1.usc.edu/apps/doc/Z2001406555/BBCN?u=usocal_main&sid=bookmark-BBCN& xid=231527c9.

24. "News," *Weekly Journal or Saturday's Post*, 13 June 1719, 4–5, *Seventeenth and Eighteenth Century Burney Newspapers Collection* (accessed 9 February 2024). https://link-gale-com .libproxy1.usc.edu/apps/doc/Z2001594101/BBCN?u=usocal_main&sid=bookmark-BBCN& xid=44ba3b97.

25. For more on the debates and upheaval surrounding calico see Eacott, 101–15.

26. *Journal of the Commissioners for Trade and Plantations from Nov 1718 to Dec 1722 preserved in the Public Records Office* (London, 1925), 82, 118; Eacott, 106; Also see BL IOR E/1/9, ff. 377, 421, 534, 536.

27. Swingen, 9.

28. For the continued worries see BL IOR D/97, E/1/201, 266–273, 307, 318.

29. Robert Raymond and Philip Yorke, 3 October 1721, BL IOR H/23, f. 136.

30. The *London Journal* reported that Gordon was a missionary in the West Indies for several years and that he discovered gold mines in Africa. "News," *London Journal* [1720], 18 June 1720–25 June 1720, no. 48, 5, *Seventeenth and Eighteenth Century Burney Newspapers Collection* (accessed 9 February 2024). https://link-gale-com.libproxy1.usc.edu/apps/doc/Z2001382005/BBCN?u= usocal_main&sid=bookmark-BBCN&xid=f9e40a8c. I can find no connection between Gordon and Africa, but there was a Reverend William Gordon in town at the time who had been a clergyman in Barbados and who was a former commissary of the bishop of London. He often attended meetings of the Board of Trade to bring forth complaints about Governor Lowther (one complaint being the loss of Gordon's living) and later to give advice on colonial matters. *Journal of*

the Commissioners for Trade and Plantations from Nov 1718 to Dec 1722 preserved in the Public Records Office (London, 1925), 48–49, 159, 179, 184, 222. For his disagreements with Governor Lowther see William Gordon, *A sermon preach'd before the governor, council, & general assembly of the Island of Barbadoes* (London, 1717) *Eighteenth Century Collections Online* (accessed 9 February 2024). https://link-gale-com.libproxy1.usc.edu/apps/doc/CB0131522347/ECCO?u=usocal _main&sid=bookmark-ECCO&xid=8cdf1919&pg=1 and William Gordon, *A representation of the miserable state of Barbadoes* (London, 1719), *Eighteenth Century Collections Online* (accessed 9 February 2024). https://link-gale-com.libproxy1.usc.edu/apps/doc/CW0106106626/ECCO?u= usocal_main&sid=bookmark-ECCO&xid=2a150f69&pg=1.

31. Papers of the Committee of Lawsuits, BL IOR H/23, f. 134; Minutes of Court of Directors, 17 June 1729, BL IOR B/56, f. 42.

32. Minutes of Court of Directors, 17 June 1729, BL IOR B/56, f. 42, 44–45.

33. For worries about unlicensed ships going to Madagascar at this time see Minutes of the Court of Directors, 4 September 1717, 8 January 1718, BL IOR B/54, f. 420, 546.

34. See Minutes of the Court of Directors, 30 October 1717, 20 November 1717, BL IOR B/54, ff. 475, 492; Minutes of the Court of Directors, 23 December 1718, 25 November 1719, 2 December 1719, BL IOR B/55, ff. 182, 437, 441; East India Company Correspondence (Letters Received), 1 July 1719, 12 September 1717, BL IOR E/1/9, f. 232, 318; Correspondence, 6 January 1720, BL IOR E/1/11, f. 9.

35. Minutes of the Court of Directors, 17 June 1720, BL IOR B/56, ff. 42–44.

36. "News," *London Journal* [1720], 18 June 1720–25 June 1720, no. 48, 5, *Seventeenth and Eighteenth Century Burney Newspapers Collection* (accessed 9 February 2024). https://link -gale-com.libproxy1.usc.edu/apps/doc/Z2001382005/BBCN?u=usocal_main&sid=bookmark -BBCN&xid=f9e40a8c. The Court of Directors' minutes also report that the decision caused "much discourse about Town and a Debate arising thereupon." Minutes of Court of Directors, 8 July 1720, BL IOR B/56, f. 61.

37. Minutes of the Court of Directors, 15 June 1720, BL IOR B/56, f. 38.

38. Minutes of the Committee of Correspondence, 2 August 1720, BL IOR D/97.

39. Memoranda of the Committee of Correspondence, 2 August 1720, BL IOR D/97. For Kent's license to go to Madagascar see Minutes of the Court of Directors, 9 October 1717, BL IOR B/54, f. 452.

40. Minutes of the Court of Directors, 5 August 1720, BL IOR B/56, f. 79.

41. Memoranda of the Committee of Correspondence, 2 August 1720, BL IOR D/97.

42. Minutes of the Court of Directors, 5 August 1720, BL IOR B/56, f. 79; "News," *London Journal* [1720], 13 August 1720–20 August 1720, no. 56, 6, *Seventeenth and Eighteenth Century Burney Newspapers Collection* (accessed 9 February 2024). https://link-gale-com.libproxy1.usc .edu/apps/doc/Z2001382043/BBCN?u=usocal_main&sid=bookmark-BBCN&xid=9014c5dc.

43. Portuguese Envoy to the East India Company, 29 September 1720, BL IOR E/1/11, f. 331.

44. In fact, they had William Gordon write a rebuttal. Memoranda of the Committee of Correspondence, 11 October 1720, BL IOR D/97.

45. Robert Raymond and Philip Yorke, 3 October 1721, BL IOR H/23, f. 137.

46. Swingen, 12.

47. This was determined by looking at the value of the stock as mentioned in the *Evening Post* and *Daily Courant* from 4 August 1721 to 31 January 1722. On 4 August 1720 East India stock stood at 365. On 17 October 1720 it was 140, the lowest it hit during the period. "News,"

Evening Post [1709], 2-4 August 1720, issue 1718, 2. *Seventeenth and Eighteenth Century Burney Newspapers Collection* (accessed May 1, 2024). https://link-gale-com.libproxy2.usc.edu/apps/doc/Z2001371204/BBCN?u=usocal_main&sid=bookmark-BBCN&xid=11027330. "News," Daily Courant, 17 October 1720, issue 5925, 2. *Seventeenth and Eighteenth Century Burney Newspapers Collection* (accessed May 1, 2024). https://link-gale-com.libproxy1.usc.edu/apps/doc/Z2000198927/BBCN?u=usocal_main&sid=bookmark-BBCN&xid=5c2308b9.

48. Minutes of the Committee of Correspondence, 18 October 1720, BL IOR D/18, f. 30v. On 17 October 1720 their stock hit 140, which was the lowest it would go during the crisis. "News," Daily Courant, 17 October 1720, issue 5925, 2. *Seventeenth and Eighteenth Century Burney Newspapers Collection* (accessed May 1, 2024). https://link-gale-com.libproxy1.usc.edu/apps/doc/Z2000198927/BBCN?u=usocal_main&sid=bookmark-BBCN&xid=5c2308b9.

49. Minutes of the Court of Directors, 25 November 1720, BL IOR B/56, f. 170.

50. Minutes of the Court of Directors, 30 October 1717, 8 January 1717/8, BL IOR B/54, ff. 475, 546.

51. Minutes of the Court of Directors, 23 December 1720, BL IOR B/56, f. 206. By mid-January they had decided on the sum of five hundred pounds for past expenses and fifteen shillings a day for the present. Minutes of the Court of Directors, 18 January 1720/1, BL IOR B/56, f. 231.

52. East India Company Directors to the Board of Trade, 15 September 1720, TNA CO 388/22, f. 138v.

53. East India Company to the Commissioners for Trade and Plantations, 1 February 1721, BL IOR D/97.

54. Eacott, 113.

55. Swingen, 2, 15.

56. In fact, when exploring the issue in October of 1721 one of the main reasons given for abandoning the opening of the trade to southeastern Africa was that "parliament would not allow the Company to carry Negroes to the West Indies." Robert Raymond and Philip Yorke, 3 October 1721, BL IOR H/23, ff. 137–38.

57. Minutes of the Court of Directors, 29 March 1721, BL IOR B/56, f. 297.

58. Minutes of the Court of Directors, 10 May 1721, BL IOR B/56, f. 352; Minutes of the Court of Directors, 17 May 1721, BL IOR B/56, f. 357.

59. Minutes of the Court of Directors, 10 May 1721, BL IOR B/56, f. 352.

60. Michael A. Gomez, *African Dominion: A New History of Empire in Early and Medieval West Africa* (Princeton: Princeton University Press, 2018), 105–9, 159.

61. James Walvin, *Black and White: The Negro and English Society, 1555–1945* (London: Allen Lane, Penguin Press, 1973), 17. In John Lok's account of his 1554–1555 voyage, he details the gold and ivory to be found in Africa. Peter D. Fraser, "Slaves or Free People? The Status of Africans in England, 1550–1750," in *From Strangers to Citizens: The Integration of Immigrant Communities in Britain, Ireland and Colonial America, 1550–1750*, ed. Randolph Vigne and Charles Littleton (Brighton, Portland, Ore.: Sussex Academic Press, 2001), 255–56.

62. Philip D. Curtin, "Africa and the Wider Monetary World, 1250–1850," in *Precious Metals in the Later Medieval and Early Modern Worlds*, ed. J.F. Richards (Durham: Carolina Academic Press, 1983), 238.

63. Curtin, 235.

64. "News," *Weekly Journal or British Gazetteer*, 16 July 1720, 5, *Seventeenth and Eighteenth Century Burney Newspapers Collection* (accessed 9 February 2024). https://link-gale-com

.libproxy1.usc.edu/apps/doc/Z2001586882/BBCN?u=usocal_main&sid=bookmark-BBCN&
xid=d9c4194e.

65. Minutes of the Bye Committee, 13 June 1721, TNA T70/142, f. 1.

66. Daniel Defoe, *Captain Singleton* (Oxford: Oxford University Press, 1990), 93–97,
126–34.

67. William Pettigrew, *Freedom's Debt: The Royal African Company and the Politics of the
Atlantic Slave Trade, 1672–1752* (Chapel Hill: University of North Carolina Press, 2013), 165.

68. C. H. Collins Baker and Muriel I. Baker, *The Life and Circumstances of James Brydges
First Duke of Chandos: Patron of the Liberal Arts* (Oxford: Clarendon, 1949), 208–11.

69. These numbers come from the Slave Voyages Database. I searched the years 1673 to
1720 and then limited it to the Royal African Company as the "vessel owner." It gave the number
of 174,667 captives embarked. Slave Voyages Database, https://www.slavevoyages.org/voyages
/TWWwmw7m (accessed 12 June 2024).

70. Pettigrew, 11–12.

71. Matthew David Mitchell, "'Legitimate Commerce' in the Eighteenth Century: The
Royal African Company of England Under the Duke of Chandos, 1720–1726," *Enterprise and
Society* 14, no. 3 (September 2013): 551.

72. Pettigrew, 162–63; Mitchell, 544–78.

73. BL Add. MS 43498, f. 12, 13; BL Add. MS 22639, f. 13.

74. Henry Newman notes that Toogood turned to Chandos because he knew him, and
Chandos introduced the princes to the Royal African Company. Henry Newman to the Rev. Dr.
Wilkins, 18 August 1721, CAM SPCK MS D4/11, ff. 18–19.

75. James Brydges to Mr. [Maurice] Pughe, 1 November 1720, HEH ST 57.18, f. 173.

76. James Brydges to Capt. N. Hereford, 23 May 1721, HEH ST 57.19, f. 73. It is interesting
to note that on 11 July 1722 the minutes of the Royal African Company's Court of Assistants
recorded this: "Captain Mitchell acquainting the Court that when he came away from Cabenda
he brought over by the King of Angoys leave a freeman of that Country on promise to carry
him or send him safe back, and desiring passage for him on board the Sherbro: Gally Capt Bul-
cock bound for Cabenda." This suggests that free Africans were not infrequently setting sail for
England. TNA T70/92, f. 151. This man appears to be the ruler's son, and he too had a difficult
return. The records state: "And that in the next letters to Cabenda, It be recommended to the Governor and Councill to put the best Construction they can upon the misfortune which befell the
King's Son who was taken by the Pirates on board the Royall African Packett assuring them that
the Company are very much concer'd at it, and will use all possible Endeavours to recover him,
and send him home." Minute Book of the Committee of Trade, 23 August 1723, TNA T70/124.

77. James Brydges to Capt. N. Hereford, 10 January 1720/1, HEH ST 57.17, ff. 318–19.
Around this same time Captain James Sharrow, who would eventually take the princes home, suggested a settlement near Cape Negro, which was close to the river that interested Chandos. Minutes of the Court of Assistants, 22 November 1720, 8 December 1720, TNA, T70/90, ff. 135, 149.

78. James Brydges to Capt. N. Hereford, 10 January 1720/1, HEH ST 57.17, ff. 318–19.

79. Durate Lopes, *A Report of the Kingdome of Congo* (London, 1597), 194, *Early English
Books Online*, http://libproxy.usc.edu/login?url=https://www.proquest.com/books/report
-kingdome-congo-region-africa-countries/docview/2240866527/se-2.

80. For European references linking Monomotapa to Solomon's mines see: Pierre
Avity, *The Estates, Empires, & Principallities of the World Represented by Ye Description of Countries, Maners of Inhabitants, Riches of Prouinces, Forces, Gouernment, Religion* (London, 1615),

1093, *Early English Books Online*, http://libproxy.usc.edu/login?url=https://www.proquest.com /books/estates-empires-principallities-world-represented/docview/2240873688/se-2., 1093; Manuel de Faria e Sousa, *The Portugues Asia*, (London, 1695), 104, *Early English Books Online*, http://libproxy.usc.edu/login?url=https://www.proquest.com/books/portugues-asia-history -discovery-conquest-india/docview/2248544242/se-2.; Patrick Gordon, *Geography Anatomized* (London, 1693), 321, *Early English Books Online*, http://libproxy.usc.edu/login?url=https://www .proquest.com/books/geography-anatomized-compleat-geographical/docview/2248547593 /se-2.; Jan Huygen van Linschoten, *Iohn Huighen Van Linschoten: His Discours of Voyages into Ye Easte & West Indies Deuided into Foure Bookes* (London, 1598), 212, *Early English Books Online*, http://libproxy.usc.edu/login?url=https://www.proquest.com/books/iohn-huighen-van -linschoten-his-discours-voyages/docview/2240950438/se-2; Lopes, 194–95; Samuel Purchas, *Purchas His Pilgrimage* (London, 1613), 576, *Early English Books Online*, http://libproxy.usc .edu/login?url=https://www.proquest.com/books/purchas-his-pilgrimage-relations-vvorld -religions/docview/2240884050/se-2. 576.

81. Purchas, 576.

82. Roland Oliver and Anthony Atmore, *Medieval Africa, 1250–1800* (Cambridge: Cambridge University Press, 2001), 203.

83. Oliver and Atmore, 201, 207.

84. Lorraine Swan, "Southeastern African Gold Mining and Trade," in *Encyclopedia of Precolonial Africa: Archaeology, History, Languages, Cultures, and Environments*, ed. Joseph O. Vogel (Walnut Creek, Calif.: AltaMira Press, 1997), 539–40; I. R. Phimister, "Alluvial Gold Mining and Trade in Nineteenth-Century South Central Africa," *Journal of African History* 15, no. 3 (1974): 447; Michael N. Pearson, *Port Cities and Intruders: The Swahili Coast, India, and Portugal in the Early Modern Era* (Baltimore: Johns Hopkins University Press, 1998), 104.

85. Curtin, 235.

86. Pearson, *Port Cities and Intruders*, 104–5.

87. Curtin, 235–38; Pearson, *Port Cities and Intruders*, 93–94, 104–5; Phimister, 447; Swan, 540.

88. Oliver, 208.

89. Walter Rodney, "Africa in Europe and the Americas," in *The Cambridge History of Africa*, ed. Richard Gray (Cambridge: Cambridge University Press, 1975), 581; Vincent Leblanc, *The World Surveyed* (London, 1660), *Early English Books Online*, http://libproxy.usc.edu/login ?url=https://www.proquest.com/books/world-surveyed-famous-voyages-travailes-vincent /docview/2240876206/se-2.

90. Herman Moll, *A new & correct map of the whole world* (1719), HEH 493935. The Dutch had a similar issue. They too thought Monomotapa was a vast kingdom extending almost to Angola. Gerhard Liesegang, "New Light on Venda Traditions: Mahumane's Account of 1730," *Africa in History* 4 (1977): 165–66.

91. Henry Newman to the Rev. Dr. Wilkins, 18 August 1721, CAM SPCK MS D4/11, f. 19.

Chapter 4

1. Dinner was served around 3 P.M. at Cannons, a bit later than was normal at the time, and so they probably would have arrived later in the afternoon. Gilly Lehmann, *The British Housewife: Cookery Books, Cooking and Society in Eighteenth-Century Britain* (Blackawton: Prospect Books, 2003), 304, 385; C. H. Collins Baker and Muriel I. Baker, *The Life and Circumstances of James Brydges First Duke of Chandos, Patron of the Liberal Arts* (Oxford: Clarendon Press,

1949), n. 193; John Macky, *A journey through England: In familiar letters from a gentleman here, to his friend abroad*, vol. 2 (London, 1722), 6, *Eighteenth Century Collections Online* (accessed 9 February 2024). https://link-gale-com.libproxy2.usc.edu/apps/doc/CW0100355103/ECCO?u =usocal_main&sid=bookmark-ECCO&xid=aff9fbf9&pg=31.

2. Daniel Defoe, *Curious and diverting journies, Thro' the whole Island of Great-Britain* (London, 1734), 252, *Eighteenth Century Collections Online* (accessed 9 February 2024). https:// link-gale-com.libproxy1.usc.edu/apps/doc/CW0102871896/ECCO?u=usocal_main&sid= bookmark-ECCO&xid=cebc7261&pg=1.

3. Macky, 5; Others did view it as too grand. Its opulence might have inspired Alexander Pope to write his satirical poem "Timon's Villa," which decried such luxury. Baker and Baker, xvi.

4. Baker and Baker, 117, 144, 170; Macky, 7.

5. Baker and Baker, 144.

6. Macky, 9.

7. Baker and Baker, 172.

8. Macky, 7.

9. Baker and Baker, 172. Since Chandos was just adding the finishing touches to his house, it is possible that this painting was not yet completed.

10. Baker and Baker, 184–85.

11. John Nott, *The cook's and confectioner's dictionary* (London, 1723), no pagination, image 455, *Eighteenth Century Collections Online* (accessed 9 February 2024). https://link-gale -com.libproxy1.usc.edu/apps/doc/CW0109868716/ECCO?u=usocal_main&sid=bookmark -ECCO&xid=0c9ae03d&pg=1; HEH HM 58283.

12. Roy Strong, *Feast: A History of Grand Eating* (Orlando: Harcourt, 2002), 231.

13. Macky, 9.

14. A list of menus served at Cannons that begins in December 1721 and goes through 1722 exists at the Huntington Library, HM 58283. The "Book of Strangers" reveals who ate at Cannons on 23 September 1722, for which date there is a corresponding menu. There were ten guests that night. HEH ST 59.

15. Lehmann, 176.

16. Vincent DiMarco, *Egg Pies, Moss Cakes, and Pigeons Like Puffins: Eighteenth-Century British Cookery from Manuscript Sources* (New York: iUniverse, 2007), 122–23.

17. Strong, 224.

18. Mark Girouard, *Life in the English Country House: A Social and Architectural History* (New Haven: Yale University Press, 1978), 139.

19. See recipes 9 and 11 under "TA," in Nott, images 521–22.

20. 23 September 1722, HEH HM 58283.

21. Lehmann, 335.

22. Thomas Bray, *Missionalia: Or, a collection of missionary pieces relating to the conversion of the heathen; both the African negroes and American Indians* (London: Printed by W. Roberts in the Year 1727), 47–48. *Eighteenth Century Collections Online* (accessed 9 February 2024). https://link-gale-com.libproxy1.usc.edu/apps/doc/CW0117415598/ECCO?u=usocal_main& sid=bookmark-ECCO&xid=89c0052b&pg=1.

23. Kate Fullagar, *The Savage Visit: New World People and Popular Imperial Culture in Britain, 1710–1795* (Berkeley: University of California Press, 2012), 1–3. Also see Coll Thrush, *Indigenous London: Native Travelers at the Heart of Empire* (New Haven: Yale University Press, 2016), 83–91.

24. Fullagar, 2; Thrush, 73–82.

25. "News," *Daily Post*, 27 April 1721, no. 491, 2, *Seventeenth and Eighteenth Century Burney Newspapers Collection* (accessed 10 February 2024). https://link-gale-com.libproxy2.usc .edu/apps/doc/Z2000264071/BBCN?u=usocal_main&sid=bookmark-BBCN&xid=ae4dcb36; "News," *Daily Courant*, May 2, 1721, no. 6093, 2, *Seventeenth and Eighteenth Century Burney Newspapers Collection* (accessed 10 February 2024). https://link-gale-com.libproxy1.usc.edu /apps/doc/Z2000200477/BBCN?u=usocal_main&sid=bookmark-BBCN&xid=ad8bb6dc; "News," *Daily Courant*, 26 May 1721, no. 6114, 1, *Seventeenth and Eighteenth Century Burney Newspapers Collection* (accessed 10 February 2024). https://link-gale-com.libproxy1.usc .edu/apps/doc/Z2000200725/BBCN?u=usocal_main&sid=bookmark-BBCN&xid=24b3e870; "News," *Daily Courant*, 3 May 1721, no. 6094, 1, *Seventeenth and Eighteenth Century Burney Newspapers Collection* (accessed 10 February 2024). https://link-gale-com.libproxy1.usc.edu /apps/doc/Z2000200491/BBCN?u=usocal_main&sid=bookmark-BBCN&xid=036a2ba0.

26. Emmett L. Avery, ed., *The London Stage 1660–1800*, part 2, vol. 1 (Carbondale: Southern Illinois University Press, 1960), cxiv.

27. For example, see "News," *Daily Courant*, 16 April 1719, no. 5455, 2, *Seventeenth and Eighteenth Century Burney Newspapers Collection* (accessed 10 February 2024). https://link -gale-com.libproxy1.usc.edu/apps/doc/Z2000194973/BBCN?u=usocal_main&sid=bookmark -BBCN&xid=2f30ce16.

28. Avery, part 2, vol. 1, cxiv.

29. Willard Connely, *Sir Richard Steele* (London: Charles Scribner's Sons, 1934), 364–66.

30. TNA T70/90, f. 223.

31. Avery, part 2, vol. 1, 26.

32. Avery, part 2, vol. 1, 34, 178.

33. Arthur H. Scouten, ed., *The London Stage 1660–1800*, part 3 (Carbondale: Southern Illinois University Press, 1961), 132.

34. Avery, part 2, vol. 2, 644.

35. Avery, part 2, vol. 2, 592–670.

36. Avery, part 2, vol. 2, 592–670.

37. George Winchester Stone Jr., ed., *The London Stage 1660–1800*, part 6 (Carbondale: Southern Illinois University Press, 1962), 95. The performance was "for the entertainment of two young Africans."

38. *Gentleman's Magazine*, vol. 19 (February 1749), 89–90, USC Libraries, Special Collections, AP4 .G34 1831 V.19.

39. Kim Hall, *Things of Darkness: Economies of Race and Gender in Early Modern England* (Ithaca, N.Y.: Cornell University Press, 2018), 2–6.

40. Andrew S. Curran, *The Anatomy of Blackness: Science and Slavery in an Age of Enlightenment* (Baltimore: Johns Hopkins University Press, 2011), 1–2; Roxann Wheeler, *The Complexion of Race: Categories of Difference in Eighteenth-Century British Culture* (Philadelphia: University of Pennsylvania Press, 2007), 22–24.

41. Winthrop D. Jordan, *White over Black: American Attitudes Towards the Negro, 1550–1812* (Chapel Hill: University of North Carolina Press, 1959), 12; Catherine Molineux, *Faces of Perfect Ebony: Encountering Atlantic Slavery in Imperial Britain* (Cambridge, Mass.: Harvard University Press, 2012), 95.

42. Molineux, 97.

43. Mark Dawson, *Bodies Complexioned: Human Variation and Racism in Early Modern English Culture, c. 1600–1750* (Manchester: Manchester University Press, 2019), 9–13.

44. Jordan, 19; Curran, 81, 107.

45. Dawson, 217–223.

46. Ania Loomba, "Periodization, Race, and Global Contact," *Journal of Medieval and Early Modern Studies* 37, no. 3 (2007): 604.

47. David M. Goldenberg, *Black and Slave: The Origins and History of the Curse of Ham* (Berlin: De Gruyter, 2017), 200; David M. Whitford, *The Curse of Ham in the Early Modern Era: The Bible and Justifications for Slavery* (Farham, U.K.: Ashgate, 2009), 103.

48. For this progression see Goldenberg, passim.

49. Curran, 76–78; Jordan, 17–20.

50. Simon Newman, *Freedom Seekers: Escaping from Slavery in Restoration London* (London: University of London Press, Institute of Historical Research, 2022), 39. There is a growing scholarship on the Black community in London. See Susan Dwyer Amussen, *Caribbean Exchanges: Slavery and the Transformation of English Society, 1640–1700* (Chapel Hill: University of North Carolina Press, 2007); Kathleen Chater, *Untold Histories: Black People in England and Wales During the Period of the British Slave Trade, c. 1660–1807* (Manchester: Manchester University Press, 2009); Madge Dresser and Andrew Hann, eds., *Slavery and the British Country House* (London: Historic England, 2013); Peter D. Fraser, "Slaves or Free People? The Status of Africans in England, 1550–1750," in Randolph Vigne and Charles Littleton, eds., *From Strangers to Citizens: The Integration of Immigrant Communities in Britain, Ireland and Colonial America, 1550–1750* (Brighton, Portland, Ore.: Sussex Academic Press, 2001), 254–60; Peter Fryer, *Staying Power: The History of Black People in Britain* (London: Pluto Press, 2010); Gretchen Gerzina, *Black London: Life Before Emancipation* (New Brunswick, N.J.: Rutgers University Press, 1995); Gretchen Gerzina, ed., *Britain's Black Past* (Liverpool: Liverpool University Press, 2020); Imtiaz Habib, *Black Lives in the English Archives, 1500–1677: Imprints of the Invisible* (Aldershot, U.K.: Ashgate, 2008); Kim Hall, *Things of Darkness: Economies of Race and Gender in Early Modern England* (Ithaca, N.Y.: Cornell University Press, 2018); Molineux, passim; Norma Myers, *Reconstructing the Black Past: Black in Britain, c. 1780–1830* (London: Frank Cass, 1996); Simon P. Newman, *Freedom Seekers: Escaping from Slavery in Restoration London* (London: University of London Press, Institute of Historical Research, 2022); Simon P. Newman, "Freedom-Seeking Slaves in England and Scotland, 1700–1780," *English Historical Review* 134, no. 570 (October 2019): 1136–68; David Olusoga, *Black and British: A Forgotten History* (London: Pan Books, 2016); F. O. Shyllon, *Black Slaves in Britain* (London: Published for the Institute of Race Relations by Oxford University Press, 1974); F. O. Shyllon, *Black People in Britain, 1555–1833* (London: Published for the Institute of Race Relations by Oxford University Press, 1977); James Walvin, *Black and White: The Negro and English Society, 1555–1945* (London: Penguin Press, 1973); James Walvin, *The Black Presence: A Documentary History of the Negro in England, 1555–1860* (New York: Schocken Books, 1972).

51. Peter Fryer, *Staying Power: The History of Black People in Britain* (London: Pluto Press, 2010), 72–74; Olusoga, 86–91; Simon P. Newman, "Freedom-Seeking Slaves," 1137; Gretchen Holbrook Gerzina, *Black London: Life Before Emancipation* (New Brunswick, N.J.: Rutgers University Press, 1995), 15–18.

52. Newman, "Freedom-Seeking Slaves," 1138.

53. For women with young black pages see Gerzina, 15–18.

54. "News," *Applebee's Original Weekly Journal,* 15 April 1721, 4, *Seventeenth and Eighteenth Century Burney Newspapers Collection* (accessed 10 February 2024). https://link-gale-com .libproxy1.usc.edu/apps/doc/Z2000105735/BBCN?u=usocal_main&sid=bookmark-BBCN &xid=33b3e97e; "News," *Daily Journal,* 13 April 1721, no. 70, 2, *Seventeenth and Eighteenth Century Burney Newspapers Collection* (accessed 10 February 2024). https://link-gale-com .libproxy1.usc.edu/apps/doc/Z2000239578/BBCN?u=usocal_main&sid=bookmark-BBCN& xid=78238772.

55. Chater, 26–27.

56. "News," *Daily Courant,* 17 March 1721, no. 6054, 2, *Seventeenth and Eighteenth Century Burney Newspapers Collection* (accessed 10 February 2024). https://link-gale-com.libproxy1.usc .edu/apps/doc/Z2000200095/BBCN?u=usocal_main&sid=bookmark-BBCN&xid=2fc75b1b; "News," *Daily Courant,* 30 March 1721, no. 6065, 2, *Seventeenth and Eighteenth Century Burney Newspapers Collection* (accessed 10 February 2024). https://link-gale-com.libproxy1.usc.edu /apps/doc/Z2000200205/BBCN?u=usocal_main&sid=bookmark-BBCN&xid=16825e3f.

57. "News," *Daily Courant,* 21 November 1722, no. 6579, 2, *Seventeenth and Eighteenth Century Burney Newspapers Collection* (accessed 10 February 2024). https://link-gale-com .libproxy1.usc.edu/apps/doc/Z2000204368/BBCN?u=usocal_main&sid=bookmark-BBCN& xid=1931c42d.

58. "News," *Daily Courant,* 29 September 1722, no. 6534, 2, *Seventeenth and Eighteenth Century Burney Newspapers Collection* (accessed 10 February 2024). https://link-gale-com.libproxy1 .usc.edu/apps/doc/Z2000204165/BBCN?u=usocal_main&sid=bookmark-BBCN&xid=f8f3adb4.

59. Imtiaz Habib, *Black Lives in the English Archives, 1500–1677: Imprints of the Invisible* (Aldershot, U.K.: Ashgate, 2008), 123. For the status of Black individuals in England also see Holly Brewer, "Creating a Common Law of Slavery for England and Its New World Empire," *Law and History Review* 39, no. 4 (2021): 789–826.; Fraser, passim.

60. Newman, "Freedom-Seeking Slaves," 54–55; Molineux, 63–67.

61. Newman, "Freedom-Seeking Slaves," 34.

62. Brewer, 820.

63. Walvin, *Black and White,* 110.

64. These individuals were found through a search of *Gale's Seventeenth and Eighteenth Century Burney Newspapers Collection,* British Library Newspapers, 1600–1950 Database, and the Runaway Slaves in Britain: Bondage, Freedom and Race in the Eighteenth Century Database (https://runaways.gla.ac.uk).

65. "News," *Daily Post,* 4 August 1720, no. 263, 2, *Seventeenth and Eighteenth Century Burney Newspapers Collection* (accessed 10 February 2024). https://link-gale-com.libproxy1.usc.edu /apps/doc/Z2000263159/BBCN?u=usocal_main&sid=bookmark-BBCN&xid=746554a3.

66. "News," *Daily Courant,* 24 February 1721, no. 6036, 2, *Seventeenth and Eighteenth Century Burney Newspapers Collection* (accessed 10 February 2024). https://link-gale-com .libproxy1.usc.edu/apps/doc/Z2000199919/BBCN?u=usocal_main&sid=bookmark-BBCN& xid=48fb43c4.

67. "News," *Daily Post,* 18 September 1721, no. 614, 2, *Seventeenth and Eighteenth Century Burney Newspapers Collection* (accessed 10 February 2024). https://link-gale-com.libproxy1.usc .edu/apps/doc/Z2000264490/BBCN?u=usocal_main&sid=bookmark-BBCN&xid=1caa4463.

68. "News," *Daily Courant,* 6 January 1722, no. 6306, 2, *Seventeenth and Eighteenth Century Burney Newspapers Collection* (accessed 10 February 2024). https://link-gale-com.libproxy1.usc .edu/apps/doc/Z2000202560/BBCN?u=usocal_main&sid=bookmark-BBCN&xid=1a7e791d.

69. "News," *Daily Post,* 2 November 1720, no. 430, 2, *Seventeenth and Eighteenth Century Burney Newspapers* Collection (accessed 10 February 2024). https://link-gale-com.libproxy1.usc.edu/apps/doc/Z2000263430/BBCN?u=usocal_main&sid=bookmark-BBCN&xid=c273785b; "News," *Daily Post,* 25 February 1721, no. 439, 2, *Seventeenth and Eighteenth Century Burney Newspapers Collection* (accessed 10 February 2024). https://link-gale-com.libproxy1.usc.edu/apps/doc/Z2000263870/BBCN?u=usocal_main&sid=bookmark-BBCN&xid=9487a2fa.

70. Newman, "Freedom-Seeking Slaves," 1139.

71. Henry Newman to Henry Hoare, 27 February 1720, Cam SPCK MS D4/9, f. 86; Henry Newman to Rowland Tryon, 22 February 1720, Cam SPCK MS D4/32, n.p.

72. Newman, "Freedom-Seeking Slaves," 1157–58; Walvin, *Black and White,* 64–66.

73. Goldenberg, 200; Whitford, 103.

74. Molineux, 94.

75. Jordan, 24; Wheeler, 7, 54–67.

76. Jordan, 29–31.

77. Molineux, 86–90.

78. Henry Newman to the Rev. Dr. Wilkins, 18 August 1721, CAM SPCK MS D4/11, ff. 19–19v; Alan Ruston, "Oldfield, Joshua (1656–1729)," *Oxford Dictionary of National Biography* (Oxford: Oxford University Press, 2004 (http://www.oxforddnb.com.huntington.idm.oclc.org/view/article/20681, accessed 3 July 2017). The inn had also been a meeting place for Presbyterians during the Restoration. Notes by Williamson, Dr. B[utler] and Ch[urch], 13 December 1671, MS SP 29/294 f.223, Records Assembled by the State Paper Office. The National Archives (Kew, United Kingdom), 294. *State Papers Online* (accessed May 1, 2024). https://link-gale-com.libproxy1.usc.edu/apps/doc/MC4328380141/SPOL?u=usocal_main&sid=bookmark-SPOL&xid=916518fc.

79. Henry Newman to the Rev. Dr. Wilkins, 18 August 1721, CAM SPCK MS D4/11, ff. 19–19v.

80. Abstract of Letter from the Archbishop of Canterbury, 14 September 1721, Cam SPCK MS D2/16, abstract 6789.

81. "News," *London Journal* [1720], 24 June 1721, no. 100, 4, *Seventeenth and Eighteenth Century Burney Newspapers Collection* (accessed 10 February 2024). https://link-gale-com.libproxy1.usc.edu/apps/doc/Z2001382378/BBCN?u=usocal_main&sid=bookmark-BBCN&xid=e86feb94.

82. "News," *London Journal* [1720], 24 June 1721, no. 100, 4, *Seventeenth and Eighteenth Century Burney Newspapers Collection* (accessed 10 February 2024). https://link-gale-com.libproxy1.usc.edu/apps/doc/Z2001382378/BBCN?u=usocal_main&sid=bookmark-BBCN&xid=e86feb94.

83. Composite register, 1720–1761, St. Mary the Virgin, Twickenham, Composite register, 1730–1761, 20 June 1721, LMA DRO/174/A/01/006.

84. "News," *London Journal* [1720], 24 June 1721, no. 100, 4, *Seventeenth and Eighteenth Century Burney Newspapers Collection* (accessed 10 February 2024). https://link-gale-com.libproxy1.usc.edu/apps/doc/Z2001382378/BBCN?u=usocal_main&sid=bookmark-BBCN&xid=e86feb94.

85. It is the minutes of the SPCK papers that include these names: Minutes of the SPCK, 5 October 1721, Cam SPCK MS A1/9, f. 195; Minutes of the Standing Committee, 6 February 1722, 27 March 1722, Cam SPCK MS A5/4, f. 87, 97. The princes would also sign their letters with the last name of Maffoom. James Chandos and John Towgood Maffoom to John Perceval, 24 January 1721, 1 February 1721/2, BL Add. MS 47029, ff. 97, 101v.

86. In the East India Company records they were referred to as the "Indian Princes of Delagoa" twice, the "Delagoa princes" five times, the "Princes of Delagoa" four times, the "Black princes" four times, and the "Black Indian princes" once. When corresponding with the Royal African Company, the East India Company called them the "African princes" four times. Toogood, when petitioning the Company, uses both "Indian princes of Delago" and "Princes of Delago," "The Memorial of Mr. Toogood in behalf of the two Princes of Delagoa to the Honourable Court of Directors of the East India Company," BL IOR E/1/11, f. 326, 378v; "Black Indian Princes" was used in the draft of a license to the Royal African Company to take the princes to Mpfumo: 2 December 1721, BL IOR D/97. For the "Black princes" see Minutes of the Committee of Correspondence, 21 September 1721, BL IOR D/18, f. 57.

87. James Brydges to Capt. N. Hereford, 23 May 1721, HEH ST 57.19, f. 74.

88. Minutes of the Court of Assistants, 9 May 1721, TNA T70/90, f. 230.

89. "News," *London Journal* [1720], 13 May 1721, no. 94, 4, *Seventeenth and Eighteenth Century Burney Newspapers Collection* (accessed 10 February 2024). https://link-gale-com.libproxy1.usc.edu/apps/doc/Z2001382327/BBCN?u=usocal_main&sid=bookmark-BBCN&xid=bd2a35e0.

90. Minutes of the Committee of Trade, 4 May 1721, TNA T70/123, ff. 24–25.

91. Minutes of the Committee of Trade, 4 May 1721, TNA T70/123, ff. 24–25.

92. Henry Newman to the Rev. Dr. Wilkins, 18 August 1721, Cam SPCK MS D4/11, ff. 18–20.

93. Minutes of the Committee of Trade, 24 May 1721, TNA T70/123, ff. 28–29; Minutes of the Court of Assistants, 25 May 1721, TNA T70/90, f. 239.

94. Minutes of the Committee of Trade, 17 May 1721, TNA T70/123, f. 25; Minutes of the Court of Assistants, 22 June 1721, TNA T70/90, f. 251. Minutes of the Court of Assistants, 11, 13, 18, 25 July 1721, TNA T70/90, ff. 260, 261, 262, 265. The records note that one Samuel Wade was to be given the money to support the princes. No more is known of Wade.

95. Henry Newman to the Rev. Dr. Wilkins, 18 August 1721, Cam SPCK MS D4/11, ff. 18–20.

96. David Wilkins to Henry Newman, 17 August 1721, Abstracts of Letters Received, Cam SPCK MS D2/16, letter 6994.

97. David Wilkins to Henry Newman, 17 August 1721, Abstracts of Letters Received, Cam SPCK MS D2/16, letter 6994; Minutes of the Committee of Trade, TNA T70/123, f. 42; Minutes of the Court of Assistants, TNA T70/91, f. 15.

98. Henry Newman to the Archbishop of Canterbury, 9 September 1721, Cam SPCK MS D4/11, f. 25; Minutes of the Committee of Trade, 30 August 1721, TNA T70/123, f. 42.

99. James Roydon to Captain Sharrow, 14 May 1724, HEH ST 57.24, f. 86.

100. Minutes of the Court of Assistants, 22 November 1720, 8 December 1720, TNA, T70/90, f. 135, 149; James Brydges to Mr. Lockwood, 27 July 1721, HEH ST 57.19, f. 139.

101. James Brydges to Mr. Lockwood, 27 July 1721, HEH ST 57.19, f. 139.

102. Sharrow's original proposal does not survive, but years later, while cutting ties with him, Chandos's secretary mentioned that part of the reason Chandos would have nothing to do with him was that Sharrow had "misled the Company by any Prospect of Trade to the Brazils." James Roydon to Captain Sharrow, 14 May 1724, HEH ST 57.24, f. 85.

103. James Brydges to [Sir John] Comyns, 7 August 1721, HEH ST 57.18, f. 259; James Brydges to Mr. Phips, 11 September 1721, HEH 57.19, f. 185.

104. James Brydges to [Sir John] Comyns, 7 August 1721, HEH ST 57.18, f. 259; Minutes of the Bye Committee, 1 February 1721/2, TNA T70/142, f. 23.

105. Minutes of the Bye Committee, 1 February 1721/2, TNA T70/142, ff. 23–24.

106. Minutes of Court of Assistants, 29 August 1721, TNA T70/91, f. 12.

107. Minutes of Court of Directors, 13 September 1721, BL IOR B/56, f. 456.

108. Minutes of Court of Directors, 20 September 1721, BL IOR B/56, f. 464.

109. In June 1721 the company received an anonymous letter about such illegal doings, and another letter from Mr. Chitwell in Virginia would be sent in November. Brittanicus to Gilbert Heathcote, 6 June 1721, BL IOR D/97, n.p.; Minutes of the Court of Directors, 21 June 1721, BL IOR B/56 f. 389; Mr. Chitwell to the Court of Directors, 26 November 1721, BL IOR E/1/12, f. 469.

110. Papers of the Committee of Lawsuits, Home Miscellaneous, BL IOR H/23, ff. 138–39. For the rejection of the Royal African Company's proposals see Minutes of the Committee of Correspondence, 21 September 1721, BL IOR D/18, f. 57; Minutes of the Court of Directors, 22 September 1721, BL IOR B/56, f. 468.

111. Minutes of the Court of Assistants, 5 October 1721, TNA T70/91, ff. 33–34.

112. The East India Company approved the license on 13 December 1721, but on the 29th of that month the Royal African Company was still asking when the final license would be ready; neither company mentions the license after this point, although a copy survives in the Royal African Company papers, so it was probably given to them in the last few days of December or in early January. Minutes of the Court of Directors, 13 December 1721, BL IOR B/56, f. 540; Francis Lynn to Mr. Woolley, 29 December 1721, TNA IOR E/1/12, f. 531. For the license see Miscellaneous Entries 1720–1744, TNA T70/1185, f. 17.

113. Instructions for Captain John Sharrow, Mr. Leonard Ely, Mr. Colin Hay and Captain Jeremiah Tinker, 1 February 1722, TNA T70/142, f. 26.

114. James Brydges to Maurice Pughe, 1 November 1720, HEH ST 57.18 f. 173; "Book of Strangers," 24 September 1721, HEH ST 59.

115. Strong, 229.

116. In Chandos's "Book of Strangers" there are separate columns for different tables. Those tables include: His Grace's, the Chaplain's, Gentleman of the Horse, Officers, Music, Servants. HEH ST 59.

117. Adam Petrie, *Rules of good deportment, or of good breeding: For the Use of Youth* (Edinburgh, 1720), 82–86, *Eighteenth Century Collections Online* (accessed 10 February 2024). https://link-gale-com.libproxy1.usc.edu/apps/doc/CW0119630551/ECCO?u=usocal_main& sid=bookmark-ECCO&xid=88fe5138&pg=1.

118. Bray, 48.

119. Petrie, 82, 84.

120. Lehmann, 332.

121. Henri A. Junod, *The Life of a South African Tribe*, 2nd edition, Revised and Enlarged, vol. 1 (London: Macmillan, 1927), 37–38, 317–18.

122. 24 September 1721, HEH ST 59.

123. 24 September 1721, HEH ST 59.

124. Henry Newman to John Toogood, 3 December 1720, Cam SPCK MS D4/33, f. 15.

Chapter 5

1. The dome of St. Paul's Cathedral had been completed more than ten years previously. The last stone was placed on the lantern in October 1708. The paintings inside, however, would have been bright and fresh, as they were finished just the month before. Jane Lang, *Rebuilding*

St. Paul's After the Great Fire of London (London: Geoffrey Cumberlege, Oxford University Press, 1956), 241; James W. P. Campbell, *Building St. Paul's* (London: Thames and Hudson, 2008), 162, 165. The fact that they met at St. Paul's Chapter House is noted in the Minutes of the SPCK, 5 October 1721, Cam SPCK MS A1/9, f. 195, and reaffirmed in William A. Bultmann and Phyllis W. Bultmann, "The Roots of Anglican Humanitarianism: A Study of the Membership of the SPCK and the SPG, 1699–1720," *Historical Magazine of the Protestant Episcopal Church* 33, no. 1 (March 1964): 42. This article also has details on the early members of the SPCK.

2. Minutes of the Standing Committee, 31 January 1721, Cam SPCK MS A5/4, f. 30.

3. For complaints about the cold see Minutes of the SPCK, 4 January 1721/2, Cam SPCK MS A1/9, f. 223.

4. This recreation is taken from the SPCK's minutes of this meeting. Minutes of the SPCK, 5 October 1721, Cam SPCK MS A1/9, ff. 195–96.

5. Subscription Book, 1698–1769, Cam SPCK MS C1/1.

6. H. P. Thompson, *Thomas Bray* (London: SPCK, 1954), 36–42; E. G. Rupp, *Religion in England, 1688–1791* (Oxford: Clarendon Press, 1986), 299.

7. Brent Sirota, *The Christian Monitors: The Church of England and the Age of Benevolence, 1680–1730* (New Haven: Yale University Press, 2014), 111–14, 150.

8. Sirota, 117–18.

9. SPCK Special Letters, 1708–1732, Cam SPCK MS D3/1, f. 1.

10. Notes by Chamberlayne and Newman on SPCK Business, 26 October 1699, 2 November 1699, 8 February 1699/1700, 9 May 1700, Bod MS Rawl C 844, ff. 6v–8, 16, 25v; Henry Newman to Mr. Tomlinson, 28 January 1719/20, Cam SPCK MS D4/9, f. 26.

11. Sirota, 70.

12. Sirota, 258.

13. Leonard W. Cowie, *Henry Newman: An American in London, 1708–43* (London: SPCK, 1956), 3–20.

14. For example, see Henry Newman to Thomas Woolley, 19 October 1715, 27 October 1715, BL IOR E/1/6, f. 197, 207; Henry Newman to Thomas Woolley, 10 December 1718, BL IOR E/1/9, f. 445; Henry Newman to Thomas Woolley, 28 December 1722, BL IOR E/1/12, f. 529.

15. Henry Newman to Mr. Woolley, 13 November 1721, Cam SPCK MS D4/11, f. 48.

16. Minutes of the SPCK, 25 January 1722, Cam SPCK MS A1/10, f. 3.

17. Henry Newman to the Rev Dr. Wilkins, 18 August 1721, Cam SPCK MS D4/11, f. 18-20.

18. Minutes of the Standing Committee, 31 January 1721, Cam SPCK MS A5/4, f. 30; Henry Newman to John Toogood, 3 December 1720, Cam SPCK MS D4/33, f. 15.

19. Minutes of the Standing Committee, 31 January 1720/1, Cam SPCK MS A5/4, f. 29; Minutes of the SPCK, 2 February 1720/1, Cam SPCK MS A1/9, f. 148.

20. For a quick overview of the Tranquebar mission see W. K. Lowther Clarke, *A History of the SPCK* (London: SPCK, 1959), 59–67. For the company's interactions see Cam SPCK MS A33/1-8. For the translation of the New Testament into Arabic see Cam SPCK MS A32.

21. Henry Newman to the Rev. Mr. Lewes, 4 January 1711, Cam SPCK MS D3/1, f. 39.

22. Henry Newman to the archbishop of Canterbury, 9 September 1721, Cam SPCK MS D4/11, f. 25.

23. Henry Newman to the Rev. Dr. Wilkins, 18 August 1721, CAM SPCK MS D4/11, f. 20.

24. Henry Newman to the Rev. Mr. King, 17 April 1722, Cam SPCK MS D4/12, ff. 14–15. For a copy of Penelope Rowland's will see Cam SPCK MS C25/1, f. 216.

25. Minutes of the Standing Committee, 26 September 1721, Cam SPCK MS A5/4, f. 65.

26. Minutes of the Standing Committee, 3 October 1721, Cam SPCK MS A5/4, f. 67.

27. Henry Newman to George Wheeler, 7 October 1721, Cam SPCK MS D4/11, f. 38.

28. Minutes of the Standing Committee, 6 February 1722, 12 February 1722, Cam SPCK MS A5/4, ff. 86–87, 89.

29. Minutes of the Standing Committee, 6 February 1722, Cam SPCK MS A5/4, f. 86.

30. Minutes of the Standing Committee, 12 February 1722, Cam SPCK MS A5/4, f. 89.

31. Minutes of the Standing Committee, 12 February 1722, 20 February 1722, Cam SPCK MS A5/4, f. 89, 90; Minutes of the SPCK, 8 February 1722, Cam SPCK MS A1/10, f. 7.

32. "Circular Letter to the Members in London about the African Affair," Cam SPCK MS D4/11, f. 65.

33. Minutes of the Standing Committee, 6 February 1722, Cam SPCK MS A5/4, f. 86.

34. Minutes of the Standing Committee, 6 February 1722, 12 February 1722, Cam SPCK MS A5/4, ff. 86, 89.

35. Henry Newman to the Rev. Dr. Wilkins, 18 August 1721, Cam SPCK D4/11, ff. 19–19v.

36. John Perceval to Charles Dering, December 1721, BL Add. MS 47029, f. 93v.

37. Minutes of the Standing Committee, 23 January 1722, Cam SPCK MS A5/4, f. 82.

38. Minutes of the SPCK, 5 October 1721, Cam SPCK MS A1/9, f. 196; Princes James and John to John Perceval, 24 January 1721, BL Add. MS 47029, f. 97.

39. David Wilkins to Henry Newman, 8 February 1722, Abstracts of Letters Received, Cam SPCK MS D2/16, Letter 6967.

40. Two candidates not discussed can be found here: Minutes of the Standing Committee, 10 October 1721, Cam SPCK MS A5/4, f. 68; John Carpender to Henry Newman, 31 January 1722, Abstracts of Letters Received, Cam SPCK MS D2/16, Letter 6943.

41. Henry Newman to the archbishop of Canterbury, 9 September 1721, Cam SPCK MS D4/11, f. 25; Wood Rogers to Henry Newman, 15 February 1721/2, Abstracts of Letters Received, Cam SPCK MS D2/16, Letter 6956; Minutes of the Standing Committee, 12 February 1722, Cam SPCK MS A5/4, f. 90.

42. Henry Newman to the archbishop of Canterbury, 9 September 1721, Cam SPCK MS D4/11, f. 25.

43. Minutes of the Standing Committee, 19 December 1721, Cam SPCK MS A5/4, f. 77.

44. Minutes of the Standing Committee, 26 December 1721, Cam SPCK MS A5/4, f. 78.

45. Joseph Adams to Henry Newman, 30 December 1721, Abstracts of Letters Received, Cam SPCK MS D2/16, Letter 6907; Joseph Adams to Thomas Bray, 24 January 1722, Abstracts of Letters Received, Cam SPCK MS D2/16, Letter 6940.

46. John Perceval to Charles Dering, December 1721, BL Add. MS 47029, f. 94.

47. Minutes of the Standing Committee, 23 January 1721/2, Cam SPCK MS A5/4, f. 82.

48. Henry Newman to John Sharrow, 5 March 1722, Cam SPCK MS D4/12, f. 3.

49. Henry Newman to the Rev. Mr. King, 16 June 1722, Cam SPCK MS D4/12, f. 23.

50. Minutes of the SPCK, 17 March 1720, Cam SPCK MS A1/9, f. 90.

51. John Perceval to Berkeley Taylor, 24 October 1724, BL Add. MS 46971, f. 96.

52. Sirota, 246.

53. John Perceval to Charles Dering, December 1721, BL Add. MS 47029, ff. 93v–94.

54. James Chandos and John Towgood Maffoom to John Perceval, 24 January 1721, 1 February 1721/2, BL Add. MS 47029, f. 97, 101v.

55. John Perceval in the margin of his letter book beside the letter from Marmaduke Penwell to John Perceval, 31 March 1722, Add. 47029, 112v.

56. John Perceval to Charles Dering, December 1721, BL Add. MS 47029, f. 94.

57. Thomas Bray, *Missionalia: Or, a collection of missionary pieces relating to the conversion of the heathen; both the African negroes and American Indians* (London: Printed by W. Roberts in the Year 1727), 47–48. *Eighteenth Century Collections Online* (accessed 9 February 2024). https://link-gale-com.libproxy1.usc.edu/apps/doc/CW0117415598/ECCO?u=usocal_main& sid=bookmark-ECCO&xid=89c0052b&pg=1.

58. John Perceval to Thomas Bray, 26 January 1721/2, BL Add. MS 47029, f. 97.

59. John Perceval to Thomas Bray, 27 January 1721/2, BL Add. MS 47029, f. 99.

60. Minutes of the SPCK, 1 February 1722, Cam SPCK MS A1/10, f. 5.

61. John Perceval to Thomas Bray, 27 January 1721/2, BL Add. MS 47029, ff. 99v–101.

62. Bray, *Missionalia*, 22.

63. Bray, *Missionalia*, 22–23.

64. James Brydges to Hans Sloane, 4 December 1721, BL Sloane MS 4046, f. 152.

65. James Brydges to Hans Sloane, 19 December 1721, HEH ST 57.20, f. 48. The company considered other men like a Mr. Goodred, but he did not end up on the voyage. Minutes of the Committee of Trade, 7 December 1721, TNA T70/123.

66. Minutes of the Committee of Trade, 4 January 1722, TNA T70/123.

67. Instructions for Captain John Sharrow, Mr. Leonard Ely, Mr. Colin Hay and Captain Jeremiah Tinker, 1 February 1722, TNA T70/142, ff. 24–25.

68. Instructions for Captain John Sharrow, Mr. Leonard Ely, Mr. Colin Hay and Captain Jeremiah Tinker, 1 February 1722, TNA T70/142, f. 24.

69. Vincent Leblanc suggested that the river went through Monomotapa as well. Vincent Leblanc, *The World Surveyed* (London, 1660), 193, *Early English Books Online*, http://libproxy.usc.edu/login?url=https://www.proquest.com/books/world-surveyed-famous-voyages-travailes-vincent/docview/2240876206/se-2.

70. Instructions for Captain John Sharrow, Mr. Leonard Ely, Mr. Colin Hay and Captain Jeremiah Tinker, 1 February 1722, TNA T70/142, f. 23-27.

71. Instructions for Captain John Sharrow, Mr. Leonard Ely, Mr. Colin Hay and Captain Jeremiah Tinker, 1 February 1722, TNA T70/142, f. 26.

72. James Brydges to Mr. Hill, 26 January 1721/2, HEH ST 57.20, f. 87; James Brydges to Captain Paul, 26 January 1721/2, HEH ST 57.20, f. 88.

73. Instructions for Captain John Sharrow, Mr. Leonard Ely, Mr. Colin Hay and Captain Jeremiah Tinker, 1 February 1722, TNA T70/142, f. 26.

74. Instructions for Captain John Sharrow, Mr. Leonard Ely, Mr. Colin Hay and Captain Jeremiah Tinker, 1 February 1722, TNA T70/142, f. 23.

75. Instructions for Captain John Sharrow, Mr. Leonard Ely, Mr. Colin Hay and Captain Jeremiah Tinker, 1 February 1722, TNA T70/142, ff. 23–24.

76. Minutes of Standing Committee, 20 February 1722, Cam SPCK MS A5/4, f. 90.

77. Instructions for Captain John Sharrow, Mr. Leonard Ely, Mr. Colin Hay and Captain Jeremiah Tinker, 1 February 1722, TNA T70/142, f. 26.

78. Minutes of the Committee of Trade, 4 May 1721, TNA T70/123, ff. 24–25.

79. "Circular Letter to Members in London about the African Affair," Cam SPCK MS D4/11, f. 65; Minutes of the Standing Committee, 27 March 1722, Cam SPCK MS A5/4, f. 97.

80. Minutes of the Committee of Trade, 4 May 1721, TNA T70/123, f. 24.

81. The first time they visited the Court of Assistants of the Royal African Company was in May of 1721. Minutes of the Court of Assistants, 9 May 1721, TNA T70/90, f. 231.

82. John Sharrow to Henry Newman, 4 October 1721, Abstracts of Letters received, Cam SPCK MS D2/16, Letter 6801.

83. John Sharrow to Henry Newman, 30 December 1721, Abstracts of Letters received, Cam SPCK MS D2/16, Letter 6908; Henry Newman to John Perceval, 1 January 1722, Cam SPCK MS D4/11, f. 62.

84. Minutes of the SPCK, 5 October 1721, Cam SPCK MS A1/9, ff. 195–96.

85. John Sharrow to Henry Newman, 30 December 1721, Abstracts of Letters received, Cam SPCK MS D2/16, Letter 6908.

86. Minutes of Court of Assistants, 13 February 1722, TNA T70/91, f. 103; Minutes of Standing Committee, 20 February 1722, Cam SPCK MS A5/4, f. 90.

87. Princes James Chandos and John Towgood Maffoom to John Perceval, 24 January 1721, BL Add. MS 47029, f. 97.

88. Princes James Chandos and John Towgood Maffoom to John Perceval, 1 February 1721, BL Add. MS 47029, f. 101v.

89. John Perceval to Charles Dering, December 1721, BL Add. MS 47029, f. 94.

90. Henri A. Junod, *The Life of a South African Tribe*, 2nd Edition, Revised and Enlarged, vol. 2 (London: Macmillan, 1927), 372–74.

91. James Brydges to Capt. N. Hereford, 10 January 1720/1, HEH ST 57.17, f. 318; James Brydges to Capt. N. Hereford, 23 May 1721, HEH ST 57.19, f. 74.

92. Minutes of the Committee of Trade, 4 May 1721, TNA T70/123, f. 24.

93. Minutes of the Bye Committee, 1 February 1722, TNA T70/142, f. 26.

94. Henry Newman to Henry Hoare, 27 February 1720, Cam SPCK MS D4/9, f. 86; Henry Newman to Rowland Tryon, 22 February 1720, D4/32, n.p.

95. Henry Newman to George Wheeler, 7 October 1721, Cam SPCK MS D4/11, ff. 37–38; John Perceval to Charles Dering, December 1721, BL Add. MS 47029, f. 93.

96. Minutes of Standing Committee, 20 February 1721/2, Cam SPCK MS A5/4, f. 90; Princes James Chandos and John Towgood Maffoom to John Perceval, 1 February 1722, BL Add. MS 47029, 101v.

97. John Perceval to Charles Dering, December 1721, BL Add. MS 47029, f. 94; Junod, 371–76.

98. For the complexity of religious conversion also see the story of Philip Quaque, the first African to be ordained a minster in the Church of England. In 1754 he was sent from Cape Coast to England to be educated by the Society for the Propagation of the Gospel (SPG). He was ordained in 1765 and returned to Cape Coast the next year to act as a chaplain and as a missionary. A number of his letters written to the SPG from 1765 to 1811 survive. See Vincent Carretta and Ty M. Reese, eds., *The Life and Letters of Philip Quaque: The First African Anglican Missionary* (Athens: University of Georgia Press, 2010).

99. "The Memorial of Mr. Toogood in behalf of the two Princes of Delagoa to the Honourable Court of Directors of the East India Company," BL IOR E/1/11, f. 326.

Chapter 6

1. Marmaduke Penwell to John Perceval, 31 March 1722, BL Add. MS 47029, ff. 112v–13.

2. Richard Allestree, *The whole duty of man laid down in a plain and familiar way for the use of all, but especially the meanest reader* (London, 1713), 207, *Eighteenth Century Collections Online* (accessed February 10, 2024). https://link-gale-com.libproxy1.usc.edu/apps/doc /CW0123206209/ECCO?u=usocal_main&sid=bookmark-ECCO&xid=dba32cc9&pg=1.

3. Marmaduke Penwell to John Perceval, 31 March 1722, BL Add. MS 47029, f. 113. This diagnosis is not quite as incomprehensible as it might seem. Melancholy and madness were both seen as connected not to mental struggles but to bodily ones. Both were often attributed to an imbalance of the humors. A physical ailment could have mental repercussions and could be cured in the same way. Roy Porter, *Mind-Forg'd Manacles: A History of Madness in England from the Restoration to the Regency* (Cambridge, Mass.: Harvard University Press, 1987), 38–54.

4. "Copy of the List of the Ship's Crews and Passengers on board the Royal African Company's Vessells for Africa," TNA T70/1439, f. 46.

5. John Sharrow to Henry Newman, 2 March 1722, Abstracts of Letters Received, Cam SPCK MS D2/16, Letter 6990.

6. James Brydges to Hans Sloane, 4 December 1721, BL Sloane MS 4046, ff. 152–53.

7. "Copy of the List of the Ship's Crews and Passengers on board the Royal African Company's Vessells for Africa," TNA T70/1439, f. 46.

8. Henry Newman to John Sharrow, 5 March 1722, Cam SPCK MS D4/12, f. 3.

9. Instructions to Captains, TNA T70/64, ff. 108–9.

10. Instructions to Captains, TNA T70/64, ff. 106–7; Marmaduke Penwell to John Perceval, 31 March 1722, BL Add. MS 47029, f. 112v.

11. Orders of the Court for Committee of Shipping, 3 April 1722, TNA T70/137.

12. James F. Imray, *Sailing Directions for the English Channel, Part I: The South Coast of England* (London: James Imray and Son, 1879), 64.

13. Marmaduke Penwell to John Perceval, 31 March 1722, BL Add. MS 47029, f. 112v.

14. Marmaduke Penwell to Henry Newman, 25 March 1722, Abstracts of Letters Received, Cam SPCK MS D2/16, Letter 7007.

15. Henry Newman to John Sharrow, 17 April 1722, Cam SPCK MS D4/12, ff. 13–14; Henry Newman to the Rev. Mr. King, 17 April 1722, Cam SPCK MS D4/12, f. 14.

16. Henry Newman to John Sharrow, 17 April 1722, Cam SPCK MS D4/12, ff. 13–14.

17. Henry Newman to the Rev. Mr. King, 17 April 1722, Cam SPCK MS D4/12, ff. 14–15.

18. Henry Newman to Marmaduke Penwell, 17 April 1722, Cam SPCK MS D4/12, f. 14.

19. Henry Newman to John Sharrow, 17 April 1722, Cam SPCK MS D4/12, f. 14.

20. Orders of the Court for Committee of Shipping, 3 April 1722, TNA T70/137.

21. James Brydges to John Sharrow, 7 April 1722, HEH ST 57.18, ff. 410–11.

22. Francis Lynn to John Sharrow, 17 April 1722, TNA T 70/46, f. 131.

23. Minutes of Court of Assistants, 29 March 1722, TNA T 70/91, f. 119. Exmouth was a much smaller town than Exeter and, thus, it is unsurprising they would look to people in Exeter to repair the ship. In fact, much of modern day Exmouth did not exist in the early eighteenth century. It was not until it became a popular beach resort that they reclaimed much of the land towards the coast. Michael Menhenitt at the Exmouth Museum and Heritage Centre, in discussion, 23 May 2024.

24. Francis Lynn to Thomas Mitchell, 29 March 1722, TNA T 70/46, f. 127; Francis Lynn to Captain Tinker, TNA T 70/46, f. 127; Francis Lynn to Mr. Veal, TNA T 70/46, f. 128; Francis Lynn to Captain Sharrow, TNA T 70/46, f. 128.

25. Minutes of the SPCK, 29 March 1722, Cam SPCK MS A1/10, f. 27.

26. Henry Newman to Richard King, 29 March 1722, Cam SPCK MS D4/12, f. 11; Henry Newman to Marmaduke Penwell, 29 March 1722, Cam SPCK MS D4/12, f. 12; Henry Newman to John Perceval, 29 March 1722, BL Add. MS 47029, f. 112v.

27. Henry Newman to John Perceval, 29 March 1722, BL Add. MS 47029, f. 112v.

28. Minutes of the SPCK, 5 October 1721, Cam SPCK MS A1/9, f. 195.

29. Henry Newman to Richard King, 17 April 1722, Cam SPCK MS D4/12, f. 15.

30. Henry Newman to Marmaduke Penwell, 29 March 1722, Cam SPCK MS D4/12, f. 12.

31. Richard King to Henry Newman, 7 April 1722, Abstracts of Letters Received, Cam SPCK MS D2/16, Letter 7045.

32. Francis Lynn to John Sharrow, 17 April 1722, TNA T 70/46, f. 131.

33. Marmaduke Penwell to John Perceval, 21 May 1722, BL Add. MS 47029, f. 122v.

34. Marmaduke Penwell to John Perceval, 21 May 1722, BL Add. MS 47029, f. 122v.

35. James Brydges to Leonard Ely, April 24, 1722, HEH ST 57.20, ff. 199–200.

36. John Perceval to Charles Dering, December 1721, BL Add. MS 47029, f. 93v.

37. Chandos used these words to Ely: "If his Crimes are such as his Brother represents them," which supports the idea that the theory that Prince James wronged the king came from his brother, Prince John. James Brydges to Leonard Ely, April 24, 1722, HEH ST 57.20, ff. 199–200.

38. James Brydges to Leonard Ely, 24 April 1722, HEH ST 57.20, f. 200.

39. Francis Lynn to John Sharrow, 3 May 1722, TNA T 70/46, f. 132.

40. Instructions to Captains, TNA T70/64, f. 108–9.

41. Marmaduke Penwell to John Perceval, 21 May 1722, BL Add. MS 47029, f. 122v.

42. Richard King to Henry Newman, 2 June 1722, Abstracts of Letters Received, Cam SPCK MS D2/16, Letter 7087.

43. Prince James's movements come from Penwell's retelling to Perceval: Marmaduke Penwell to John Perceval, 21 May 1722, BL Add. MS 47029, f. 122v.

44. Henry A. M. Smith, "The Colleton Family in South Carolina," *South Carolina Historical and Genealogical Magazine* 1, no. 4 (October 1900): 327.

45. Smith, "The Colleton Family in South Carolina," 334–35; Elizabeth Jane Brabazon, *Exmouth and Its Environs* (Exmouth, 1866), 54.

46. Marmaduke Penwell to John Perceval, 21 May 1722, BL Add. MS 47029, f. 122v.

47. Marmaduke Penwell to John Perceval, 21 May 1722, BL Add. MS 47029, f. 122v.

48. Marmaduke Penwell to John Perceval, 21 May 1722, BL Add. MS 47029, f. 122v.

49. Marmaduke Penwell to John Perceval, 31 March 1722, BL Add. MS 47029, ff. 112v–113.

50. Marmaduke Penwell to John Perceval, 21 May 1722, BL Add. MS 47029, f. 122v; Thomas Bray, *Missionalia: Or, a collection of missionary pieces relating to the conversion of the heathen; both the African negroes and American Indians* (London: Printed by W. Roberts in the Year 1727), 45. *Eighteenth Century Collections Online* (accessed 9 February 2024). https://link-gale-com.libproxy1.usc.edu/apps/doc/CW0117415598/ECCO?u=usocal_main&sid=bookmark-ECCO&xid=89c0052b&pg=1; Minutes of Court of Assistants, 9 May 1722, TNA T 70/91, f. 138.

51. For the time see Marmaduke Penwell to Henry Newman, 4 May 1722, Abstracts of Letters Received, Cam SPCK MS D2/16, Letter 7062.

52. C. Willett Cunnington and Phillis Cunnington, *Handbook of English Costume in the Eighteenth Century* (London: Faber and Faber, 1957), 83.

53. Marmaduke Penwell to John Perceval, 21 May 1722, BL Add. MS 47029, f. 122v; Henry Newman to John Perceval, 8 May 1722, BL Add. MS 47029, f. 121v; 9 May 1722, Minutes of Court of Assistants, TNA T 70/91, f. 138.

54. Terri L. Snyder, *The Power to Die: Slavery and Suicide in British North America* (Chicago: University of Chicago Press, 2015), 24.

55. Snyder, 52.

56. Hans Sloane, *A voyage to the islands Madera, Barbados, Nieves, S. Christophers and Jamaica*, vol. 1 (London, 1707), xlviii, *Eighteenth Century Collections Online* (accessed 10 February 2024). https://link-gale-com.libproxy1.usc.edu/apps/doc/CW0101368735/ECCO?u=usocal_main&sid=bookmark-ECCO&xid=e369e9a9&pg=1.

57. Isaac Lamego to Henry Barham, 4 May 1739, Bod. MS. Clar Dep c. 376.

58. Snyder, 4, 17.

59. Emile Durkheim, *Suicide: A Study in Sociology*, trans. John A. Spaulding and George Simpson (Glencoe, Ill: Free Press, 1951), 208–16.

60. Henri A. Junod, *The Life of a South African Tribe*, 2nd Edition, Revised and Enlarged, vol. 2 (London: Macmillan, 1927), 372–74.

61. William Wake, *The principles of the Christian religion explained*, 3rd ed. (London, 1708), 115, *Eighteenth Century Collections Online* (accessed 10 February 2024). https://link-gale-com.libproxy1.usc.edu/apps/doc/CW0118188343/ECCO?u=usocal_main&sid=bookmark-ECCO&xid=4b9167d4&pg=1.

62. Minutes of Standing Committee, 20 February 1722, Cam SPCK MS A5/4, f. 90.

63. Matthew Hole, *A practical exposition of the church-catechism*, 2nd ed., vol. 2 (London, 1715), 461, *Eighteenth Century Collections Online* (accessed 10 February 2024). https://link-gale-com.libproxy1.usc.edu/apps/doc/CW0120301912/ECCO?u=usocal_main&sid=bookmark-ECCO&xid=ec961ec6&pg=1.

64. Hole, 461–62. Other tracts echo these beliefs: see Peter Newcome, *A Catechetical Course of Sermons*, 3rd ed., vol. 1 (London, 1712), 45, *Eighteenth Century Collections Online* (accessed 10 February 2024). https://link-gale-com.libproxy1.usc.edu/apps/doc/CW0120086800/ECCO?u=usocal_main&sid=bookmark-ECCO&xid=c35a2ad5&pg=1; John Ollyffe, *A Practical Exposition of the Church-Catechism*, vol. 2 (London, 1710), 475, *Eighteenth Century Collections Online* (accessed 10 February 2024). https://link-gale-com.libproxy1.usc.edu/apps/doc/CW0119783885/ECCO?u=usocal_main&sid=bookmark-ECCO&xid=01732462&pg=1.

65. Allestree, 208.

66. Ollyffe, 474.

67. Lawrence Fogg, *An Entrance into the Doctrine of Christianity, by Catechetical Institution* (Chester, 1712), 150, *Eighteenth Century Collections Online* (accessed 10 February 2024). https://link-gale-com.libproxy1.usc.edu/apps/doc/CW0120935705/ECCO?u=usocal_main&sid=bookmark-ECCO&xid=00d2ff75&pg=1.

68. Michael MacDonald and Terence R. Murphy, *Sleepless Souls: Suicide in Early Modern England* (Oxford: Clarendon Press, 1990), 154–56.

69. MacDonald and Murphy, 165.

70. MacDonald and Murphy, 123.

71. John Shaw, *The Fundamental Doctrines of the Church of England*, vol. 2 (London, 1720), 345, *Eighteenth Century Collections Online* (accessed 10 February 2024). https://link-gale-com.libproxy1.usc.edu/apps/doc/CW0118277814/ECCO?u=usocal_main&sid=bookmark-ECCO&xid=3cc1f4ee&pg=363.

72. Francis Lynn to John Sharrow, 10 May 1722, TNA T 70/46, f. 132.

73. Henry Newman to the archbishop of Canterbury, 10 May 1722, Cam SPCK MS D4/12, f. 16–17.

74. Bray, *Missionalia*, 45–46.

75. MacDonald and Murphy, 126–27.

76. Michael Macdonald, *Mystical Bedlam: Madness, Anxiety, and Healing in Seventeenth-Century England* (Cambridge: Cambridge University Press, 1981), 128; Porter, 41–46.

77. Robert Burton, *The Anatomy of Melancholy* (London: 1621), quoted in MacDonald and Murphy, 136–37.

78. Marmaduke Penwell to John Perceval, 21 May 1722, BL Add. MS 47029, f. 123.

79. Brabazon, 51. The church was later torn down to help widen the road and the bodies found were relocated. The lot is still vacant though and can be found. Michael Menhenitt at the Exmouth Museum and Heritage Centre, by email with author, 23 April 2024, and in discussion, 23 May 2024.

80. Henry Newman to Richard King, 16 June 1722, Cam SPCK MS D4/12, f. 23.

81. Marmaduke Penwell to John Perceval, 21 May 1722, BL Add. MS 47029, f. 123.

82. Junod, 166.

83. "Mr Penwells Account of Delagoa given me by himself," BL Add. MS 27990, f. 67.

84. Marmaduke Penwell to John Perceval, 21 May 1722, BL Add. MS 47029, f. 123; Francis Lynn to John Sharrow, 3 May 1722, TNA T 70/46, f. 132.

85. Minutes of the SPCK, 29 March 1722, Cam SPCK MS A1/10, f. 27.

86. James Brydges to Mr. Hill, 24 May 1722, HEH ST 57.20, f. 221; James Brydges to Mr. Ely and Hay, 28 May 1722, HEH ST 57.20, f. 227.

87. James Brydges to Mr. Ely and Hay, 28 May 1722, HEH ST 57.20, f. 227.

88. James Brydges to John Sharrow, 28 May 1722, HEH ST 57.20, f. 229.

89. List of Ships and Their Voyages in the Service of the Royal African Company of England, TNA T70/1225, f. 30.

Chapter 7

1. Marmaduke Penwell to John Perceval, 21 May 1722, BL Add. MS 47029, f. 123; Francis Lynn to John Sharrow, 3 May 1722, TNA T 70/46, f. 132.

2. "Capt Pauls Journal of his Voyage to Delagoa Anno. 1722," HEH ST 9, ff. 69–71.

3. Day Register, 23 June 1722 to 31 May 1723, DNA VOC Archives 1.04.02, Part 1/E.5.b, 4367, ff. 283–350; translated by Julie van den Hout; Day Register, 18 January 1723 to 31 May 1723, DNA VOC Archives 1.04.02, Part 1/E.5.b, 4367, ff. 588–99v; translated by Jason Perlman.

4. Instructions for Captain John Sharrow, Mr. Leonard Ely, Mr. Colin Hay and Captain Jeremiah Tinker, 1 February 1721/2, TNA T70/142, ff. 23–27.

5. List of Ships and Their Voyages in the Service of the Royal African Company of England, TNA T70/1225, f. 30; for more on Madeira see David Hancock, *Oceans of Wine: Madeira and the Emergence of American Trade and Taste* (New Haven: Yale University Press, 2009).

6. "Capt Pauls Journal of his Voyage to Delagoa Anno. 1722," HEH ST 9, ff. 69–70.

7. "Capt Pauls Journal of his Voyage to Delagoa Anno. 1722," HEH ST 9, ff .69–70.

8. Instructions for Captain John Sharrow, Mr. Leonard Ely, Mr. Colin Hay and Captain Jeremiah Tinker, 1 February 1722, TNA T70/142, f. 24.

9. Instructions for Captain John Sharrow, Mr. Leonard Ely, Mr. Colin Hay and Captain Jeremiah Tinker, 1 February 1722, TNA T70/142, f. 24; C. R. Boxer notes that an English name that frequently surfaces with regard to Minas Gerais is Maynard and that the family may be related to the former English envoy at Lisbon, Thomas Maynard, who was there from 1655 to 1689. C. R. Boxer, *The English and the Portuguese Brazil Trade, 1660–1780* (Bundoora, Australia: Institute of Latin American Studies at La Trobe University, 1981), 3–4.

10. C. R. Boxer, "Brazilian Gold and British Traders in the First Half of the Eighteenth Century," *Hispanic American Historical Review* 49, no. 3 (August 1969): 456–59.

11. Boxer, "Brazilian Gold," 460–63.

12. "Capt Pauls Journal of his Voyage to Delagoa Anno. 1722," HEH ST 9, f. 70.

13. Marmaduke Penwell to John Perceval, 30 November 1722, BL Add. MS 47029, f. 155.

14. "Capt Pauls Journal of his Voyage to Delagoa Anno. 1722," HEH ST 9, f. 70.

15. H. C. V. Leibbrandt, *Precis of the Archives of Cape Town: Journal, 1699–1732* (Cape Town: W. A. Richards and Sons, 1896), 292.

16. Leibbrandt, 292. 10 December 1722, Resolutions of the Council of Policy of Cape of Good Hope, Cape Town Archives Repository, South Africa, Reference code: C. 61, pp. 62–87; translated by Jason Perlman. It does appear that the *Northampton*'s papers were tweaked a bit. The Dutch at the Cape included a transcription of the papers Sharrow possessed in their resolutions, where it states that the ship paid its duty coming out of Dover but was bound for "Guinea." Its certification from the Customs House in London also said it was bound for Barbados. The instructions from the Royal African Company, which the Dutch also had access to, did give the correct itinerary. So perhaps the Dutch were right to be suspicious. Sharrow's instructions from the company do note, however, that Sharrow had the license from the East India Company. Instructions for Captain John Sharrow, Mr. Leonard Ely, Mr. Colin Hay and Captain Jeremiah Tinker, 1 February 1722, TNA T70/142, f. 26.

17. Marmaduke Penwell to John Perceval, 30 November 1722, BL Add. MS 47029, f. 155.

18. A. K. Smith, "The Struggle for Control of Southern Mozambique, 1720–1835" (Ph.D. diss., UCLA, 1970), 52.

19. Leibbrandt, 295.

20. Marmaduke Penwell to John Perceval, 30 November 1722, BL Add. MS 47029, f. 155.

21. Marmaduke Penwell to John Perceval, 30 November 1722, BL Add. MS 47029, f. 155; Minutes of the Court of Directors, 29 February 1722/3, BL IOR B/57, f. 267.

22. "List of the Names of the Officers and Seamen belonging to the Nightingale mustered in the Downes, 26 February 1721," BL IOR E/1/201, f. 407.

23. Leibbrandt, 288.

24. Leibbrandt, 288-289.

25. Leibbrandt, 289; Dispatch Books, BL IOR E/3/101, f. 161.

26. Minutes of the Court of Directors, 4 December 1723, BL IOR B/57, f. 490.

27. Marmaduke Penwell to John Perceval, 30 November 1722, BL Add. MS 47029, f. 155.

28. Minutes of the Court of Directors, 23 September 1720, 6 January 1721, 24 November 1721, BL IOR B/56, f. 119, 218, 524.

29. Minutes of the Court of Directors, 25 November 1720, BL IOR B/56, f. 170.

30. Marmaduke Penwell to John Perceval, 30 November 1722, BL Add. MS 47029, f. 155.

31. Marmaduke Penwell to John Perceval, 30 November 1722, BL Add. MS 47029, f. 155; Marmaduke Penwell to John Perceval, 2 December 1722, BL Add. MS 47029, f. 155v.

32. Marmaduke Penwell to John Perceval, 2 December 1722, BL Add. MS 47029, f. 155v.

33. "Capt Pauls Journal of his Voyage to Delagoa Anno. 1722," HEH ST 9, f. 70. Later Chandos told his correspondent, Mr. Lockwood, that he hoped the crew of the *Northampton* had followed the "Captains advice" to continue; this captain was probably Captain Mabbot, the East India captain who helped the *Northampton*. James Brydges to Mr. Lockwood, 25 February 1722/3, HEH ST 57.22, f. 182.

34. "Capt Pauls Journal of his Voyage to Delagoa Anno. 1722," HEH ST 9, f. 70. The date is confirmed in Dutch East India Company (VOC) records, 18 January 1723, Day Register, 23 June 1722 to 31 May 1723, f. 324; translated by Julie van den Hout. It should be noted that the British still adhered to the Julian calendar at this point, while the Dutch accepted the Gregorian, so the British dates are thirteen days behind the Dutch. The Julian dates are given in the text to provide continuity with the rest of the text.

35. "Directions for the Bay of Delagoa and the River therein, with some Memorandums concerning the Trade of that Place," TNA T70/1185, f. 18; List of Ships and Their Voyages in the Service of the Royal African Company of England, TNA T70/1225, f. 30.

36. "Capt Pauls Journal of his Voyage to Delagoa Anno. 1722," HEH ST 9, f. 70. The Dutch East India Company Day Registers report that the British did not show their passes until 11 January; 22 January 1723, Day Register, 23 June 1722 to 31 May 1723, DNA VOC Archives 1.04.02, Part 1/E.5.b, 4367, f. 328; translated by Julie van den Hout; 22 January 1723, Day Register, 18 January 1723 to 31 May 1723, DNA VOC Archives 1.04.02, Part 1/E.5.b, 4367, f. 588; translated by Jason Perlman.

37. "Capt Pauls Journal of his Voyage to Delagoa Anno. 1722," HEH ST 9, f. 70.

38. Smith, 52–53.

39. Smith, 57–58.

40. Smith, 51.

41. Smith, 53–55.

42. Smith, 55–57.

43. 24 January 1723, Day Register, 18 January 1723 to 31 May 1723, DNA VOC Archives 1.04.02, Part 1/E.5.b, 4367, f. 589; translated by Jason Perlman.

44. 24 January 1723, 24 January 1723, Day Register, 18 January 1723 to 31 May 1723, DNA VOC Archives 1.04.02, Part 1/E.5.b, 4367, f. 589; translated by Jason Perlman. Other sources refer to the ruler of Mpfumo as Biri. Smith, 53–54.

45. 24 January 1723, Day Register, 23 June 1722 to 31 May 1723, DNA VOC Archives 1.04.02, Part 1/E.5.b, 4367, f. 329; translated by Julie van den Hout.

46. 25 January 1723, Day Register, 23 June 1722 to 31 May 1723, DNA VOC Archives 1.04.02, Part 1/E.5.b, 4367, f. 329v–31; translated by Julie van den Hout.

47. In 1727, Thomas Bray published an account that has Prince John instantly turning against the British. Bray stated: "Being arrived at *Delagoa*, Mr. *Penwell*, his Instructor went with him to his Mother's Hutt, where the Rascal having entered, shut himself up, the poor Tutor standing at the Door six Hours before he would come forth to him; and when at length he came out, with great Reluctancy, he gave him such Frowns and looked so Surly upon him, that the Man thought it concern'd him speedily to on Ship-board, if he would save his Life." Thomas Bray, *Missionalia: Or, a collection of missionary pieces relating to the conversion of the heathen; both the African negroes and American Indians* (London: Printed by W. Roberts in the Year 1727), 46, *Eighteenth Century Collections Online* (accessed 9 February 2024). https://link-gale-com.libproxy1.usc.edu/apps/doc /CW0117415598/ECCO?u=usocal_main&sid=bookmark-ECCO&xid=89c0052b&pg=1.

48. "Capt Pauls Journal of his Voyage to Delagoa Anno. 1722," HEH ST 9, f. 70.

49. 27 January 1723, Day Register, 18 January 1723 to 31 May 1723, DNA VOC Archives 1.04.02, Part 1/E.5.b, 4367, f. 589; translated by Jason Perlman; 30 January 1723, Day Register, 23 June 1722 to 31 May 1723, DNA VOC Archives 1.04.02, Part 1/E.5.b, 4367, ff. 333v–34; translated by Julie van den Hout.

50. 5, 7 February 1723, Day Register, 18 January 1723 to 31 May 1723, DNA VOC Archives 1.04.02, Part 1/E.5.b, 4367, f. 590; translated by Jason Perlman; 7 February 1723, Day Register, 23 June 1722 to 31 May 172, DNA VOC Archives 1.04.02, Part 1/E.5.b, 4367, f. 335v; translated by Julie van den Hout.

51. The Dutch Day Registers have them trading at what is probably Manisse, which they spell Menisse, Mainisse, and Maijnisse. This would be to the north of the bay. Smith, 223; "Capt Pauls Journal of his Voyage to Delagoa Anno. 1722," HEH ST 9, f. 70; 8, 10, 18 February 1723, Day Register, 18 January 1723 to 31 May 1723, DNA VOC Archives 1.04.02, Part 1/E.5.b, 4367, f. 591; translated by Jason Perlman; 7, 8, 12, 20, February 1723, Day Register, 23 June 1722 to 31 May 1723, DNA VOC Archives 1.04.02, Part 1/E.5.b, 4367, ff. 335v, 336, 337; translated by Julie van den Hout.

52. "Capt Pauls Journal of his Voyage to Delagoa Anno. 1722," HEH ST 9, f. 70.

53. Smith, 61–62.

54. 20 January 1723, Day Register, 23 June 1722 to 31 May 1723, DNA VOC Archives 1.04.02, Part 1/E.5.b, 4367, f. 326; translated by Julie van den Hout.

55. "Directions for the Bay of Delagoa and the River therein, with some Memorandums concerning the Trade of that Place," TNA T70/1185, f. 18v-19.

56. "Directions for the Bay of Delagoa and the River therein, with some Memorandums concerning the Trade of that Place," TNA T70/1185, f. 19.

57. "Directions for the Bay of Delagoa and the River therein, with some Memorandums concerning the Trade of that Place," TNA T70/1185, f. 18v.

58. John Perceval to Thomas Bray, 27 January 1721/2, BL Add. MS 47029, ff. 99–101.

59. John Perceval to Thomas Bray, 27 January 1721/2, BL Add. MS 47029, f. 100v.

60. There is one surviving reference to the dictionary after the *Northampton*'s return. Henry Newman sent Erasmus Philipps "a copy of the Names of the Numbers us'd by the Natives of Delagoa," and noted this information came from Penwell's Journal. Henry Newman to Erasmus Philipps, 16 October 1723, Abstracts of Letters Sent, Cam SPCK MS D2/17, Letter 9223. I assume that the journal the members of the SPCK discuss upon the *Northampton*'s return is the same as the document containing answers to Perceval's queries found in his papers entitled "Mr Penwells Account of Delagoa given me by himself, part ye 2d." There could, however, have been another journal, or a first part to this account, but no copies of one have been found. BL Add. MS 27990, ff. 63–70.

61. "Mr Penwells Account of Delagoa given me by himself," BL Add. MS 27990, f. 68.

62. "Mr Penwells Account of Delagoa given me by himself," BL Add. MS 27990, f. 69.

63. "Mr Penwells Account of Delagoa given me by himself," BL Add. MS 27990, f. 68.

64. "Mr Penwells Account of Delagoa given me by himself," BL Add. MS 27990, ff. 68v, 69v.

65. "Mr Penwells Account of Delagoa given me by himself," BL Add. MS 27990, ff. 65–65v.

66. "Mr Penwells Account of Delagoa given me by himself," BL Add. MS 27990, ff. 65v-70. The main crop does seem to be what we refer to as corn, as Penwell states: "They make both Rice & Corn of two sorts, Indian Corn & a small Corn which they call Maise." BL Add. MS 27990, f. 69.

67. "Mr Penwells Account of Delagoa given me by himself," BL Add. MS 27990, ff. 65v, 69v-70.

68. "Mr Penwells Account of Delagoa given me by himself," BL Add. MS 27990, f. 66.

69. "Mr Penwells Account of Delagoa given me by himself," BL Add. MS 27990, f. 68.

70. "Capt Pauls Journal of his Voyage to Delagoa Anno. 1722," HEH ST 9, ff. 70–71.

71. 2 March 1723, Day Register, 23 June 1722 to 31 May 1723, DNA VOC Archives 1.04.02, Part 1/E.5.b, 4367, f. 338v; translated by Julie van den Hout.

72. 13 February 1723, Day Register, 18 January 1723 to 31 May 1723, DNA VOC Archives 1.04.02, Part 1/E.5.b, 4367, f. 591; translated by Jason Perlman.

73. 3 March 1723, Day Register, 18 January 1723 to 31 May 1723, DNA VOC Archives 1.04.02, Part 1/E.5.b, 4367, f. 592; translated by Jason Perlman. The other day register does not mention this justification.

74. 5 March 1723, Day Register, 23 June 1722 to 31 May 1723, DNA VOC Archives 1.04.02, Part 1/E.5.b, 4367, f. 340; translated by Julie van den Hout.

75. 3 March 1723, Day Register, 23 June 1722 to 31 May 1723, DNA VOC Archives 1.04.02, Part 1/E.5.b, 4367, f. 338v; translated by Julie van den Hout. This claim is mentioned in the other day register as well. 3 March 1723, Day Register, 18 January 1723 to 31 May 1723, DNA VOC Archives 1.04.02, Part 1/E.5.b, 4367, f. 592; translated by Jason Perlman.

76. 3 March 1723, Day Register, 23 June 1722 to 31 May 1723, DNA VOC Archives 1.04.02, Part 1/E.5.b, 4367, f. 338v; translated by Julie van den Hout; 3 March 1723, Day Register, 18 January 1723 to 31 May 1723, DNA VOC Archives 1.04.02, Part 1/E.5.b, 4367, f. 592; translated by Jason Perlman.

77. 5 March 1723, Day Register, 23 June 1722 to 31 May 1723, DNA VOC Archives 1.04.02, Part 1/E.5.b, 4367, f. 340; translated by Julie van den Hout.

78. "Capt Pauls Journal of his Voyage to Delagoa Anno. 1722," HEH ST 9, f. 71.

79. 7 March 1723, Day Register, 23 June 1722 to 31 May 1723, DNA VOC Archives 1.04.02, Part 1/E.5.b, 4367, ff. 340v–41; translated by Julie van den Hout.

80. "Capt Pauls Journal of his Voyage to Delagoa Anno. 1722," HEH ST 9, f. 71.

81. In the 1720s the Dutch East India Company exported only three hundred enslaved people from Maputo Bay. Robert Ross, "Khoesan and Immigrants: The Emergence of Colonial Society in the Cape, 1500–1800," in *The Cambridge History of South Africa*, vol. 1, ed. Carolyn Hamilton, Bernard K. Mbenga, and Robert Ross (Cambridge: Cambridge University Press, 2009), 187.

82. O. F. Mentzel, *Life at the Cape in Mid-Eighteenth Century: The Biography of Rudolph Siegfried Allemann*, trans. Margaret Greenless (Cape Town: Van Riebeeck Society, 1919), 59–62; Robert C.-H. Shell, "The Twinning of Maputo and Cape Town: The Early Mozambican Slave Trade to the Slave Lodge, 1677–1732," in *History, Memory and Identity*, ed. Vijayalakshmi Teelock and Edward A. Alpers (Reduit, Moka: University of Mauritius and Nelson Mandela Centre for African Culture, 2001), 183.

83. Shula Marks and Richard Gray, "Southern Africa and Madagascar" in *The Cambridge History of Africa, Volume 4, c. 1600–c. 1790*, ed. Richard Gray (Cambridge: Cambridge University Press, 1975), 408; Malyn Newitt, *A History of Mozambique* (Bloomington: Indiana University Press, 1995) 159. The Austrians were there from 1778 to 1781, and the Portuguese attempted their first permanent settlement in 1781.

Epilogue

1. "Capt Pauls Journal of his Voyage to Delagoa Anno. 1722," HEH ST 9, f. 71; Instructions for Captain John Sharrow, Mr. Leonard Ely, Mr. Colin Hay and Captain Jeremiah Tinker, 1 February 1722, TNA T70/142, f. 26.

2. Minutes of the Court of Assistants, 13 February 1724, TNA T70/92, f. 44; Matthew David Mitchell, "'Legitimate Commerce' in the Eighteenth Century: The Royal African Company of

England Under the Duke of Chandos, 1720–1726," *Enterprise and Society* 14, no. 3 (September 2013): 572; for the later history of this area see Daniel B. Domingues da Silva, *The Atlantic Slave Trade from West Central Africa, 1780–1867* (Cambridge: Cambridge University Press, 2017).

3. List of Ships and Their Voyages in the Service of the Royal African Company of England, TNA T70/1225, f. 30; Hereford and Reed to the Royal African Company, 18 May 1723, Abstracts of Letters Received, TNA, T 70/7, f. 46.

4. James Brydges to Mr. Lockwood, 25 February 1722/3, HEH ST 57.22, ff. 182v–83.

5. John Perceval to Henry Newman, 2 March 1722/3, BL Add. MS 47029, f. 156.

6. Henry Newman to John Perceval, 30 March 1723, Cam SPCK MS D4/12, ff. 77–78.

7. James Brydges to Gov. Hereford, 22 August 1723, HEH ST 57.21, f. 328; Hereford and Reed to the Royal African Company, 18 May 1723, Received 19 August 1723, TNA T70/7, f. 46.

8. List of Ships and Their Voyages in the Service of the Royal African Company of England, TNA T70/1225, f. 30.

9. List of Ships and Their Voyages in the Service of the Royal African Company of England, TNA T70/1225, f. 30.

10. Minutes of the SPCK, 24 September 1723, Cam SPCK MS A1/10, f. 196.

11. Henry Newman to Mr. Witham, 15 October 1723, Cam SPCK MS D4/13, f. 58; Treasurer's Cash Book, Cam SPCK MS C1/5, f. 34v.

12. Minutes of the SPCK, 15 October 1723, Cam SPCK MS A1/10, f. 200.

13. Henry Newman to Erasmus Philipps, 16 October 1723, Abstracts of Letters Sent, Cam SPCK MS D2/17, Letter 9223; Henry Newman to Richard King, 19 October 1723, Cam SPCK MS D4/13, f. 61.

14. Richard King to Henry Newman, 24 February 1724, Abstracts of Letters Received, Cam SPCK MS D2/17, Letter 7740, f. 44. A note was made of the need to make a copy for him. Notes by Chamberlayne and Newman on SPCK Business, 7 January 1724, Bod MS Rawl C 844, f. 107v.

15. Henry Newman to Edmund Gibson, Bishop of London, 8 January 1739/40, Cam SPCK MS D4/51, f. 35.

16. Thomas Bray, *Missionalia: Or, a collection of missionary pieces relating to the conversion of the heathen; both the African negroes and American Indians* (London: Printed by W. Roberts in the Year 1727), *Eighteenth Century Collections Online* (accessed 9 February 2024). https://link-gale-com.libproxy1.usc.edu/apps/doc/CW0117415598/ECCO?u=usocal_main&sid=bookmark-ECCO&xid=89c0052b&pg=1. He says this on the second page of the dedication (no pagination).

17. Bray, *Missionalia*, 46.

18. He noted this on a slip of paper added to his letter book. See BL Add. 47030, f. 55. For information on Barrett see letters between him and Perceval dated between 23 April 1722 and 23 March 1722/3, BL Add. 47029 and letters between 30 March 1723 and 25 August 1724, BL Add. 47030.

19. George Berkeley to John Perceval, 4 March 1722/3, BL Add. MS 47029, ff. 156–57.

20. Daniel Dering to John Perceval, 31 January 1725/6, BL Add. MS 47031, f. 91; George Berkeley to John Perceval, 10 February 1725/6, BL Add. MS 47031, f. 104; John Perceval to Daniel Dering, 12 February 1725/6, BL Add. MS 47031, f. 106; Daniel Dering to John Perceval, 28 February 1725/6, BL Add. MS 47031, f. 112; William Byrd II to John Perceval, 10 June 1729, BL Add. MS 47032, f. 117; George Berkeley to John Perceval, 2 March 1730/1, BL Add. MS 47033, f. 32.

21. Paul M. Pressly, *On the Rim of the Caribbean: Colonial Georgia and the British Atlantic World* (Athens: University of Georgia Press, 2013), 12, 30–32.

22. List of Ships and Their Voyages in the Service of the Royal African Company of England, TNA T70/1225, f. 30.

23. Minutes of Court of Assistants, 20 February 1724, TNA T70/92, f. 48.

24. Orders of the Court for Committee of Shipping, 20 February 1724, TNA T 70/137.

25. James Roydon to John Sharrow, 14 May 1724, HEH ST 57.25, f. 85.

26. Minute Book of the Committee of Trade, 23 October 1723, TNA T70/124. Ely and Hay were paid as well: Minutes of Court of Assistants, 17 December 1723, TNA T70/92, f. 21.

27. Minute Book of the Committee of Trade, 6 Nov 1723, TNA T70/124; Minutes of Court of Assistants, 7 November 1723, TNA T70/92, f. 6; Minutes of Court of Assistants, 31 December 1723, TNA T70/92, f. 28.

28. Minute Book of the Committee of Trade, 26 February 1724, TNA T70/124.

29. List of Passengers, TNA T70/1437, f. 68.

30. Henry Newman to John Sharrow, 5 March 1722, Cam SPCK MS D4/12, f. 3.

31. William Gower to the Royal African Company, 26 October 1725, Abstracts of Letters Received, TNA T70/7, f. 78v.

32. Henry Newman to the Rev. Mr. King, 16 June 1722, Cam SPCK MS D4/12, f. 23; William Gower to the Royal African Company, 26 October 1725, Abstracts of Letters Received, TNA T70/7, f. 78v.

33. Walter Charles to the Royal African Company, 10 December 1726, Abstracts of Letters Received, TNA T70/7, f. 82v-83.

34. Walter Charles to the Royal African Company, 12 December 1726, Abstracts of Letters Received, TNA T70/7, f. 83v. He added a postscript on the 13th relaying this information.

35. Walter Charles to the Royal African Company, 8 April 1727, Abstracts of Letters Received, TNA T70/7, f. 83v.

36. The Royal African Company to Walter Charles, 6 July 1727, Letters Sent to Sierra Leone, T 70/60, ff. 55–56.

37. "A List of all the Persons Living and Dead who have been and now are in the Service of the Royal African Company of England in the District of Sierraleone from November 2d 1726 to January 31st 1728," TNA T 70/1447, f. 16.

38. "A List of all the Persons Living and Dead who have been and now are in the Service of the Royal African Company of England in the District of Sierraleone from November 2d 1726 to January 31st 1728," TNA T 70/1447, f. 16.

39. The Royal African Company to Walter Charles, 18 July 1728, Letters Sent to Sierra Leone, TNA T 70/60, ff. 68–70.

40. Sean M. Kelley, *The Voyage of the Slave Ship* Hare (Chapel Hill: University of North Carolina Press, 2016), 66; Kevin MacDonald, *Pirates, Merchants, Settlers, and Slaves: Colonial America and the Indo-Atlantic World* (Oakland: University of California Press, 2015), 115.

41. Walter Charles to the Royal African Company, 12 December 1726, Abstracts of Letters Received, TNA T70/7, f. 83v.

42. Kelley, 63; Penwell mentions Lopez's debts in a letter: Marmaduke Penwell to Sierra Leone, 25 January 1725/6, Abstracts of Letters Received, TNA T70/7, f. 78v.

43. Kelley, 63.

44. The Royal African Company to Walter Charles, 6 February 1728/9, Letters Sent to Sierra Leone, TNA T 70/60, f. 90.

45. Henry Newman to Edmund Gibson, bishop of London, 8 January 1739/40, Cam SPCK MS D4/51, f. 35.

46. K. G. Davies, *The Royal African Company* (London: Longmans, 1960), 344.

47. Davies, 345; William Pettigrew, *Freedom's Debt: The Royal African Company and the Politics of the Atlantic Slave Trade, 1672–1752* (Chapel Hill: University of North Carolina Press, 2013), 193–205.

48. Minutes of the Committee of Seven, 15 September 1725, TNA T70/103, ff. 51–52.

49. 22 August 1726, Resolutions of the Council of Policy of Cape of Good Hope, Cape Town Archives Repository, South Africa, Reference code: C. 75, pp. 159–61. Translated by Jason Perlman.

50. 22 August 1726, Resolutions of the Council of Policy of Cape of Good Hope, Cape Town Archives Repository, South Africa, Reference code: C. 75, pp. 159–61. Translated by Jason Perlman.

51. Alan K. Smith, "The Struggle for Control of Southern Mozambique, 1720–1835," (Ph.D. diss., UCLA, 1970), 83–86.

52. Smith, 102–4.

53. Smith, 111.

54. For the establishment of the Austrian settlement and the struggles of the Portuguese to maintain their post until the 1830s, see Smith, 153–353.

55. Allan D. Austin, *African Muslims in Antebellum America: Transatlantic Stories and Spiritual Struggles* (New York: Routledge, 1997), 50–61; Sylviane A. Diouf, *Servants of Allah: African Muslims Enslaved in the Americas* (New York: New York University Press, 1998), 164–66. For a contemporary account of his life see T. Bluett, *Some memories of the life of Job, the son of the Solomon high priest of Boonda in Africa* (London, 1734), *Eighteenth Century Collections Online* (accessed 10 February 2024). https://link-gale-com.libproxy1.usc.edu/apps/doc/CW0100361018/ECCO?u=usocal_main&sid=bookmark-ECCO&xid=9860abf1&pg=1.

56. Randy Sparks, *Where the Negroes Are Masters: An African Port in the Era of the Slave Trade* (Cambridge, Mass.: Harvard University Press, 2014), 1–3, 45–52, 56–67, 256. For a contemporary account of Sessarakoo's life see [Anon.,] *The royal African, or, Memoirs of the young prince of Annamaboe* (London, 1749).

57. Randy Sparks, *The Two Princes of Calabar: An Eighteenth-Century Atlantic Odyssey* (Cambridge, Mass.: Harvard University Press, 2004).

INDEX

The index entry *"Maffoom, James and John"* contains the princes' shared experiences. Their individual experiences can be found in the entries *"Maffoom, James"* and *"Maffoom, John."* Page numbers in italic type indicate illustrations.

Adams, Joseph, 83
Addison (ship), 113
Africa: eighteenth-century map of, *55*, 56; enslavement of elites of, 11, 62, 152n96; European ties cultivated by the elite in, 12; gold in, 5, 46, 48–49, 51–56, 70, 88–89, 91–93, 130; power exercised over European colonists and traders in, 5, 9, 109, 115–16, 122, 130–31; slave trade role of the elite in, 142n52; trade role of the elite in, 40. *See also* East Africa; Maputo Bay area; West Africa
ambergris, 10, 11, 117, 126
Anglican Church, 67, 76–79, 81–82, 92, 104

Baldwin, Robert, 41
Barbados, 34
Barrett, John, 125
Bartholomew, Manuel, 36
Becket, Rosamond, 47
Behn, Aphra: *Emperor of the Moon*, 61; *Oroonoko*, 11, 31–32, 40
Berkeley, George, 125
Bermuda, 125
Bialuschewski, Arne, 143n66, 146n118
Bible, 63, 68, 81, 118
Blount, Lady, 68, 75
Bowes, John, 38
Bowes, Joshua, 38–42, 44, 97
Bowrey, Thomas, 14, 140n28
Bray, Thomas, 73, 78, 81, 85–86, 90, 105, 118, 124–25, 134n3, 177n47; *Catechetical Lectures*, 78
Brazil, 71, 88–89, 108, 110–11, 115
Britain: class etiquette in, 73; enslaved persons in, 65–67; imperialism of, 3–4; and Maputo Bay area, 1–2, 5, 9–10; and Mpfumo, 1–2, 4, 115–22; Portuguese treaty with, 111; Privy Council, 36; race in, 4, 62–66; reception of elite non-Europeans in, 59–62, 130–31; and the slave trade, 15, 29, 130, 153n96; travel and education undertaken by the elite of, 12–13. *See also* London
Brodrick, William, 36
Brooking, Charles, *Shipping in the English Channel*, 96
Brydges, James. *See* Chandos, James Brydges, first Duke of
Burton, Robert, *The Anatomy of Melancholy*, 106
Butts v. Penny (1677), 66

Cabinda, 54, 87–88, 110, 123–24, 126
Caesar (ship), 113
Cain (biblical figure), 68, 94
calico, 46–47, 50
Cannons, Middlesex, England, 57–60, *58*, 73–75, *74*
Canterbury, archbishop of, 71, 81
Cape of Good Hope, 8–9, 15, 18, 28, 49, 70, 72, 108, 111–15, *112*, 122, 128, 176n16
Catalan Atlas, 51
cattle, 8
Cavendish, James, *65*
Chamberlayne v. Harvey (1696), 66
Chandos (ship), 113
Chandos, James Brydges, first Duke of, 45, 52–60, *53*, 68, 71, 73, 77, 80, 86–88, 91, 95–96, 98, 100–101, 107–8, 110–11, 123–24, 126, 129–30, 135n16
Charles, Walter, 127

ACKNOWLEDGMENTS

Tracing the journey of Prince James and Prince John took me into uncharted waters, and I needed a lot of pilots to help steer my ship home. To tell the princes' story I had to build up my knowledge on many areas and topics from scratch, and I depended a lot of people to do so. Writing this book has made me truly grateful for the generosity of my fellow scholars and the patience of my family and friends.

This book would not have been possible without the constant support of Peter Mancall, who is not only the editor of the book series this monograph appears in but also a mentor and friend. Bob Lockhart also deserves a very emphatic thank-you. He has been supportive since I told him about this project and gave me the encouragement needed to complete it.

I could not have written this project without massive assistance from my fellow scholars. A number of people helped me to tackle the documents that were in Dutch: Alison Games and Susanah Shaw Romney, who have both been constant supporters, helped me translate small bits, and both Lydia Sigismondi and Anne Goldgar gave translation a go. Susanah also connected me to both Jason Perlman and Julie van den Hout, who were translators extraordinaire. Christine Walker helped me find Jamaican archival resources. Kate Blackmer made the beautiful maps for the book. The folks at the Exmouth Museum and Heritage Centre, especially Michael Menhenitt, took the time to talk to me about eighteenth century Exmouth and direct me the churchyard where Prince John was probably buried. John Demos and Lori Anne Ferrell read whole drafts of the manuscript, one at the beginning of the project and one at the end. A number of people read whole chapters to keep me on the straight and narrow. Thank you Alejandra Dubcovsky, Admire Mseba, Abby Swingen, and Dan Livesay. I owe you all drinks, coffee, desserts, and eternal gratitude. Also, thanks to the two anonymous readers for the Press. This is a better book because of you.

Then there is my coterie of supporters at USC, the Huntington Library, and beyond. Vanessa Wilke and Tawny Paul could probably write this book now. Roy Richie not only inspired me with his own work, he was always there to support me and the project. The same goes for Keith Wrightson, Bill Deverell,

Deb Harkness, Steve Pincus, Karen Halttunen, Joan Flores-Villalobos, Alice Baumgartner, Amy Braden, Carole Shammas, Keith Pluymers, Karin Amundsen, Amy Watson, Amy Froide, Asheesh Siddique, Lisa Cody, Daniel Richter, Michael Bloch, Mark Hanna, Dana Murillo, Julie Lewandoski, Susan Amussen, James Davey, Nicholas Radburn, Karen Harvey, Amy Dunnigan, Chris Kyle, and Tim Harris. This book also had me cold-calling scholars I had never met, and the number of people who actually responded was heartening, so thank you, Ettore Morelli, Malyn Newitt, Arne Bialuschewski, Heather Hughes, Richard Woodward, Margaret Makepeace, Mark Horton, Carolyn Hamilton, and Ralph Austen. Also, thanks go to my students who read parts of this in my methodology course—especially those who read the whole thing and gave comments in fall semester 2023: Jacob Ballon, Haige Chen, Ramon Garza, Ben Rana, Ethan Shamoeil, and Hugo Vogel. Thanks too to Himani Boompally, Sean Silvia, and Jack Green, who always asked about the book.

I also want to thank all the institutions that have supported me. The USC Huntington Early Modern Studies Institute has been invaluable with its support. The institute has provided me with funds to research, places to present, and shoulders to lean on. Big thanks also to Steve Hindle, Susan Juster, Catherine Wehrey-Miller, Juan Gomez, and others the Huntington Library, my home away from home. The Huntington also provided me with a short-term fellowship and the opportunity to do research in Cambridge through the Trinity Hall–Huntington Exchange Fellowship. Thanks as well to the Center for Religion and Civic Culture at USC for financial support early on in the project.

And, finally, to my friends and family who kept this project afloat. Many of you have been mentioned above, know you are in this group as well. But I also want to mention Heather Richardson Kuljurgis, Pat Richardson, Don and Sue Hartley, Maria Garcia, Katherine Mannheimer, Rachel Bond, Chris Bond, Oleg Sindiy, and Heather Adams. If you aren't listed here it just means you probably don't ask me about my book, which is appreciated too. My family has had to listen to me struggle with the book for years, so thank you, Heather, Josh, Caleb, and Wesley Brown, Melissa and Steve Landau, Charis and Joey Armstroff, and Violet, Rowan, and Blake. And thanks to my parents, John and Jan O'Neill, who kept asking about the book even though I was nasty and cranky when they did. Also, to the band the Spin Doctors, who gave me a soundtrack for the book. But most of all to Damon, who heard this story on our first date and who could tell it himself by now. Thanks for putting up with me through the whole process and for making sure I also had a life outside it. This book's for you.

www.ingramcontent.com/pod-product-compliance
Lightning Source LLC
Chambersburg PA
CBHW020334100426
42812CB00029B/3118/J